THE DEVIL RIDES OUT

www.**rbooks**.co.uk

Also by Paul O'Grady

AT MY MOTHER'S KNEE . . .
AND OTHER LOW JOINTS

THE DEVIL RIDES OUT

Paul O'Grady

BANTAM PRESS

LONDON · TORONTO · SYDNEY · AUCKLAND · JOHANNESBURG

TRANSWORLD PUBLISHERS
61–63 Uxbridge Road, London W5 5SA
A Random House Group Company
www.rbooks.co.uk

First published in Great Britain
in 2010 by Bantam Press
an imprint of Transworld Publishers

This book is a work of non-fiction based on the life, experiences and recollections of
Paul O'Grady. In some limited cases names of people, places, dates, sequences or the
detail of events have been changed solely to protect the privacy of others. The author
has stated to the publishers that, except in such minor respects not affecting the
substantial accuracy of the work, the contents of this book are true.

A CIP catalogue record for this book
is available from the British Library.

ISBNs 9780593064245 (cased)
9780593064252 (tpb)

Addresses for Random House Group Ltd companies outside the UK
can be found at: www.randomhouse.co.uk
The Random House Group Ltd Reg. No. 954009

The Random House Group Limited supports the Forest Stewardship
Council (FSC), the leading international forest-certification organization. All our
titles that are printed on Greenpeace-approved FSC-certified paper carry the FSC logo.
Our paper procurement policy can be found at
www.rbooks.co.uk/environment

Mixed Sources
Product group from well-managed
forests and other controlled sources
www.fsc.org Cert no. TT-COC-2139
© 1996 Forest Stewardship Council

Typeset in 11.5/15.5pt Sabon by
Falcon Oast Graphic Art Ltd.
Printed and bound in Great Britain by
CPI Mackays, Chatham, ME5 8TD

2 4 6 8 10 9 7 5 3 1

In memory of
Buster Elvis Savage.

The greatest canine star since Lassie.

CONTENTS

PROLOGUE

Saturday night. The big night out, the one you started preparing for the moment you opened your eyes on a Saturday morning, asking yourself, as you contemplated the pattern of cracks across the bedroom ceiling that looked like Barbara Castle in profile, 'What am I going to wear tonight?' This question would later prompt a trip into town to buy a new top, a garment that would invariably turn out to be a skin-tight, Omo-white, cap-sleeved T-shirt, exactly the same as all the others that lay in my wardrobe drawer. Didn't matter, there was something about a brand new T-shirt that made you feel 'dressed up' and dazzling.

There was a hysterical queen on the club scene known as 'Suicide Lee', so-called for the many wrist-slashing escapades and overdoses of paracetamol he put his body through each time he was dumped by the latest boyfriend. Since this happened every other weekend, the sight of a comatose Lee being carried out of a club by a posse of agitated queens became quite a regular feature on the late night streets of Liverpool. These futile suicide attempts never took place in the privacy of his own home. They were always carried out in

1

public, usually in the toilets of a pub or club where he knew that he would be quickly discovered by his long-suffering friends and saved yet again from the jaws of death. He probably got off on the adrenalin rush of all this high drama and the subsequent attention, which he mistook for sympathy when in reality it was ridicule and piss-taking on a grand scale.

One Saturday teatime he awoke on a friend's bed from a drug-induced coma, the result of another attempt at self-harm the previous night, and asked his anxious pal wanly, in his best Camille voice, what the time was.

'Half six,' came the gentle reply.

'Oh my Christ,' Suicide Lee screeched, sitting bolt upright in the bed and springing into action. 'What am I going to wear tonight?'

I never socialized with Suicide Lee – I couldn't stand him, to be honest, and thought he should abandon any further botched attempts on his life and instead entrust the task of dispatching him to one of the many people, myself included, who would be only too happy to volunteer for the job – but in a way I sort of empathized with him when I heard the 'what am I going to wear' story. Even the debilitating after-effects of an attempted suicide couldn't stop this queen's primeval urge to find the all-important something to wear and get out there clubbing. Every self-respecting young person went out on a Saturday night regardless of circumstances. To stay in was unthinkable; it meant you were a social outcast, a disgrace, a complete loser forced to sit in his bedroom listening to records and fretting while the rest of the town was out clubbing and having a ball.

I was going out tonight though and looked friggin' gorgeous, or so I believed. My skin-tight jeans had been freshly washed in the bath that afternoon and then spun and tumble-dried in the launderette on Church Road, where sometimes, in my haste to get ready, I forgot to ask or rather to grovel pathetically before the unpredictable pit bull who ran the launderette for her kind dispensation to use the drying machines. This faux pas would result in my being shown the door with a sharp reminder that the 'use of dryers was strictly for those who had done a full load in the shop previous'. Like a mantra she read this out from a handwritten sign sellotaped to the wall over the spin dryer, as if it gave her declaration some sort of official authority. It was just one of the many rules and regulations written out on the inside of empty soap-powder boxes and then stuck on machines, walls and even windows of the launderette that either she or the other fifteen-stone piece of officialdom – similarly encased in a uniform of polyester overall and battered slippers – who ran the show when she wasn't there had conjured up between the service washes in their little cubby hole that they grandly referred to as 'the Office'. A refusal to be allowed to use the dryer meant running home to perform the laborious ritual known as 'ironing your jeans dry', a process that was never 100 per cent successful and meant enduring a damp crotch, arse and pockets all evening.

No damp jeans tonight though: a brand new pair of brushed denim Sea Dogs were about to make their debut, as was the ubiquitous cap-sleeved T-shirt bought that afternoon in Birkenhead Market. Hair blow-dried viciously until the top resembled a guardsman's busby with back and sides nicely curled under by torturing my naturally wavy hair with a round hairbrush. Any imperfections such as a pimple, spot or love bite would be amateurishly disguised with a generous daub of Rimmel's Hide and Heal that was the colour of magnolia emulsion and glowed unnaturally under the fluorescent lights of a club. After checking myself in my ma's dressing-table mirror I descended the stairs, leaving an eye-watering smog of Aqua Manda for Men in my wake. My mother, sat on the bottom step talking to my aunty on the phone, scrunched up her face and fanned it frantically with her hand like a panto dame who's just found out that the slipper fits Cinderella.

'What in God's name have you covered yourself in?' she moaned. 'It smells like a gas attack, and I hope you're going to wear a coat, you'll catch your death going out like that.'

A coat? She had to be kidding. Only nesh old people wore coats. I had my brown leather bomber jacket – trendy enough to be considered acceptable outdoor wear. It had an elasticated waist that rode up at the back and I wore the sleeves pushed up to the elbow. It was also a size too small for me and therefore could never possibly be mistaken for anything as enveloping and shameful as a coat.

'I won't be late,' I lied, 'and if I'm not home it means that I've stayed at one of me mates.'

'Mates? Which mates?' she asked suspiciously. 'Ooh, I'd like to be behind you to see what you're up to with these mates, my lad.'

'You wouldn't,' I thought.

'He's off out tomcatting it again, Annie,' my mother sighed resignedly down the phone to my aunty. 'I don't know what he's up to, but I can tell you one thing,' she added, giving me the once-over as she spoke, 'the devil rides out. Oh, the devil rides out tonight, Annie.'

CHAPTER I

The Ghosts of Holly Grove

'I WONDER WHAT I DID IN A PAST LIFE THAT WAS SO EVIL TO BE cursed with a lunatic like you for a son,' my mother sighed. 'I must've been the one who said to the Gestapo, "Anne Frank? Oh, she's behind the wardrobe." Why else would I have to suffer a big soft ciss who at eighteen years of age has to sleep with his mother because he's scared of ghosts?'

Personally I saw her more as a Madame Defarge than an informer but whatever sins she fancied she'd committed in a past life, she was right. I was scared of ghosts. Bloody well petrified.

I'd been to see *The Exorcist* at the Futurist Cinema in Liverpool and had wound myself up on the journey home to such an extent that when I got in and scuttled up the stairs to bed I lay 'like a big soft ciss' unable to sleep, fully convinced that an abomination similar to what I'd seen earlier on the screen was lurking somewhere in the room waiting to pounce the moment I dared to close my eyes. Pulling the blankets over my head, I tried to blot out the image of that possessed child with the obscene black tongue and nice line in projectile vomiting.

My heart was thumping. I knew it was infantile to allow my imagination to conjure up these nightmares but I'm afraid common sense had been left behind at the Futurist and nothing could dissuade me from the idea that something unholy was in the room. I just knew it. I could feel it. An unspeakably evil entity from the very bowels of hell was hunched at the bottom of my bed, watching me silently through malevolent red eyes, biding its time before the inevitable attack. There was nothing else for it but to abandon ship, summon up the courage to brave the dark open space of the landing and make a mad dash for the safe harbour of my mother's bed. I took a deep breath, closed my eyes and charged, leaping into the bed beside her. Not a wise move.

'Jesus, Mary and Joseph!' she screamed, waking up most of Tranmere, 'do you want to give me another heart attack?'

Quite rightly outraged at this unwelcome intrusion, she began belting me with her library book and lashing out with her feet as she tried to kick me out of bed. Dodging the blows from a large-print Jean Plaidy I attempted to explain my peculiar behaviour, hoping that she'd show a bit of mercy. She was having none of it.

'Well, serves you right,' she crowed, suddenly remembering to keep her voice down to a respectable level in case Dot-Next-Door heard her, 'going to see such rubbish when you know full well that the Pope himself has condemned it. You reap what you sow, my lad. You can't expect to get a good night's sleep when you mess around with the devil, you know.'

She was chuckling to herself as she leaned out of the bed to drop her library book on to the floor, pausing to squint at the travel alarm clock on the cabinet beside her.

'It's gone midnight, you big fool,' she yawned, attempting another jab at me with her foot. 'And if you think you're lying in my bed stinking the place out with the smell of fags and that pappy-poo you've squirted yourself with then you've another think coming, mate.'

'It's Musk.' I'd given up on the Aqua Manda after Aunty Chrissie had sniffed the fruit bowl, complaining that she could smell a rotten orange.

'More like Muck, you mean. Go on, sling your hook, you're making the place smell like a whore's garret.'

I lay on my back resignedly folding my arms across my chest as I listened to her prattle on. I was at her mercy: it was either stay here with my ma or face Linda Blair hiding under the bed with a host of incubi and succubi next door. Linda Blair was beginning to look like the hot favourite.

'People have become possessed by demons after sitting through that filth, you know,' she went on, warming to her theme. 'Mind you, not that there's much room left inside your soul for any more of Lucifer's henchmen, the place must be chock-a-block by now.'

She was enjoying herself, wringing every last drop that she could get out of the situation.

'You want to get yourself down to church instead of sitting in picture houses that show films that are not only blasphemous but downright pornographic.'

'It wasn't pornographic.'

'Not pornogra . . .' she spluttered, raising her voice a couple of octaves. 'Well then, kindly tell me what you'd call the sight of a young girl effing and blinding and shoving a holy crucifix up her you-know-what?'

Her outraged face was shiny from the use of one of Avon's night-time preparations and her hair was wrapped carelessly in a chiffon headscarf, with a blue plastic roller that had been randomly attached to a strand of hair poking out in front. She never slept with the curtains drawn or the door closed. Both were always left wide open, not that the curtains would have been of much use to block out the light if she'd bothered; they were made of thin fibreglass and failed to meet in the middle by a good six inches. She'd bought them off the peg in Birkenhead Market to replace the heavier ones that kept the sun out when my dad was on nights and trying to sleep during the day, but she'd got the measurements wrong. However, since she quite liked the 'mod' design (black squares and oblongs on a turquoise background) she'd kept them.

'I'll have to take another Valium now,' she snapped. 'Me other one's worn off thanks to you waking me up, you know I haven't slept well since your father died.'

My father had been dead six months. My mother had been rushed to hospital after suffering a near-fatal heart attack and my father, on being told by the doctor that there wasn't much chance that she'd survive, had had one himself and died that night. On the day of his funeral my mother, still seriously ill and forbidden by the doctors to make the journey to Landican Cemetery to bury her husband, lay numb with shock in her hospital bed, her sister Chrissie tight-lipped and grim-faced in a chair beside her. His funeral had been quite an affair. St Werburgh's church was packed to the rafters, the Knights of St Columba had turned out in force as had half of Ireland, or so it seemed, and it was touching to see so many of the elderly people he'd visited regularly over the years as a Knight present as well.

After the funeral I'd gone to live with the aunties, Annie and Chrissie, in Prenton, not being trusted to live on my own in 23 Holly Grove. I didn't object as I no longer cared, going about my daily business like an automaton. My clubbing days were behind me, my mood too bleak to even begin to contemplate a night out at Sadie's or the Bear's Paw. I had a peculiar yet, to my mind, satisfactory sensation that I was fading, all colour and light slowly bleeding away from me until I was nothing more than a grey shadow, a monochrome ghost that would very soon evaporate into thin air.

My boss, Joe Black at the Magistrates' Courts, must have noticed that something was wrong, judging by the number of times he called me into his office to ask if everything was OK. He'd been particularly solicitous since my father's death and was aware of rumours that I'd got a woman in the Court Collecting Office pregnant.

'You're going around with the weight of the world on your shoulders, lad,' he said, 'and I find it unsettling that these days I always know where you are. I no longer have to tell you to stop chattering and get on with your work. It's so not like you, Paul, you seem to have lost your spark, so if there's anything at all, anything that you want to get off your chest, you know you can always talk to me. I'm pretty unshockable, you know.'

I contemplated this invitation to look upon Joe's office as the confessional for a moment before uncharacteristically deciding to spill the beans, so to speak.

'Well . . .' I started slow, 'I know my mum, who's still in hospital, blames me for my dad's heart attack and subsequent death, as does my aunty Chrissie, other members of the family and indeed myself. The rumours doing the rounds are all true. Diane from the Court Collecting Office is pregnant and I'm the father.'

'Yes, I was aware of the situation,' he said, sitting back in his chair and taking his glasses off while he had a think. 'Have you two any intention of getting married?'

'No, Mr Black, there's no chance of that happening. You see, I'm . . . erm . . . well, I'm gay.'

You know that noise that Catherine Tate's Nan character makes? A sort of *Huuup!* Well, that perfectly describes the sound that Joe made on hearing that piece of information. He sat forward smartly in his chair and suddenly became totally preoccupied with the task of polishing his glasses with the end of his tie.

'I'll get back to work then, thanks for the chat.'

'Yes, yes, you do that.'

Poor Joe, well, he did offer a sympathetic ear for me to offload my woes into.

My mother was in hospital for quite some time. Before returning home she spent a few weeks convalescing at Arrowe Hall, a beautiful mansion in the middle of Arrowe park. When she was finally discharged she stayed with Annie and Chrissie, and living under the same roof as the three of them was akin to sharing lodgings with the three witches from the Scottish play that a superstitious nature inherited from the same three women forbids me to name. My mother's grief had turned to fury and it felt as though I'd become her whipping boy. Chrissie was as brittle as spun sugar and snappier than a turtle with toothache and it was best to try and keep out of her way, while Aunty Anne sat quietly reading her *Sunday Post* engulfed in a pervading cloud of doom. Butlin's it wasn't but however uncomfortable and tense the atmosphere became at times it was infinitely preferable to going back to Holly Grove and being alone with my ma.

When she finally felt it was time to go home I tried desperately to be the model son, even going so far as to decorate the small front bedroom a somnolent shade of lilac to match a poster I'd bought in a trendy new shop on Borough Road. I discovered as I lashed emulsion haphazardly around the walls that painting and decorating wasn't my forte – it probably took less time to paint the ceiling of the Sistine Chapel than it did that tiny bedroom – nevertheless my mother was delighted with it, remarking that the shade reminded her of Lent. Inspired by my bout of home improvement, she took a trip to this trendy little shop that I was forever singing the praises of to buy a very modern white cabinet for the middle room on which she arranged a few iridescent orange fruit dishes and plates – all that was left of a Carnival Ware tea set my uncle Hal had brought back from Hong Kong – a plastic statue of Our Lady filled with Lourdes water and her pots of medication ('me tablets') in a neat little line.

We were getting on better now. At first I could do no right and we fought constantly until eventually with the passing of time we settled into an uneasy truce, her anger finally abating as gradually she began to search for some form of normality and adapt to life without my father. Now here we were in bed together. The last time I'd done this I was a small boy on New Year's Eve, listening to the ships on the river sounding their foghorns to welcome in the new year. It was a reassuring yet melancholy sound to my young ears as I drifted off to sleep dreaming of Popeye. Nowadays the river was a lot quieter, the only foghorn to be heard coming from the battleship lying next to me.

She yawned violently. 'You'll never guess who I bumped into in Birkenhead Market,' she said, recovering from the ferocity of the yawn and gently smacking her lips.

'Who?'

'Go on, guess.'

'I can't be bothered, Mam. Who?'

'That's your trouble, you can't be bothered. Well, I'll tell you who it was. It was Eileen Henshaw.'

* * *

Eileen Henshaw and her husband George had run the local grocers-cum-newsagent for as long as I could remember. I must have gone in that shop every day of my life, running messages for my ma and various neighbours. The interior of their shop was as familiar as my own front room and I envied their son, who I imagined had access to an unlimited sweet and comic supply – except for an educational one called *Look and Learn* which bored me to tears.

Eileen was extremely proud of her son and would sing his praises in the shop, much to my ma's annoyance. At the age of eight, with the confidence born of a precocious brat, I naturally assumed that every adult I came into contact with would fall instantly in love with me. If I sensed that I didn't quite have them in the bag then there was a range of tricks up my sleeve to bedazzle and charm . . . that beautiful smile, that face of a cheeky angel. How could the suckers resist? Eileen could, and did. She was impervious to my charms, probably because each time she looked at me she saw my ma's perpetually overdue paper bill.

I can instantly recall those excruciating moments spent squirming in front of the refrigerated counter while Eileen enquired in a voice that could be heard down in Cammell Laird's workshop if my mother had any intention of paying her paper bill in the near future. My mother was not very good when it came to managing money. It slipped through her fingers like water, not that there was an abundance of it in the first place. She could never seem to balance the books and, as she admitted herself, 'As soon as I've got me wages off your dad and in me purse it vanishes like fairy gold.' Consequently the paper bill at Henshaw's slowly mounted up until eventually Eileen, quite justifiably, snapped and felt compelled to tell me to pass on a reminder of the outstanding debt to my mother. At the time I'd crawl out of the shop, all eyes upon me, or so I imagined, my face burning with shame, to convey Eileen's message to my ma. It would have an effect on her similar to lighting the blue touch paper on an atomic bomb.

As a means of revenge my mother, on the occasions when her paper bill was up to date, meaning that she could enter the shop in the knowledge that she was, albeit temporarily, in the black, would slyly make disparaging remarks about George's succulent home-boiled ham and roast beef. Pointing towards the offending objects and sniffing disdainfully, she would enquire of Eileen, 'Is that ham fresh?'

The gauntlet thrown down, Eileen would take up the challenge and a gentle battle of eyebrows arched and teeth clenched would commence. There was no love lost between them, particularly after I was sacked from my job as their paper boy. When I broke that news to my ma, she stood at the kitchen stove like Eleanor of Aquitaine with a chip pan, furiously shaking it as she ranted. Eventually there was nothing left of the crinkle-cut chips inside but cremated splinters that took the roof of your mouth off even though you'd softened the blow by slathering them in Daddie's Sauce and vinegar and then wrapping them inside half a slice of buttered Mother's Pride.

'She was sympathetic about your dad, said how sorry she was,' she said quietly. 'We had quite a nice chat.'

She lay on her side with her back to me, thinking and looking up at the window.

'She's a decent woman, Eileen Henshaw,' she said after a moment. 'Grafted hard every day of her life running that shop.' She sighed long and deep before picking up the thread again. 'And I don't bloody blame her for sacking you as her paper lad when I think about it now,' she added. 'That could have been a job for life if you'd played your cards right.'

I nearly fell out of the bed. Was I hearing clearly? Could my mother actually be showering Eileen Henshaw, the very same woman who had been her sparring partner since my time began, with such glowing and tender accolades? Even taking her side and agreeing with her? Yes, she could and she was, and, being as contrary as the rich woman's cat, she did.

'A job for life? A paper boy?' I sat up and stared at her, wondering if she could possibly mean what she'd just said and if she did then I was having her certified.

'You know what I'm getting at. A job you could've had until you grew up and got a proper job ... whenever that great day is finally going to dawn.'

I lay down, not wishing to reply to this in case it provoked further discussion on the highly contentious matter of the 'career', ruminating instead over how my dad's death seemed to have healed old wounds between her and some of her fellow warhorses. Arriving home from work not long after we'd moved back into Holly Grove, I'd found Rose Long, our next-door-but-one neighbour and who my ma had fought the odd battle with over the years, washing a cup at the kitchen sink.

'Before you take your coat off,' she said authoritatively, putting her hand up like a border cop, 'run up the shop and get your mam a pint of milk, she's nearly run out, and while you're there get a bit of something to make a butty with.'

I came back bearing the milk and a quarter of corned beef for the butty to find Rose and my ma, old grievances and rows discreetly put behind them like the cushions on the sofa on which both ladies now sat, enjoying their tea and each other's reminiscences as they played 'remember when'.

'Remember when your tortoise went missing, Rose?'

'Remember when your Paul went missing?'

'I got some corned beef,' I said lamely, in the vain hope of getting a word in, and was acknowledged with a brief nod of both women's heads.

'Remember that terrible air raid when the bomb went off and half a ton of soot came down the chimney and covered your Sheila and Brendan in their cots?' Rose said cheerily.

'They looked like a pair of Al Jolsons,' my ma replied, laughing. 'but remember the mess! Soot everywhere.'

'Yes, but we soon got it cleared up in the end,' Rose said, getting up. 'Where's that corned beef? I'll make your mam a little butty.'

'It's all right, Rose, I can do that,' my mother said, pulling herself up off the sofa.

'No you won't, Molly, you just stay where you are, you've just had a bloody heart attack.' Talk about the Friendly Ladies Society. I took a sly look at my ma's face for any signs of annoyance or resentment that Rose had taken charge and was in her kitchen, but there was not a trace. Instead she drank her tea contentedly and continued her conversation with Rose by shouting from the sofa.

'There's a bit of piccalilli in the cupboard, Rose. If you fancy it. Help yourself.'

Making my excuses I went upstairs for a quick kip, leaving them to it.

As I was drifting off I heard Rose saying as she left, 'I'll get you those few messages in the morning and if you want anything – anything at all – then give me a shout or send him round.' I could hear lots of 'thanks', and 'take care' as I dozed off. Curiouser and curiouser . . . They'd known each other for a lifetime, during which there'd been many a battle fought, accompanied by all the usual intrigues, rows and petty vendettas that can escalate out of all proportion, inflaming the blood dangerously to feudal levels. One wrong word or selfish act, one whiff that you were the subject of doorstep gossip or being suddenly 'blanked' in the street or given a look that could be interpreted as a dirty one and tempers would ignite and flare up, sweeping across doorsteps, hedges and backyard fences quicker than a bush fire.

Rose and her husband didn't get on particularly well with Dot, our next-door neighbour and her husband George. They never spoke except to row. My ma was very friendly with Dot but if Dot saw her speaking to Rose, however briefly, then Dot would blank her for a couple of days for what she considered to be an act of treachery. If Rose ever called to the house then Dot would send my ma into purdah. This would last until something interesting occurred and then you'd hear the familiar knock on the wall which meant 'quick, come round'. If Mary, who lived on the other side of us, appeared to be getting overly friendly, or 'thick' as my ma called it, with Rose and spent more time gossiping at the bottom of Rose's steps than was considered acceptable, then my ma would view Mary with deep suspicion and consequently blank her. Sometimes nobody spoke at all as everyone was busy blanking each other, as if an order of Carmelites who communicated by slamming doors and banging windows had taken over the Grove.

Reflecting on the past now, I realize just how much of an indelible imprint these uniquely different women left on me and how important a role they played in my impressionable formative years contributing enormously to the sense of security that I felt while growing up. I'll never forget Rose's homemade toffee apples when the entire Grove got together on bonfire night or when her dog gave birth to puppies or the caravan holidays in North Wales. I can taste Dot's roast potatoes now and hear her budgie reciting nursery rhymes and the memory of trips with Mary to the Plaza Cinema on Borough Road to see the latest James Bond 'fillum' is as vivid as if it were yesterday. It was in Mary's kitchen that I first had bread and dripping. Wild horses couldn't get me to eat dripping today but back then I'd happily wire into a doorstop of white bread smeared with the stuff while I listened to Mary's husband Frank telling me tales of his childhood as he shaved over the kitchen sink with a cut-throat razor.

Years later, when I eventually discovered the books of E. F. Benson, in particular his monstrous creations Mapp and Lucia, I realized just how much the day-to-day politics of Holly Grove paralleled Tilling, the domain of Benson's harpies. The ladies of Tilling went about their public business seemingly uninterested in the private affairs of their good friends and neighbours, and the same applied to the goodwives of Holly Grove. It was a different story behind closed doors. You'd find that the ears that feigned deafness on the street were now in all probability pressed against walls, and eyes that looked purposefully ahead, supposedly minding their own business, were now veiled behind a pair of net curtains, surveying their manor and their neighbours' affairs with the intensity of a hawk. As in most small working-class communities of the time, their lives became interwoven, as they argued, snubbed, laughed and cried with each other down the years. The first time I watched *Coronation Street* I was hooked as I could instantly relate to the characters. Why, didn't we have an Elsie and Dennis Tanner and a Hilda and

Ena and a Len Fairclough and Annie Walker on our own doorstep? Holly Grove was a daily soap opera in itself, one that ran for years until inevitably the original cast died, moved on or just vanished.

'You know that the ghost of some poor woman is said to haunt the Grove?' my mum said, a little inappropriately, I thought, considering I was clinging on to the bedclothes like an electrocuted cat.

'Who told you that?'

'It's true. Ask Rose Long if you don't believe me. These houses are built on the site of an old quarry, Davies Quarry I think it was called. Anyway, it was around the early 1900s and this poor woman, she lived just at the back in Holt Road. Well, her son went missing and believing that he'd fallen into the quarry she went round there looking for him, frantic the poor soul was, like a woman possessed.

'And? What happened then?'

'Well, if you'll stop interrupting, I'll tell you,' she snapped, momentarily dropping the funereal tones she'd adopted to tell her tale.

'As I was saying, she was demented and ran around the quarry screaming, "Cuthbert, Cuthbert".'

'Cuthbert?'

'Yes, Cuthbert. It was a very popular name in them days, like Cedric and Walter.'

'Have you been reading *The Beano*?'

'Don't talk daft. Anyway, she fell into the quarry. Broke her neck and died later that night in Birkenhead General. Ever since, folk have claimed to have seen her spirit, staring in the window at them, looking for her little boy,' she said, finishing this dramatic monologue with a theatrical shudder.

'Folk? What folk? Who are these people who are supposed to have seen her?'

'Lots of people. Mary, Dot, Rose Long, Aunty Chrissie. Proper doubting Thomas, aren't we?'

'Well, what happened to Cuthbert, then?'

'Oh, him. He was found alive and well and playing in Mersey Park, the little tinker. I think the woman's name was Ellen.'

Oh dear, she'd really succeeded in putting the heebie-jeebies up me now. I really wished I had the guts to go back to my own room but that was impossible at the moment as I knew in my heart of hearts that my bedroom – the same familiar room that my mother had decorated years earlier in violent shades of red and mustard to resemble Tara King of *The Avengers*' apartment – the room I'd slept in for all of my eighteen years, had for the time being turned into one of the portals of hell and was best left alone.

'Have you been taking drugs?'

'No, I haven't.'

'Then what has you so terrified? It's the DTs or Purple Hearts if you ask me.'

'You don't normally get delirium tremens from half a pint of cider, which by the way is all I've had tonight,' I told her, trying to muster what was left of my dignity.

'Oh, don't you now? You're very knowledgeable on the subject all of a sudden, aren't you?'

'And I certainly haven't taken the Tardis back to the sixties to get myself some Purple Hearts either.'

'Oh, haven't you now, Mr Smarty Arse?'

'No.'

'Then why are you behaving like a bloody great wet nelly then, too scared to sleep in your own bed?'

I had to agree with her, my display of childish terror was irrational behaviour even by my standards, but I didn't care. I wasn't moving if I could help it and thought it best to stay here with this she-devil rather than the one that had taken up residence next door.

'And I'll tell you something else,' my ma said, picking up where she'd left off earlier, 'since the Henshaws sold up and moved on you can't get a decent bit of boiled ham for love nor money.'

I sat up again, forgetting my fears momentarily to turn and look at her, amazed at her ability to switch from the ghost of Ellen to George Henshaw's boiled ham.

'Anyone can boil a ham,' she went on, 'but it requires great skill to do it properly and when all's said and done George Henshaw was a master of his craft. You won't taste boiled ham like his again in a hurry, more's the pity.'

I wanted to answer her but stunned confusion had rendered me momentarily speechless. It appeared that my father's death had softened her attitude towards everyone but me. I asked her what had brought on this change of heart towards George's ham and if she remembered the sniping matches she'd indulged in over the years with his wife.

'What are you talking about?' she asked, her voice rising towards the high dudgeon level. 'I was a valued customer of theirs for years, we got along fine, thank you very much,' adding, as if in proof of her loyalty, 'I was in their Christmas Club, for God's sake.

'I could just go for a nice slice of his ham right now, on a nice floury bap from Stubbs with a scrape of mustard and a nice cup of tea.' Everything was suddenly 'nice'. The two Valium must have kicked in.

'Run down and make a cup of tea, will you?' she pleaded,

turning over and heaving herself up on to a pillow. 'Go on, you've woke me up now good and proper, you bloody nuisance.'

I quickly reminded myself that the reason I was in my ma's bed in the first place was because I was terrified to sleep in my own in case *The Exorcist* got me. I was less terrified now, still scared, but at least my hair was no longer standing up on end. However, I didn't think I was quite brave enough to go downstairs and face the back kitchen just yet and considered suggesting we leave the cup of tea till the morning.

'Well, go on then,' she prompted. 'What are you waiting for? The dawn?'

'You don't want tea at this hour of the morning, surely?'

'I know why you won't go down and put the kettle on. You're scared, aren't you?'

'No.'

'You are! You're terrified, admit it.' She was like a cat with a mouse.

'I'm not.'

'Then kindly tell me what the bloody hell you're doing in my bed?'

'Shh, keep your voice down, Dot-Next-Door will hear you.' I didn't want her knowing I was sleeping with my mother.

'Well, honest to God,' she crowed, leaning across the bed and giving me a little shove, 'you should be ashamed of yourself at your age, scared of ghosts. Don't you know that the dead can't hurt you, it's the living you've got to worry about? Now get down those stairs and put the kettle on and mind out for Ellen.' Reluctantly I crept out of the room and felt for the landing light in the dark, holding my breath and resisting the urge to run for cover.

I could hear her laughing behind me. 'Wait till I ring our Annie first thing,' she cackled. 'Wait till I tell her about this bloody carry-on, disturbing your poor mother in the middle of the night, *who*, by the way, is still recovering from a heart attack in case you'd forgotten . . .'

I went for it and ran down the stairs, moving quickly into the front room and turning the light on as I went, not daring to look left or right as I made my way to our freezing kitchen.

By the light of the fluorescent tube that I normally hated but was now extremely grateful for, as it illuminated the tiny kitchen like a football pitch, I quickly filled the kettle, lit the gas and put it on to boil. So far I'd managed to avoid looking out the window and into the darkness of the back yard by busying myself with the complicated process of putting teabags into mugs and getting the milk out. But however hard I tried to free my mind of all matters spiritual, I couldn't ignore the unsettling feeling that I was being observed from the shadows of the yard – and then, typically, right on cue, the lights inexplicably went out, plunging the kitchen into darkness and rooting me to the spot, terror-stricken.

I was aware that the pounding sound I could hear was my heart furiously beating and the tidal wave of blood rushing to my ears, and as my eyes slowly became accustomed to the moonlight I could see to my horror that, quite clearly, something that looked very much like a face partially covered by a white caul was staring in at me. I screamed, or at least I opened my mouth but nothing seemed to come out. The ghost of Ellen might have mistaken me for 'The Scream' by Munch.

My jaw relaxed as it slowly began to dawn on me that the apparition that had me in such a state was not the ghost of Ellen but was in fact a tea towel hanging on the washing line. It was one that my ma had brought back from the Isle of Man and I'd mistaken the Laxey Wheel for a face. Fool, I told myself, get a grip, there's no such thing as ghosts . . .

What was that then? I distinctly heard it, there was no imagining the shuffling and scratching slowly approaching from behind. Unable to turn round and look behind me, I could hear something feeling its way at the top of the step that led down into the kitchen. The urge to scream and run was now overpowering, and yet I couldn't. I was still rooted to the spot with fear. I could hear it plainly now – a rush of breath from whatever it was that was hovering behind me, just audible above the blood pounding in my ears and the roar of the gas jets and the hiss of the kettle as it began to boil.

I swallowed hard. The noise I produced sounded as if I'd dropped a brick in a swamp. A voice suddenly came out of the darkness and I levitated at least three feet in the air

'Don't just stand there in the dark like one of Lewis's, you soft bugger,' the demon said through a yawn. 'Turn that kettle off and come in here and find me purse, the ten bob for the meter's run out.'

CHAPTER 2

Wine Lodges and Babies

SURPRISINGLY, AS IT IS NOT THE FAMILY TRADITION TO BE anything other than a little crabby first thing in the morning, my ma was in a party mood and having a smashing time as I passed her sat on the stairs, phone in hand, filling her sister Annie in on the night's shenanigans.

''ey up, Lazarus has just risen, Anne,' she remarked, laughing as I slithered past her, 'although he still looks half dead to me.'

It was good to hear her laugh again even if it was on me and just for that moment it felt like life was back to normal. I half expected to see my dad sat in his armchair studying his pools coupon. Taking my fags off the mantelpiece and lighting one, I sat on the sofa and stared at his empty chair. From out of the blue a mawkish verse that I'd read in the In Memoriam column of the *Liverpool Echo* came to mind:

> An empty chair,
> A silent prayer,
> Always wishing you were there.

I could hear it being recited by an old woman with a broad Scouse accent that had a slightly pious tone to it and I grinned in spite of everything as I slowly eased myself into the day, idly blowing plumes of smoke into the broad shaft of sunlight cutting across the room from the window. Listening to my mother chatting away cheerfully on the phone made me hope optimistically that she was learning at last to come to terms with her grief and allow the anger that she still felt deep inside to subside.

It was an anger that she directed full blast at me, a rage that spurted furiously and unexpectedly when the frustration, born out of the panic that came from the overwhelming realization that her loved one really was gone for good and would not be coming through the front door looking for his tea ever again, rose to the surface. She felt that my past skirmishes with the police and general tomcatting (as she put it) of late had contributed to the stress that had brought on the fatal coronary. I was inclined to agree with her. The burden of guilt that I was carrying on my back was growing heavier by the day as I quietly mourned the loss of my dad's reassuring presence.

For my mother his absence was still a raw gaping wound, and sometimes in the night I'd hear her sobbing in bed and calling out my father's name. I'd bury my head in the pillow to try and drown out her cries. It was the loneliest sound in the world.

I was slow and lazy that morning as I mooched sleepily out of the house and made my way down to Green Lane Station to catch a train to work. I'd eventually gone back to my own bed but hadn't slept very well and felt that a nice lie-in of, say, another ten hours wouldn't come amiss.

Walking slowly past what had been Henshaw's shop, I saw the windows were now empty, like an East German grocer's, the shelves bare apart from a few tins of soup dotted about here and there, reminding me of a mouth full of missing teeth. Normally I was used to moving swiftly past the shop in case the sight of me reminded Eileen of unpaid paper bills. But there was no Eileen in her white overall marking up papers, no George with a pencil behind his ear cutting a neat wedge out of a round of Cheshire cheese with a wire. They'd moved on and out of my life, as had their son, who had sat in the back room and was now, to quote my mother, 'doing well' and most likely holding down a fabulous job while I was off to do another day in Yates's Wine Lodge.

Everyone seemed to have moved on. Tony, my bosom pal from the Bear's Paw who had opened my eyes to the gay scene and introduced me to a slice of life that I had previously thought only existed in films, had been promoted by HM Customs and Excise and transferred to Southend. Friends from school were training to be nurses or learning a trade, some had married and settled down, others had simply vanished. And where was I? Eighteen years of age, living at home with my grieving mother, going nowhere fast and working in a wine lodge that was one of the roughest drinking holes in Liverpool for lousy pay and to cap it all, the cherry on top of the steaming, stinking mound of dog doo-doo that currently represented my life, there was A Baby on The Way. Great, just what I wanted. In short, I was up shit creek without a paddle. But even though my prospects didn't look that good there was still a trace of optimism lurking in the background leading me hopefully to believe that opportunity was waiting somewhere in the wings.

I'd resigned from the Magistrates' Courts. I wasn't really

cut out to be a trainee court clerk, and like every other job I'd had so far the wage wasn't up to much and besides, I was bored with it all and it showed. A few of the magistrates had complained about my appearance, in front of a packed court-room. The stipendiary magistrate had leaned over the bench to stare in disbelief at my red corduroy jacket and pink tie and enquired sarcastically if my job description had read court clerk or court jester. It was a case of jump now or wait to be pushed, so I did the decent thing and handed in my resignation to my long-suffering boss. It was a relief for both of us. I'd gone back to my old ways, my timekeeping was atrocious and I frequently skived off and went missing in the endless tunnels that ran from the back of the courts and seem-ingly went on for miles. They were full of ancient court ledgers filled with charge sheets in which a long-dead clerk had recorded the past crimes and misdemeanours of Merseyside in a beautiful copperplate hand. 'Kathleen Kelly. Fined five shillings for allowing her chimney to catch fire.'

Another reason I was keen to leave the courts was the gossip going around about Diane's pregnancy. We'd become the topic of much speculation in the office and I wanted out. I wasn't really bothered about what job I did just as long as I got one and seeing that Yates's Wine Lodge in Moorfields, just around the corner from the courts, was looking for a bar-man I'd applied for the job.

The wine lodges of the seventies were bleak, basically empty halls with bare walls and wooden floors and a few chairs and tables dotted about. A long high bar ran the length of the room with four enormous wooden barrels behind con-taining the various wines and sherries that were served to the customers in 'docks' – plastic beakers as opposed to glasses. Diane and I would frequently pop in, thinking it was camp to knock back a couple of large Aussie whites before hitting the clubs, living life a little dangerously, or so we thought, by drinking in a Yates. It's not unfair to say that Yates's wine lodges had the reputation for being rough, last chance saloons frequented by alcoholics and hardened drinkers who could get hammered on the potent wine at not too much expense, the Moorfields lodge was considered one of the roughest.

This establishment was run by Molly and her sister Jean, the latter deeply suspicious when I offered my services as Yates's new barman. She couldn't comprehend why I would want to leave a 'respectable' job in the Magistrates' Courts for one behind the bar in a wine lodge and told me to come back when her sister was in. I duly returned the next day to meet her and was interviewed by a woman with coal-black ringlets and a face covered in a deep olive pan-stick. She wore a plain black dress and a lot of old gold rings and bracelets with a pair of bomb-shaped heavy gold earrings that swung back and forth from her lobes each time she took a pull of one of the many fags that she smoked. She had a hacking cough that made the building shake and I liked her on sight, a cross between Anna Magnani and Edith Piaf, laid-back and worldly wise. The interview was brief and informal and I managed to make her laugh with a few tales about life working in number three court and the regular clientele of winos and prozzies who passed through its doors.

'You won't find it much different working here then, lad,' she croaked. 'Start on Saturday morning, half nine prompt and we'll see how you go.'

And so, after a very boozy leaving do, I said goodbye to a career in law on Friday evening and hello to a life in the licensing trade behind the bar of Yates's on the Saturday morning, some of the bemused patrons asking if I knew there was a fellah working in the Magistrates who was a dead ringer for me. Predictably, my mother went crazy when she found out about my change of employment and 'took to her bed', demanding to know why I was hell-bent on breaking her heart.

Molly's sister Jean was tall and slim with eyes like a hawk and seemed quite imperious until you got to know her, when she'd give you a ciggy and chat with you at the end of the bar. I only ever saw her lose her cool when Wally the rat-catcher visited, a born comic with a purple face and a club foot who came by in an official capacity once a month. He'd brought a brace of drunken rats up from the cellar, holding his catch aloft by their tails before slapping them down on the bar, sending Jean and the rest of the women screaming out into the street, leaving Pete the barman unsure if he should stay with the grinning Wally and his inebriated vermin or risk a dent to his masculine pride and leg it after the women. It was no contest for me. I was the first one out of the building.

Every morning the floor was religiously swept out and mopped, the toilets scoured with bleach until the air made your eyes sting and the bar tops, with what little brass there was, polished. Not that there was much varnish left on the bar top as it had supposedly been eaten away over the years by the spillage of Yates's fine Australian white. By the time Jean was satisfied that the place was up to her high standards, the air was 95 per cent Jeyes Fluid and 5 per cent oxygen. Yates's Wine Lodge, Moorfields, might have looked bleak but its startling cleanliness was a testimony to the powers of industrial-strength detergents and a lot of elbow grease, and had the occasion arisen we could have performed open-heart surgery on the bar top without any risk of infection to the patient.

Before the doors were opened to the public I was sent out to a tiny café on Dale Street to buy the crusty cobs filled with chips for our mid-morning break. These were washed down with mugs of Peggy's super-strength tea and after a quick fag the doors would be opened and the first of our punters would trickle in for their mid-morning livener. Yates's customers were a real mixed bag. As in any pub there were a few lairy arseholes, but on the whole the majority of the punters were agreeable. I had my favourite alcoholics. An extremely pleasant and highly intelligent middle-aged woman who had the misfortune to teach in a school with a notorious reputation, would arrive promptly each evening at five thirty and proceed to drink her way through one of the barrels of white until by closing time, when her lips had turned blue, she would be having a heated argument with herself. A smart city type, who although he was a regular rarely spoke to anyone except to furtively order his wine, would become extremely agitated at the approach of closing time, knocking back large docks of white wine with a whisky chaser as if Prohibition was about to be enforced. I worried about him and the teacher and used to wonder what sort of home life they went back to each night, if any at all, until Jean would tell me not to be so bloody soft and get them docks washed.

The Irish workmen who were building the new metro station over the road spent their wages across the bar each night, skilfully avoiding the clutches of Tattoo Pat and Taxi Annie, two geriatric working girls so named because the former's body was rumoured to be a mass of tattoos, ranging from crude Indian ink lettering to elaborate professional jobs, and the latter as she allegedly took care of her punters in the back of a cab. Not that either of them had witnessed that many eager customers beating a path to their red-lit doors in

31

recent years, but like the troupers they were they carried on regardless, prowling the pubs and the streets for prospective and hopefully none too picky clients. Leaning on the bar half pissed, they'd mourn the good old days when pickings were rich, concluding that business was slack for professionals like themselves because 'too many friggin' scrubbers were giving it away free'. I'd nod sympathetically, politely ignoring their advancing years and grubby appearance.

Annie, with her frizzy ginger hair stuffed under a hand-knitted tartan tam-o'-shanter, probably wouldn't see seventy again and put me in mind of Super Gran, while Pat, with her greasy black locks, straight as a yard of pump water, pulled back severely from her waxen face and held in place by two hair clips, had a look all of her own that said 'I've just come back from a funeral'. Indeed, she could've easily passed for the corpse. Her usual ensemble consisted of a strangely perverse 1950s black gaberdine mac, shiny with age, which she wore buttoned up to the neck with a little black beret gripped to the back of her head. Ed D. Wood, the director/writer responsible for gems such as *Plan 9 from Outer Space*, would've loved Pat. They certainly fascinated me, these two old brasses. Women like that always have and the little snippets of their conversations that I'd catch I'd relate back to Molly, perched on a stool at the end of the bar with a mug of tea and a fag, studying the racing page.

I enjoyed my time at Yates's. It might have had a reputation for being dog rough but in my six months working there I only ever witnessed one fight. Even so, on slow days I'd lean across the bar and gaze out of the open door at people passing by on the street outside and couldn't help thinking that maybe I really had missed the boat.

I still worked the occasional night at the Bear's Paw. I'd

given up my job behind the bar after my father died, but strapped for cash as always I'd asked Gordon, the owner, to take me back on. He let me have a few weekends, even allowing me to start late as I didn't get out of Yates's till gone eleven. I was grateful for the work but secretly not happy to be back pulling pints behind the bar; as usual, I wanted to be out front drinking them with my mates.

One of my favourites was a student from Plymouth, where he had been known as David but had been rechristened Nina la Roche since his arrival in Liverpool. He was as tall and gangly as a beanstalk, rapier thin. Trailing scarves and waving arms covered in bangles, he would stand on his toes in his wooden clogs like a giant praying mantis and frighten the 'straight' queens off the dance floor. He rented one large room in an eccentric old household on Canning Street and you never knew which one of his many personas would answer the door. Sometimes he was a member of the Russian aristocracy and, answering the door first as the maid, he would tell you to wait in the hall, and then rush into his room to prepare himself for the role of a Romanov princess.

'Come in,' he would shout imperiously after what he considered a respectable passage of time and I'd enter to find him draped across his chaise longue, engulfed in shawls and with a papier-mâché sculpture belonging to his landlady, Helen, on his head that we'd nicknamed the Conch. 'What makes you think you are suitable for the position of personal maid? Do you speak Russian and Japanese?' And the game would begin. Most of the time when he wasn't being Russian or a ballet mistress we'd eat his homemade spaghetti bolognese, drink cider and dance like maniacs to his collection of 78 LPs.

*

33

It's not true that pulling pints gives you the advantage of pulling customers. Most of the customers hardly even notice you; they just want to get their drinks in and return to their mates. Well, that was more or less the case for me anyway. Choices of romance were limited to the dregs and drunks who were left hanging around at closing time as I went round the tables collecting the empties. Needless to say I preferred the long wait for the bus that went through the Mersey Tunnel to a tail home with any of that lot even though it meant not getting home till the early hours of the morning. I'd gingerly slide my key into the front-door lock and slowly, ever so slowly, open it, taking care that it didn't stick and make the knocker rattle so as not to disturb my ma. Like Buzz Aldrin landing on the moon every move was done in slow motion, barely hovering over the stairs, taking infinite care to avoid the bottom two that creaked and hardly daring to breathe all the while in case I should wake the Kraken, which I invariably did.

'Where've you been till three in the morning? Out tom-catting it?'

'No, I've been working, Mam. Go back to sleep.'

'I'd like to know what kind of work keeps you out till this hour of the morning, nothing respectable that's for sure. I wish you'd go and find yourself digs instead of creepin' in here like Marley's Ghost at all hours. There's a nice slice of beef in the fridge if your hungry.'

After Diane's phone call, that hateful morning after my father died, to announce the unwelcome news that I was going to be a father, I sat on the stairs unable to comprehend the enormity of what was happening to me. I had no idea what to do but an increasing sense of panic told me that I had to get out of the house. It was still fairly early and I had no idea where I was going. I headed off across the park, stunned by the way my life had been turned upside down in a matter of hours, walking around in a daze asking myself a thousand questions.

Top of the list was 'How the bloody hell am I going to explain this one to my mother?' I felt sick at the mess I was in, and dry retched on what was probably the twentieth fag I'd smoked that morning. This was it. Life over. The end of my world as I knew it. Sitting on what was left of a bench I weighed up my situation. Dad dead, mother seriously ill in hospital, and to cap it all I'm about to be saddled with a baby – a piece of news that I really could've done without, especially on today of all days.

For a moment I contemplated 'doing a runner', following a white rabbit who would lead me down a hole, vanishing forever from my increasingly complicated life, or curling up in a ball somewhere and going to sleep, pretending none of this had ever happened.

I thought about my father and my devastated mother and the tears came again.

Oh, the sheer hopelessness of it all. And yet I knew deep down, no matter what my tears, that I'd never be able to run away as, apart from a genuine affection for Diane, good old guilt would step in the way and prevent me from doing so. No, I'd stay and face the music. It was the first sensible solution to my problems that had entered my head that morning and I felt instantly more relaxed for it.

Lighting up yet another cigarette, I watched as a man crossed by the children's swings, a canvas bag swinging from his shoulder that almost certainly contained his 'carry out' – a lunchtime meal of cheese or egg sandwiches and a flask of tea – no doubt lovingly prepared by his wife this morning.

An alarming thought sent me panicking again as I watched him vanish down the hill and in the direction of Cammel Laird.

Jesus tonight! What if I was expected to do the decent thing and marry Diane? No, that was definitely out of the question. I could see us, unhappily married and living in her flat in Bootle, pushing a pram around Stanley Park, skint and miserable and hating each other as we played Mummy and Daddy for the baby's sake, a baby I'd bitterly resent.

The notion that I would be a father in nine months' time did nothing to awaken any paternal urges that might be lying dormant. I loved kids, I'd been ecstatic when I first became an uncle and was never away from my sister's house. I'd spend a good part of my wages each week on books and toys for my nephews and nieces and had happily babysat nearly every weekend. I was crazy for them, yet the idea of having one of my own did not appeal in the slightest. Maybe I'd change my mind when I saw it, I thought. I might just fall instantly in love with it, but then again I just might not. As for a full-time relationship, should I give it a go? Millions of others do it, I thought, so why not me and Diane? Probably something to do with the fact that I was gay and saw Diane more as a friend than a lover. No, it just wouldn't work and I was determined to 'have it out' when we met up the next day in Liverpool, sitting at an out-of-the-way table in the Lisbon pub to discuss what we were going do.

Diane was as shell-shocked as me at the news she was going to have a baby as she'd foolishly believed that it was impossible for her to conceive. I was too naive to believe otherwise. Ha. If only I'd listened to my aunty Chrissie's warning to make sure that I always put a rubber on it. Having sowed my wild oats I'd prayed for crop failure, as some old drag queen once said, but my prayers had obviously fallen on deaf ears as the bloody crops had gone and flourished this year.

'Are you absolutely sure the baby's mine?' I blurted out.

'Of course it's yours. There's been nobody else. Cheeky sod.'

A lad came down the steps carrying a wicker basket on his head and began moving amongst the tables, shouting, 'Prawns, cockles, whelks.'

'You don't want to get married or anything, do you?' I asked her hesitantly after the seafood seller had passed by.

'No, I don't,' she replied, a little too quickly for my liking. 'What do you think I am? Mad?'

'That's all right then. In that case are you having ...'

'No, I'm not having an abortion!'

'Who mentioned abortions? I was only going to ask if you where having another drink.'

And so on 16 May 1974 I became a father.

I rang the hospital as soon as I got into work.

'Can I ask who's calling?'

I hesitated before replying, 'I'm the . . . er . . . father.'

It sounded strange admitting to a complete stranger that I was the father as so far I'd kept the news of impending fatherhood to myself. My mother had no idea. Ignorance is bliss was my maxim as far as she was concerned. My sister Sheila was about to drop her fifth child and thankfully her constant visits with the children had kept my ma preoccupied and her suspicious mind off me. If there was one thing my mother worshipped above all else it was her grandchildren.

There was a woman at the Citizens Advice Bureau I'd spent an hour with, pouring my confused heart out to her in her little office in Hamilton Square. She was sympathetic and very kind but in the end she was unable to tell me anything that I didn't already know. I was grateful to her though, then and now, but failed to keep my promise to stay in touch and let her know what the sex of the baby was. She knows now if she's reading this.

'Mother and baby are doing well.'

'Great. Can you tell me what she had?'

'A little girl.'

Well, it would hardly be a six-footer, would it, I wanted to say but chose not to. Instead I answered flatly, 'Oh, that's nice,' my tone of voice lacking any conviction or enthusiasm whatsoever.

'You can visit any time after lunch . . . and oh, congratulations,' she said somewhat doubtfully as I thanked her and placed the phone slowly back on the receiver, returning to the bar unsure of just how I should be reacting to this news. Worried and scared were the top notes, but surprisingly there was also a slight whiff of pride lurking in the background. Maybe I'd enjoy being a daddy after all? Unable to resist the urge to break the news to someone, I told Jean.

'I'm a father, Jean.'

'You're a what?' she asked, slightly irritated at being bothered by what she considered nonsense. I tried to explain the saga as she poured wine from a tap in the barrel into a dock.

'You mean you've got a girl into trouble.' She shook her head as she tried to make sense of it, and after serving her customer went off to tell Molly, who was sat as usual at the end of the bar perusing the *Echo*.

'Bloody fool' was Molly's only comment, and she didn't even bother to look up from her paper. She let me go early though to visit mother and child. 'Here,' she said as I was leaving, pushing a tenner into my hand, 'a bit of luck for the baby. You're going to need it, lad.'

A smiling nurse showed me into a shiny ward where Diane lay in the middle bed of a row of three, beside which the tiny newborn babies lay in their cots. Nervously approaching the cot next to Diane's bed, I felt the blood rush to my cheeks as I became conscious that the eyes of all the new mothers and nurses in the ward were on me. All of them were waiting to get a kick out of seeing a young father's reaction to the first sight of his newborn child.

Diane, sitting on the bed, her face flushing a bright red to equal mine, was just as embarrassed by the situation as I was. She quickly said, 'Why don't you have a look at her?' I noticed she avoided my eyes as she spoke.

Leaning over the crib I tried to adopt the *Little House on the Prairie* approach as was obviously expected of me by the mums. Look at baby, look up and around at the eager faces, my own face a mask of incredulous joy, pick baby up and examine it closely, cradling it gently and making suitable cooing noises to convey a first greeting to the child, then kiss mother tenderly on the forehead to an audience of blissed-out women. Tears optional.

'You're looking at the wrong baby, mate. That one's mine, yours is over there.' The kid's mother was pointing to a cot on the other side of Di's bed. This went down a treat with the mums and nurses, setting them off screaming with laughter and me scuttling over to take a peep at my own child, feeling more like Carabosse than a loving father.

'Well, what do you think?' Diane asked, still unable to look at me.

I wasn't sure what to think. Amazed? Confused? Or just

nothing? Could this minuscule object with the scrunched-up face and the tight little fists really be my own flesh and blood? I kept waiting, hoping for a rush of fatherly love as I lifted her nervously out of the cot. She was a sweet little thing, yet I felt distant. I was ashamed of myself. What was wrong with me? Didn't I come from a loving, stable family? My father had been an excellent role model and yet here I was, a false grin fixed firmly on my face, hoping that it would mask my true inner feelings as I stared with blank eyes down at this cuckoo in my nest. The answer is clear to me now. I was a very immature and scared teenager who didn't want the responsibility of a child – simple, but back then I thought myself to be unnatural, an abomination against the laws of nature, a freak who was incapable of bonding with his own daughter, heaping more shovelfuls of guilt into that already overloaded sack that I seemed to be permanently carrying around. I remember tentatively sniffing her scalp. She smelled nice although it has to be said that all babies smell the same really, a mixture of milk, sick and Johnson's Baby Powder – providing the heart-stopping stench of a full nappy doesn't assault your nostrils first.

'Why are you sniffing her?' Diane asked.

'I don't know, it's obviously a primeval instinct to react this way, inhaling the scent of your child to see if you recognize it.'

'Oh, for God's sake, and do you?'

'Not particularly.'

I felt awkward and wished that this moment could've been a private one. No mothers, nurses or Diane gawping at me, eagerly waiting to see my reaction. Why couldn't it be just me and the baby left on our own for a while to quietly get to know each other during these important first moments?

'Well, what do you think?' Diane asked again, a note of anxiety in her voice. I did my duty and grinned at the mums, kissed Diane clumsily, telling her unconvincingly that the baby was beautiful before quickly handing her over as she'd woken up and was starting to cry.

'She wants her feed,' Diane said, taking her off me.

No she doesn't, I thought. She knows, she sensed it. I don't know what to do with her.

When the time came for them to leave hospital I collected them both and we went back to Diane's flat on the bus.

I stayed over those first few days and nights. Sharon cried non-stop, an exhausted Diane seemed to be forever pressing the baby on me, eager that I got to know my daughter, but every time I went near her she screamed the place down. She reckons today that the reason she cried for such long periods was down to croup, but back then I was convinced she could sense my fears.

Diane and I were used to spending long periods together and on the whole we would have a good time. Not surprisingly, the arrival of the baby put a load of new stresses on our relationship and I was now with her not because I wanted to be, but out of a begrudged sense of duty. Nevertheless, while we may have had our differences (wow, and that's the understatement of the year) for the moment we were still good friends.

When the baby was old enough we took her to be registered. There had been some dispute between us over a suitable name. I wanted to call her Gypsy, Diane had other ideas and understandably put her foot down, adamant that she was to be called Sharon, which I thought was boring.

'I can just hear you,' I sneered. '"Sharrrin, gerrin fer ya tea."'

'I don't talk like that as well you know and I don't care what you say, I'm not calling her Gypsy, it sounds like a poodle's name.'

So Sharon it was but as a consolation prize I was allowed to pick her middle name, providing it was sensible. I chose Lee, whether it was after Lee Remick, who I had the hots for at the time, or Gypsy Rose Lee I can't really remember.

Diane could make a pound stretch all week if she had to; she was thrifty and put money aside for that rainy day. Since she'd been hit by a tsunami, she quite rightly worried about her future finances. I was an idiot with money. Even though I religiously handed over my housekeeping each Friday to my ma out of my wages, the rest would be spent by midweek and I'd end up borrowing it back. Diane wanted to come to some sort of legal arrangement to make sure I contributed to Sharon's care, and without hesitating I agreed. She took out an affiliation order against me and I was summoned to appear along with Diane at Bootle Magistrates' Court.

Stupidly I was under the misapprehension that we'd sit around a table with a kindly member of the legal profession and have a friendly discussion until both parties reached an amicable agreement. Instead I found myself in the dock again, standing in front of an elderly female magistrate who, judging by the look she was giving me over her pince-nez, had a very low opinion of errant fathers who evaded their duties. Even though I'd gone to court voluntarily I felt as if I were on trial. Obviously in Madame Beak's jaded eyes I was just another low-life scally, dragged before the courts to be forced to contribute to his child's upkeep.

Diane sat opposite me holding the baby in her arms, looking suitably pathetic, the picture of the eternal martyr who at that moment could've passed for a survivor of the Irish Potato Famine. All she needed was a raggedy shawl. I could've killed her. Following a lengthy character assassination, in which the Beak denounced me as the archetypal yob incapable of keeping his pecker in his pants, she made her decision.

'You will pay three pounds a week towards the support of this child. If you fail to do so then you will go to prison. You, young man, need to be made to face up to your responsibilities.'

Three pounds sounds such a pitiful amount, laughable now, but it's a sizeable chunk of your income when your take-home pay is eleven quid a week, five of which goes to your ma for board and keep, then a couple of quid a week to pay off the catalogue, and train fare to work, ciggy and dinner money to find. There was hardly any change to play with.

I left the court annoyed that I'd found myself in such a situation, for having worked in the courts it had been naive of me to think that the procedure would be as jolly and simplistic as I'd assumed. Now I'd been made to feel like a criminal and was seriously pissed off with Diane for what I considered to be a masterful stroke of duplicity, although, to be fair, she was as ill informed about the procedure as I was.

'You coming back to the flat?' she whined, as I marched on ahead of her.

'No,' I shouted, not waiting for her to catch up. 'The only place I want to go back is in time.' Standing sulkily at the bus stop, my shoulders hunched against the miserable drizzle of rain that had started to fall, I watched Diane pushing the pram across Stanley Road and felt sad for us all. I felt, rather dramatically as usual, that I was part of a particularly depressing scene from *Love on the Dole*, only in this instance it was all very real and I'd better do something about earning some cash.

Since this was my day off I indulged myself in the luxury of taking to my bed as soon as I got home, wallowing in self-pity and angry at the injustice of it all. I hadn't been, as the magistrate had accused me, an absent father. I'd spent a lot of time with Diane. Even if it was after extreme pressure on the guilt rack, hadn't I even babysat on the odd occasion? And on a Saturday night! The Greatest Sacrifice! Mother of God, the abject misery of babysitting a screaming child on a Saturday night when you want to be in town, stood in the middle of a packed club with your mates, knows no bounds.

If I was looking for sympathy then quite rightly there was none forthcoming from Diane.

'Now you know how I feel,' she said smugly, going upstairs to check that Sharon had survived the night in my care.

My ma hadn't questioned my absences from home as my sister Sheila had given birth to a boy, Martin, and she was in her element, helping with the new baby and having the children over at weekends. I was in the way, she'd complain, and she couldn't be bothered with a troublesome teenager under her feet and prayed for the day when I'd finally leave home for good. If I arrogantly assumed that this was just another of her fanciful rants and she didn't really mean a word of it, then I was about to find out otherwise.

'That's it, pack your bags and sling your hook,' she roared, bursting into my bedroom and waving a bit of paper at me. To my bowel-dropping horror I could see that it was my summons, the damn thing must have fallen out of my pocket when I threw my jacket on the sofa.

'Who is she?' my apoplectic ma demanded. 'Who is this poor girl that you've gone and got into trouble, you dirty little sod? Well, God love her, that's all I can say, getting mixed up with a lying cowboy like you.'

I tried to interrupt but it was pointless attempting to stem the tide of abuse.

'You fornicating, no-good, dirty big who-er, how old is this poor girl?'

Diane was older than me. It made no difference to us or anyone else, for she certainly didn't look or act her age.

'Twenty-seven.'

'She's how old?'

'Twenty-seven.'

I didn't like the tone of her voice nor the way things were going.

'What?! Twenty-bloody-seven, nine years older than you? Nine years!' she squawked. 'And pray tell me who is this Jezebel preying on daft young lads?'

Oh good, she's changed her tune, I thought as it began to dawn on me that there might be a way of getting out of this mess relatively unscathed. I was swiftly going from villain to victim, the wronged son seduced by the older vamp.

'Oh Paul, fancy letting some predatory middle-aged woman get her claws into you. Where did you meet her, the She Club?'

'I've never been in the She in my life,' I protested. 'It's full of desperate old divorcees looking for a fellah.'

'Exactly.'

'C'mon, you can hardly call twenty-seven middle-aged, can you? She's nice, me dad met her.'

That did it.

'Don't be bringing your poor father into this,' she yelled, laying into me with her fist. 'Just as well he's not alive to hear all this carry-on because if he was he'd be in his grave.'

'Eh?'

'Bloody fool, getting caught out like this. You've ruined your life, d'ya hear me, you've ruined your life.'

She sat down on the chair under the window, putting her head in her hands and sighing loudly, exhausted for the moment by her anger.

'It's not the first time I've sat in this room with a silly fool and had a conversation not dissimilar to the one we're having now, you know.'

'When was the last time then?' I foolishly asked.

'When do you think, soft lad?' She looked at me pityingly. 'When our Chrissie was sent home pregnant with John in the war.'

'Well, that turned out all right in the end, didn't it? Look at our John, he's the most well-adjusted of all of us.'

'The things he comes out with,' she said, directing her conversation towards the wardrobe. 'Well-adjusted, like he'd know anything about that, the bloody lunatic. Now straighten that bed then come downstairs pronto, I want to investigate this carry-on further.'

I told her everything and except for the odd flare-up of temper she took it quite well on the whole – apart, that is, from the court order demanding three pounds a week for sixteen years.

'Why oh why did you have to go like a lamb to the slaughter into a court? Why couldn't you just do a runner like everyone else?' she wailed, throwing me completely off my guard by this unexpected change in attitude. 'If anyone had come looking for you I'd have just said that I didn't have a clue about your whereabouts. I wish you'd told me, you daft bugger, I'd have helped you.'

This was so out of character for my mother, thinking of covering up for me, condemning herself to a lifetime of confession to atone for the lie she'd told to protect me. My ma, honest as the day was long, was actually prepared to lie for me, even though she considered it to be a mortal sin. I was amazed. But then she never ceased to amaze me.

'Well, I've got to pay me way, haven't I?' I said, not trying to curry favour with her but acknowledging that I had a responsibility to help support the kid.

'Yes, but did you have to go and settle it through the courts?' She got up from the sofa and shut the window in case any of the neighbours heard us. 'They'll be on your back for sixteen years, that's a long time. If you miss a payment you'll have the worry of being put away hanging over you like the Sword of Damocles. Honestly, son, you're so daft I'm beginning to think that you shouldn't be allowed out on your own.'

I was praying that she wouldn't want to go over to Liverpool and have it out with Diane but thankfully for the moment she expressed no interest in getting involved with Diane or the baby and chose to let the matter simmer on a back burner until she felt able to deal with it.

'If I were you I'd get myself down to the Labour Exchange and have a look for a decent job with a proper wage instead of that hell-hole of a wine lodge. You've got maintenance to find now.'

She was right, I couldn't exist on the wages I was earning at Yates's and the occasional night at the Bear's Paw, but there didn't seem to be much going in the way of well-paid jobs on Merseyside for an unqualified barman. Maybe it was time to venture forth again and give London another try. Chris and Billy, a couple of gay guys I'd stayed with for a few nights in their Maida Vale flat, had offered to put me up on their sofa as a paying lodger if I ever returned to London to look for work. They'd thrown me out the last time I'd stayed with them for bringing a girl back from an Irish club one night. It had been a purely platonic affair – she didn't have her cab fare back to whatever outer region of north London she lived in so I'd offered her a bed, or rather a floor for the night. Chris and Billy – a pair of dyed-in-the-wool misogynists unless of course you happened to be Rosalind Russell or Mae West – were not amused the following morning when they found a hearty Irish girl sprawled across their front-room floor and slung us both out.

We'd made up since then and I gave them a ring to see if their offer still held. Thankfully it did, and so that night I gave Molly a week's notice. I'd have left for London immediately but I'd grown fond of Molly and Jean and didn't want to run out on them, and besides, I had yet to break the news to Diane. Jean wasn't very happy at my leaving, nor was Molly, and had I known that my going would upset them so much I might have been tempted to stay.

Diane was surprisingly philosophical at the news that I was off again but wondered what I was going to do for a living down there. Chris had told me over the phone, in all serious-ness, that if I ever considered stripping as a way of earning a living then he knew of an agent he could have a word with who booked male strippers for the pubs.

'You don't have to go all the way,' he added as an incentive, 'or be hung like a horse.'

I considered the offer for all of a second. An image of me swishing around the altar of St Joseph's as an altar boy to the imaginary beat of a kettledrum and a blaring trumpet sprang to mind. Here was the chance to do it for real, but I knew that I'd be laughed off the stage if I started to get 'em off. Revealing my skinny, pasty white frame to a paying crowd was out of the question; I'd rather be horsewhipped than take my clothes off in public, or so I thought at the time. I didn't know my attitude towards appearing on stage barely clothed was about to change.

Sharon, now four months old, still screamed like the banshee if she suspected that I was about to go anywhere near her, let alone, horror of horrors, attempt to pick her up. I suspected I wouldn't be missed. In fact, as soon as the whistle was blown at Lime Street Station and my train pulled out, she'd probably get the bunting out and hang it round her cot.

I said goodbye to friends and lovers and went up to see the aunties before I left. 'Trust you to get things arse about face' was Aunty Chrissie's only comment on my situation. 'Aren't you supposed to bugger off to London before the courts get you? Not the other way round?'

Aunty Anne adopted her priest's housekeeper voice and an enfeebled manner and hinted darkly that she hoped she'd see me next time I was home, if she were spared, that is, but I was not to hold my breath.

'Jesus, is she in one of her "one foot in the grave" moods? Take no notice of her,' Aunty Chrissie snorted, rooting around in her purse. 'Here, take this ten bob and buy yourself some chips from Billy Lamb's and get a fishcake for the Grim Reaper here, she's getting on my bloody nerves.'

I was going to miss my sister's kids. The latest addition to the family was only a few weeks younger than Sharon and I questioned myself as to why I could feel such affection for my nephew but not for my own flesh and blood. I began to agree with my mother that I was indeed 'odd'.

My mother insisted on coming over with me to Lime Street to see me off on the train. She was unusually solicitous as she said goodbye to me on the platform.

'Look after yourself, son, and for God's sake be a good lad and try and keep away from any trouble, eh?'

I kissed her and boarded the train quickly so she wouldn't see my eyes welling up. I waved at her from the open window of the door as she stood on the platform watching the train pull out until finally she vanished from sight, then I popped into the toilet for a quick cry before I found my seat.

CHAPTER 3

In Which I'm Introduced to the Finer Art of Drag Artistry . . .

CHRIS AND BILLY'S FLAT WAS ABOVE A NEWSAGENT'S SHOP IN Formosa Street, Maida Vale. It was a shrine to every female star who ever graced the stage and silver screen. Movie posters and photographs of their idols adorned every wall. They kept a rabbit in a hutch at the bottom of their bed and a couple of cats. One of them, a petulant Siamese, was known as 'the Baby', not due to the urge to satisfy any latent yearnings they may have had for fatherhood but because that's what Madame Rose called Baby June in the musical *Gypsy*. Like me they were devotees of *Gypsy*, but on reflection I doubt they were so keen on the soundtrack after I'd been there for a while as I played it every chance I got.

Chris had the biggest LP collection of obscure movie soundtracks and musicals I'd ever seen, some of them extremely rare and worth a fortune. They were his pride and joy. He was very camp, tall and thin with a mop of frizzy hair that he occasionally 'threw a rinse through'. His partner Billy was a small and officious Scot with the unsettling habit of flying off the handle at the slightest provocation. He'd furiously swish about the flat in a grubby kaftan with the Baby

51

yowling at his feet, leaving a trail of French cigarette smoke in his wake. I usually went for a walk or over to the neighbours' flat when Billy was throwing a hissy fit.

The neighbours had been a revelation. Chris had taken me across the street to meet them not long after I arrived. The door was opened by a tall friendly bloke who Chris greeted as Mrs Page.

'Hello, dear, nice to meet you,' he said, extending his hand and inviting me in. 'Tony Page, singer, compère in or out of drag, available for bar mitzvahs, private functions and cock and hen, especially the cock, dear.'

As he chivvied me down the narrow hall I noticed every coat peg on the wall had a wig of a different colour and size hanging from it. In a clear polythene bag on the peg nearest to the kitchen door a teased-out wig of frizzy grey hair rested on a polystyrene wig block that someone had drawn a face on. An image of a decapitated pensioner flashed across my mind.

'We've got company, Alice,' Mrs Page sang out as we entered the back room. 'It's Mrs Scott come to introduce her niece from the country.'

Alice, all smiles, was standing in the middle of the room modelling a strapless cocktail gown that had seen one too many parties, the zip of which was undone at the back. 'Hello, dear, I'm Alistair. I take it you've already met my mother?' he said, nodding towards Tony Page.

'New frock?' Chris asked.

Alistair blinked his enormous eyes and went into mock coquette mode, holding the dress close to him, his arms crossed coyly over the bust in case it fell down. 'What, this tatty old rag?' he simpered. 'Just a little something I threw on.'

'And missed,' Tony snorted, dragging on a fag and coughing violently as he laughed at his own joke.

'Those things are going to kill you one day,' Alice snapped back, emulating my ma, 'hopefully sooner than later. Now give the jaw a rest and let's have another go at pulling this zip up.'

Tony squinted and contorted as he attempted to pull up a zip on a dress being worn by a man at least three sizes bigger than its original owner. Alistair was optimistic though and kept up a running commentary concerning the dress's origins, wincing in discomfort as Tony struggled.

'Got it in a charity shop near Westbourne Grove . . . Pull it then, dear . . . Wanted a fiver, got it for three . . . Careful! Mind the flesh, you nearly had me fucking back off then, Mrs Page . . . I'll wear it with that naff wig for "I Hate Men" . . . Uuugh. Come on, you're nearly there, dear. Pull it hard.' Chris went to give a hand and between them they miraculously got the zip to go up.

'There you go, ladies,' Alistair gasped, unable to breathe or move, 'a perfect fit.'

The dress was so tight that two fleshy rolls of his flabby chest oozed over the top of it. Alistair pushed them together so that they met in the middle and looked like a real cleavage.

'Varda,' he smiled proudly, holding his arms up and bending his knee in an Ethel Merman pose. 'Look at the size of those balloons.'

'If I were you I'd have a couple of panels put in that frock before you go on stage,' Tony said, eyeing the bursting seams dubiously, 'because if you don't mind me saying, dear, and I know you won't, there's simply no way that delicate little zip is going to cope with the tonnage it's expected to hold in.'

'Go to work, dear, before they see sense and cancel you.' Alistair grunted, admiring the enormous cleavage he'd created. 'She was the cabaret at the Last Supper, you know, her act's so old,' he added in a stage whisper to me.

'You should know, dear, you were the barmaid,' Tony jumped in, roaring with laughter, delighted with himself at the speed of his comeback.

'Sad, isn't it?' Alistair smiled, patting Mrs Page on the arm in a gesture of mock concern and staring intently into his face. 'Look at that eek, those bags, those lines, poor old thing. She's as old as her gags, and they're ancient.'

'Hark at her, that's a bit rich coming from a mime act who can't even fart unless it's on tape.'

'Why don't you make yourself useful and put the kettle on, Lime Street Sadie here looks like she could do with a cup of tea after the shock of seeing you in daylight.'

I was already known as Lil in certain circles, now here I was being rechristened as Sadie. I had an Aunty Sadie, my dad's sister, and I didn't think of it as a particularly funny or unusual name. Mrs Page, Chris and Alistair did though, and so Sadie I became. Alistair called me nothing else from that day on.

He was extremely easy to get on with, warm and good-natured, as was Tony Page. I sat round the table smoking and drinking tea, listening to them gossip and bitch. I felt a little out of my depth at first which made me come over shy, but eventually, prompted by Chris, I stirred myself and fed them a few highly salacious and grossly exaggerated titbits about the prolific sexual activity that was available to any queen who fancied a stroll down the Liverpool dock road. Their eyes stood out like chapel hat pegs as I described the hordes of sex-mad sailors from the four corners of the globe who frequented the gay bars of Liverpool and were just ripe for the picking.

'Who'd have thought it?' Tony said, whistling through his teeth and looking me up and down. 'She's like the League of fucking Nations!'

The more they laughed the more I loosened up and started to enjoy myself. Making people laugh is a potent drug that gives you a real buzz, whether it's on a stage or in a west London kitchen. I liked these people and wanted them to like me.

They were different from anyone else I'd ever met. They were showbiz. Not the showbiz of the blues clubs of Long John Baldry or the classical world that Sir John Pritchard lived in – these being the only two people I'd previously met who were famous and worked within the entertainment industry. No, Alistair and Tony Page were something else entirely. They were a different breed, lairy, funny, brave and ever so slightly devious and the world they inhabited sounded daring, exciting and extremely appealing. I felt that I'd found my tribe.

'You should be on the stage, wack,' Tony said, getting up from the table, 'and talking of which that's just exactly what I should be preparing to do.'

'It takes her a long time, you see. It's tricky getting that iron lung in the back of the car,' Alistair simpered, smoothing his hair and pursing his lips.

'I shall clean you when I get back, madam, but right now your mother has got more important matters on her mind, like getting to work. I'm resident compère at the Black Cap, you know.' Tony looked into the mirror over the fireplace and, licking his finger, ran it over his eyebrows. 'Got to bring the shekels in, so thank God I'm very busy and working every night, twice on Sundays. Can't complain, dear.'

'Neither can we,' Alistair chipped in so as not to appear

outdone. 'We're more or less fully booked for months.' He turned his attention to a wig that sat on top of the telly, and gently ran a hand across it to see if its heavily back-combed and tortured surface could do with a bit more lacquer.

Alistair was one half of a mime drag double act called the Harlequeens. His partner Phil and he hadn't been doing the rounds of pubs and clubs for very long but they were quickly becoming extremely popular. Alistair was the larger of the two both in height and girth. Phil was smaller, very funny and like Alice could go from gross caricature to high glamour. They did a 'tarts' routine at first, made up of bits of recognizable songs cleverly edited together on a reel-to-reel tape. They had a wealth of songs to choose from courtesy of Chris's extensive record collection and between them had concocted a very funny montage. The tarts had gone down a treat when the Harlequeens made their debut. They had planned on calling themselves the Harlequins until someone suggested the funnier alternative, then with a new name they had extended the act into the requisite two twenty-minute spots and successfully gone on the pub circuit.

There was a drag boom on. Every pub in London, gay or straight, seemed to have a drag act. Mime acts were extremely busy too. They could work any pub, no matter how small, and were cheaper as the landlord was spared the expense of the drummer and pianist required to accompany live acts. All the mime acts needed was a record player or a tape machine plus a speaker to play them through. The Harlequeens had their own sound system, not exactly high tech but nevertheless effective and worth the initial expense as it allowed them greater scope.

'What are you doing tonight, Sadie?' Alistair asked. 'Why

don't you come and watch us? We're working a pub in the East End.'

I couldn't wait. I'd read about the famous East End and seen it depicted in films on telly. It was home to the Krays and Jack the Ripper, Limehouse opium dens and the white slave trade. Gaslit alleys crawled with whores who lurked in the shadows and said, 'Wanna good time, duckie?' to every passing male. And fog, lots and lots of fog. Oh, I knew all about the East End all right, so it was not surprising that after an unremarkable journey squashed in the back of Alistair's sister's Mini with the speaker on my lap I was more than a bit disappointed when we pulled up outside an ordinary-looking pub on a main road. No fog, no opium dens, just a couple of girls outside a kebab shop.

Inside was equally unremarkable. The stage was a little carpeted platform with a bit of silver and red slash curtain tacked to the back wall for theatrical effect. A small organ and a set of drums completed the scene and at the side of the stage a chenille curtain had been hung for the acts to change behind. I sat at the bar while Alistair and Phil set their costumes up behind the curtain. They had no need to get made up as they'd arrived in full slap, hiding their heavily painted eyes behind dark glasses in the vain hope that it made them less conspicuous.

The changing facilities in most pubs ranged from appallingly squalid to non-existent. Very few had what could be described as a proper dressing room; at best the manager might allow them to change in the kitchen or at a push in the living accommodation over the bar, but it was more than likely the act could be found in the ladies' toilet trying to apply an elaborate make-up in a dirty mirror lit by a forty-watt bulb while standing in two inches of pee. It was usually a wise move to arrive fully made up to save the hassle and abuse from the women who were, quite rightly, annoyed at finding their lav taken over by a couple of fellahs.

'Get us two bevvies, Sadie,' Alistair shouted, waving a couple of pound notes from behind the curtain. 'And get one yourself.'

As I waited to be served I studied a poster that was pinned to the wall at a jaunty angle. *'This Week's Cabaret,'* it proclaimed in shaky black felt-tip. *'Saturday, the Fabulous Harlequeens! with Compère the Lovely Shane!'* This was accompanied by a black and white ten-by-eight photo of Philip dressed as a baby, complete with bonnet and teddy bear, and a deranged Alistair advancing towards him wearing a fright wig, bovver boots and clutching a lavatory brush. Underneath this, written in a smaller hand, it said, *'Comedy, mime drag. Not to be missed!'*

There were lots of photographs of drag queens pinned to the wall of the bar, the majority of them sporting enormous wigs and huge eyelashes. A few were dressed in corsets and negligees trying to look like fifties sex kittens, candyfloss wigs, one leg in front of the other, knee slightly bent, heavily painted lips pouting as if blowing a kiss at the camera. An act called Derek Reece was even dressed as a pregnant bride.

My attention was diverted by the arrival of a woman behind the bar. I was transfixed by this glamorous creature in an elegant full-length, low-cut black velvet gown dispensing drinks and holding court. She was extraordinary, her features chiselled and hard yet not unattractive, her movements slow and deliberate as she daintily poured a gin into a glass from one of the optics.

'Ice and a slice, love?' She weighed me up from behind a heavy blonde fringe as she popped an ice cube into the drink.

'Are you waiting to be served,' she asked in a husky voice, 'or are you just gonna stand there gawping at my tits all night?'

My face slowly turned scarlet as I realized that I'd been staring at her chest. It was hard not to, they were hanging out of the top of her dress. I muttered my order.

'You one of the act's bit of trade?' she asked casually, pulling a pint of lager. 'How far do you go for a quid then?'

I wanted the floor to open up as she took the money Alistair had given me out of my hand and glided off towards the till laughing.

'Who's that woman behind the bar?' I asked Phil, taking the drinks behind the curtain and trying to find somewhere to put them in the cramped space.

'What woman's that then, love?' Phil asked in his strong Welsh accent, quickly moving a ratty-looking feather boa before I spilled the drinks on it.

'The blonde one behind the bar in the long black frock.'

'You mean Shane?' Alistair pulled the curtain back so he could take a look. 'She's not a woman,' he laughed, 'Shane's a drag queen.'

'But she's got tits and real hair, and she's hardly got any make-up on,' I protested.

'The tits are taped up but the hair's her own. She pins it up and backcombs it,' Alistair said, laughing at my ignorance. 'Didn't you twig that she was drag? Honestly, Sadie, open your eyes, dear. This is London, you're not in Berkhamsted now.'

'Birkenhead.'

'If you say so, dear.'

I hadn't had a lot of experience when it came to drag queens. The first time I ever saw a man in a frock was on the *Royal Variety Performance*, when I must have been about eleven.

'Paul, leave your homework for a minute and come down here and have a look at this on the telly,' my mother shouted up the stairs to me. She was ironing pillowcases in the front room. 'What do you think of her then?' she asked, pointing to a voluptuous woman on the screen with lots of hair and a very fancy dress. I leaned on the ironing board and watched her for a moment. She had a strange voice and was flamboyant, painted up like one of the elegant mannequins in Robbs' windows.

'Is it Fanny Cradock?'

'Of course it's not. Have a good look. Can't you tell what's different about her?'

'She's very tall?'

'No, soft lad, she's not a she, she's a he. He's called Danny La Rue. He's a man! And stop picking that asbestos at the end of me ironing board, will you.'

I remember wondering if he dressed like that all the time, and if so, did people mind? How did he do his shopping? I couldn't imagine him running around Birkenhead dressed like that or anywhere else for that matter.

I'd since run into trannies in Sadie's and the Bear's Paw. There was a six-foot-six heterosexual builder by trade who called himself Carol and liked to drink in Sadie's dressed in the tiniest of miniskirts and the highest of heels. Carol was not the prettiest girl in the chorus. She was built like a brick shithouse, thick neck with an Adam's apple the size of a King Edward potato and a masculine face, cowpat craggy, that made Ernest Borgnine look cute. When this was covered with a thick application of greasy cosmetics it could be quite startling to the uninitiated.

Despite her intimidating appearance we treated Carol like a lady. It wasn't just the knowledge that a punch from one of her Desperate Dan-sized fists might put you in hospital that stopped you tittering in her face, it was her quiet dignity and almost regal composure that commanded respect and consequently we treated her with the reverence she deserved. Even so, I was still a comparative neophyte when it came to the world of cross-dressing but I was learning fast.

'Wait till I tell her you thought she was a real palone,' Phil chuckled, violently shaking out an Afro wig before putting it on his head. He bent down to get a better look in the minuscule mirror propped up against the piano, an instrument recently made redundant by the arrival of the Bontempi organ that now proudly sat on the other side of the curtain.

'She'll be delighted, absolutely bloody delighted,' he said, tucking his hair into the sides of the wig. 'Now do us a favour, love, get lost and leave us to get changed, will you? We're on soon.'

Shane was indeed absolutely delighted on hearing that I thought she was the real McCoy, and consequently made frequent use of me during her opening act by gently sending me up.

I stood rooted to the spot, a fixed grin on my burning face, wishing I were somewhere else. Shane didn't have a bad singing voice. She seemed to prefer ballads and torch songs to up-tempo numbers, probably seeing herself more as a sophisticated chanteuse than a raucous pub drag act. She reminded me of the Gladys George character in the movie *The Roaring Twenties* and both terrified and fascinated me at the same time.

Eventually she finished her spot with a dramatic Shirley Bassey ballad that had the devotees in the audience cheering the roof off and, satisfied that she had the crowd warmed up sufficiently, she introduced the Harlequeens. They opened with the tarts routine. Alistair was the battered old bag with a fag hanging from her mouth wearing a short plastic mac and tatty wig and miming along to Marlene Dietrich's 'Lili Marlene', while Phil played the lip-smacking, sly-eyed sexy little scrubber. They were very funny. Alistair galumphed around the tiny stage to Joyce Grenfell's 'Stately As A Galleon' while Phil, dressed in a bonnet and romper suit, mimed to Helen Kane's 'I Wanna Be Loved By You' sung in her poop-doop-a-doop baby voice.

Reality was temporarily suspended. For a time I forgot that the precocious brat on stage was in reality the grown man I'd been speaking to a moment earlier. There was more to this than just standing there miming to records, I reasoned, as I watched them both at work. You had to act the number out, make the audience believe that the disembodied voice you were mouthing along to was really your own.

By the time Alistair dropped me off back at Formosa Street it was past midnight. I helped him unpack the wigs, costumes and equipment and carry them into the flat.

'I'll have to go for a slash, Sadie, I'm burstin',' he shouted, making a dash for the lav. 'Put those wigs on the hooks in the hall, will you.'

I looked at the blond crash helmet of a wig that I was holding and felt an overwhelming urge to put it on. I couldn't resist wigs and still can't, if I see one it has to go on my head. Alistair was audible through the wall, groaning with relief as he peed. It sounded like it was going to be a long one so I was safe for the moment. Going to the mirror and gazing at my reflection, I was amazed to see how different a wig could make you appear. Tugging the fringe down further so it just sat over one eye, I pulled the same face that my aunty Chris called her Marlene Dietrich, letting my fag dangle from the side of my mouth and sucking my cheeks in. I peered at myself in the glass through hooded eyes. I looked ridiculous. The wig was fixed in the shampoo-and-set style that old ladies went in for when they got their hair done for half price on a Wednesday afternoon and it made me look like a skull who needed a shave. Still, I thought, admiring myself in the mirror, with a different style and the right make-up I reckon I could look half-way decent . . .

'Sadie, you're very quiet out there. What are you up to?' Alistair shouted from the lav. 'You're not trying my wigs on again, are you?' The raging torrent that had rumbled against the bowl was calming down into a light stream, heralding the fast-approaching end of Alistair's marathon pee. I took the wig off and hung it on one of the hat pegs in the hall as I heard him pull the chain.

'Ooh, I needed that,' he said, coming out and looking around to see if I'd put the wigs away or dumped them on the floor. 'What you been up to?'

'Nothing,' I replied, 'I was just thinking.'

CHAPTER 4

Formosa Street

WHAT LITTLE MONEY I'D ARRIVED WITH SOON RAN OUT AND by the end of a fortnight in Formosa Street I woke up to the realization that I was now totally destitute. Chris and Billy had gone to work so I had the flat to myself. Before he'd left Billy had put his head round the front-room door and barked a list of instructions at me as I lay semi-conscious, wrapped in a blanket, on the floor.

'I want to come home and find this flat cleaned from top to toe, Sadie, or there will be trouble. You're not pulling your weight, dear, and if you're not job-hunting then at least you can clean up.'

I pretended not to hear and rolled over, preferring to concentrate on running my big toe through the shagpile carpet rather than getting up and cleaning it. I didn't blame Billy. I was a lazy sod when it came to housework, believing that somehow it did itself.

After a while hunger drove me to rouse myself from my bed on the floor and go down to the kitchen in search of sustenance. It suddenly occurred to me that the last meal I'd eaten had been over twenty-four hours ago and that had only been sausage and chips. A bit of bacon on toast and maybe some cornflakes plus a nice pot of tea, I mused, putting the kettle on and inspecting the contents of the fridge while I waited for it to boil. My vision of crispy bacon slathered in Daddie's Sauce evaporated in a flash as, apart from an empty tube of cream cheese spread that looked as if it had been there since the Crimean War and half a tin of cat food, the fridge was bare. Not even a drop of milk for a cup of tea, let alone cereal. I searched every cupboard in the kitchen for something to eat but the only remotely edible thing on offer seemed to be an ancient slice of French toast and a vegetable stock cube. What was wrong with these queens? Didn't they eat? Oh well, as my ma would say, 'Needs must when the devil drives,' and making the best of the paltry ingredients I rustled up breakfast.

Petit Déjeuner à la Formosa Street
Take one vegetable stock cube, preferably slightly battered and past its sell-by date, add boiling water and stir. A little pepper may be added if required. Take a pinhead of dehydrated cream cheese hanging out of the end of the flattened tube and dab carefully on the corner of a slice of ten-year-old French toast and voilà! Soupe de Légumes et Croque Monsieur. Extremely suitable as breakfast for a prisoner in the Bastille.

Delia would've been proud of me.

Next on the agenda was a ciggy. My packet of Cadets was empty, which meant there was nothing for it but to go through the ashtrays and bins for a respectable-sized stump. A search of Chris and Billy's bedroom proved fruitless as every single butt in there had been smoked right down to the filter. The miserable bastards, I cursed, going through every coat pocket, scouring the living room, kitchen and bathroom and then searching again, driven like a mad thing by my craving for nicotine. Eventually I got dressed and ran over the street to Alistair's to see if either he or Tony Page could 'give us the loan of a fag'. I hated asking as I'd not known them that long and was loath to reinforce the stereotypical image of residents of Merseyside as scrounging scallies, constantly bumming cigs. As for borrowing money from them, forget it, I'd sooner starve than ask for a loan and it seemed that in my current predicament I was about to find out just what that felt like.

Neither Alistair nor Tony Page was at home. Oh Lord, I'd have sold a kidney for ten Cadets, both of them for a pack of twenty, and as I was putting my key in the door a woman came out of the newsagent's and lit a cigarette. The whiff of smoke that assailed my nostrils as she strolled past made my craving for the dreaded weed unbearable. I had to have a fag, just had to and if it meant swallowing my pride and asking for a packet on tick from the newsagent that we lived above then so be it.

'Hello, I've just moved into the flat above with Chris and Billy.'

'Oh yes, you mean the two pouffes?'

'I don't know about that, I'm just the lodger.'

'And?'

'I was wondering if it would possible to get ten Cadets on tick? I can pay you back tonight.' God knows how but I'd cross that bridge when I came to it.

'Sorry, mate, no can do. I don't give credit and you know what they say.'

'No?'

'If you can't afford to buy 'em then you can't afford to smoke 'em.'

'Do you know a woman called Molly O'Grady by any chance?'

'Who?'

'Doesn't matter.'

Feeling very sorry, for myself I went back up to the flat and sat on the stairs to have a think, not very easy when your mind is fixed on ciggies and food. Was this what living in London was all about? Sat on a staircase surrounded by pictures of Betty Grable and June Haver, starving and skint?

Even if I'd wanted to give up and go back home, which at this moment I did, how was I going to find the money for the fare? Plus there was the added worry of not being able to keep up the dreaded maintenance payments. Did this mean the worry over food, fags and a roof over my head would soon be taken care of by HM Prisons? A job would bail me out of this mess but it seemed no one wanted to give me one. Even though I'd scoured the Situations Vacant section of the *Evening Standard* each evening, I'd been unsuccessful with every job I'd applied for.

I'd been fairly confident that I'd get the job at the Coleherne, a gay pub in Earls Court that had always been our first port of call when my friend Tony and I took the weekend saver down from Liverpool. It was predominantly a leather bar and at first glance the clientele, with their shaved heads, walrus moustaches and leather outfits, could be quite intimidating. But when I eavesdropped on their conversations it seemed they were more interested in opera than beating me up. The queens who carried crash helmets around with them, leading prospective trade to believe that there might be a

Harley Davidson parked on the pavement outside, invariably went home on the tube. The helmets were more a fashion accessory than of any practical use.

I reckoned I was just what the Coleherne needed – a tasty young bit of Birkenhead fluff in among all that ageing leather – and felt sure the job was in the bag. What I hadn't reckoned with was the landlord, an Irishman called Pat McConnon, who took one look at me and turned me down flat. He was a surly bugger and dismissed me with a grunt and a wave of his hand. 'Nuttin' here for you,' he muttered, showing me the door. 'Stick your job,' I shouted over my shoulder, 'I wouldn't work for a narky old bastard like you in a million years.' I got that one badly wrong, as time will reveal.

The phone rang, causing me to leap out of my skin. Jesus, nicotine withdrawal makes you jumpy.

'I hope you're up and out of that bed, dear, and giving the flat a good clean.' It was Billy. 'I don't want to come home to a mess.'

'Yes, yes, I was just cleaning the kitchen when you rang,' I lied. 'What time will you be home?'

'And why do you need to know?'

Because I want to get my hands on your ciggies, French or not, and smoke my bloody head off.

'No reason. Just wondered, that's all.'

'Aye, dear, you may well wonder. I'll be home to find a clean flat, that's when I'll be home. And don't forget to clean out the cat-litter tray. The Baby won't use it if it's full.'

The prospect of picking out the Baby's turds from sodden cat litter on an empty stomach didn't appeal to me in the least, but then maybe a bit of housework would take my mind off the hunger pains and the craving for a cig. It would also get Chris and Billy off my back and put me in their good books. Perhaps they'd even bring food home and cook something to eat? No, that was going too far.

Starting in the bathroom and making my way down to the kitchen, I became rather over-zealous in my quest for cleanliness as I hoovered the staircase and thought it'd be a good idea to give the posters on the wall a bit of a light run-over as well. They were coated in a film of dust, particularly a faded old thing for a movie called *The Women*. I watched in horror as Joan Crawford vanished down the nozzle, followed closely by Norma Shearer and Paulette Goddard. Instead of switching the Hoover off, I stood transfixed as I saw *The Women*, one of Chris and Billy's all-time favourite films and, I dare say, posters, crumble and tear like ancient parchment and disappear into the machine. Snapping out of my trance, I managed to turn the damn thing off just in time to see a large strip bearing the words 'All Star Female Cast' get sucked away. What the bloody hell was I going to do now? They'd kill me.

I carted the Hoover up the stairs and flung it into their bedroom, narrowly missing the Baby, who leaped on the bed and spat at me. How was I going to tell them that I'd destroyed, albeit accidentally, one of their prized movie posters?

'Hello, you two. Had a nice day at work? If you're wondering why there's a big gap on the staircase wall, it's because the poster that used to be there is now in the belly of the Hoover. OK? Good. I just knew you wouldn't mind.' Rearranging the other posters on the wall in an attempt to fill the gap left empty by *The Women*, of which all that now remained was the letter N and a half of Rosalind Russell's face, I quickly tore this evidence down and buried it along with the contents of the cat-litter tray at the bottom of the kitchen bin. I hated that litter tray, its acrid stench always hit the back of my throat and made me retch. Chris and Billy were immune to the smell but it was always the first thing that hit me whenever I came in the front door.

The craving for a cigarette had lessened; it was hunger that gnawed away at me now. Cleaning the kitchen I prayed that I'd come across a morsel of something fairly edible that I might have missed on my cupboard search earlier. I did. It was a bag of oats, only trouble was they were for the rabbit. Sitting on the kitchen floor I thought about my mother and her daily bowl of muesli. Rabbit oats never harmed her. Following her heart attack my ma seriously changed her diet. From information she'd gleaned in the *Reader's Digest*, the *Nursing Mirror* and books about coronary heart disease in the reference library, she took to eating muesli to lower her cholesterol. She'd buy a large bag of oats from the health food shop on Argyle Street and, mixing some with a little water or fruit juice and leaving it overnight in the fridge, she'd make a bowl of muesli for her breakfast, adding apple or prunes depending on her mood and the state of her bowels.

'Paul! Pop down and get us some oats from the health food shop, will you?'

It was a bit of a schlep to trail all the way down Birkenhead just for a bag of oats, so I used to buy them from the pet shop on Church Road instead. It was a lot nearer and they looked exactly the same as the oats in the health food shop, the rabbits seemed to thrive on them, so why not my mother? It was a while before she found out and that was only after the pet shop changed their bags. Whereas they'd once been plain brown-paper bags, they now had a jolly rabbit on the front proclaiming 'Oats! Bunnies Love 'Em'. I think the only suitable word to describe my mother's reaction after she'd uncovered my deception is 'ape-shit'.

If she could only see me now, pouring a decent handful of rabbit food into a bowl and adding some warm water, then setting it aside to soften. Divine retribution. Yum, yum!

Going back upstairs, I cleared a load of junk mail from the lid of the record player and put a record on. I tackled their bedroom while I waited for my lunch to turn to mush, and lifting the end of the mattress up off the floor to tuck the bed-sheet in I spotted it. Half a smoked Gauloise stuck to the side of a well-used tube of KY Jelly. This was no time to be fussy, I told myself, peeling the stump off the tube, refusing to con-sider how long it had lain there or what condition it might be in. Instead I took the precious, lovely little stump and lit it off the gas stove. French cigarettes didn't taste like a real ciggy, they were too strong for a start and I found it impossible to inhale the smelly things without coughing and inevitably dry-retching. This time I wasn't so particular and took a long drag and inhaled deeply to the bottom of my lungs, feeling instantly light-headed and blinded by a blaze of colored lights as my legs buckled under me and I slid down the side of the gas stove and hit the floor in a dead faint.

When I came to, it took me a little while to work out what, who and where I was. Hauling myself up from the floor, the first sight to greet me was the Baby. She'd jumped on to the work surface and was eyeing my muesli, sniffing it suspiciously and giving it little dabs with her paw. 'You're welcome to it,' I said, reeling over to the sink to get myself a glass of water. Upstairs, the phone was ringing. I ignored it. Let it bloody ring. It was probably Billy checking to see if I was 'hard at it, dear'. I was now past caring and taking myself off upstairs I lay on the front-room floor to recover. The phone started ringing again. Bollocks. I crawled along the floor and picked it up.

'What!'

'Is that any way to answer a phone?' It was my mother. 'I don't know what kind of manners you're picking up down there. You're not on drugs, are you?'

'No, Mam, I'm not.'

'And I certainly hope you're not hanging around those amusement arcades in Piccadilly Circus either. I've read about them. They're magnets for dirty old men who are looking for lads.'

At that moment in time if I could've found a dirty old man I'd have done it for the price of a bag of chips and a ciggy.

'You've had a tax refund,' she chirped down the line. I could imagine her in the hall looking through the nets on the front-door window to see if there was any activity outside. 'Forty-seven pound.'

The words were music to my ears.

'I paid it into my bank account as I can imagine what state yours is in. You probably owe them a fortune, don't you? Anyway, I've sent the money down to you, well wrapped up inside a card. There's two twenties and a ten. You owe me three pounds, by the way.'

'Fifty quid! When? When did you post it?' I was as happy as a sandboy, whatever one of those is.

'On Thursday afternoon. I meant to ring you but I had the kids down to give our Sheila a break, not that they're any trouble, God love them, but it should have arrived by now. Mind you, the post is probably different down there. Are you sure you haven't had it? Oh, don't tell me it's gone missing, you can't trust any bugger these days.'

I could hear the rising panic in her voice. This could go on all afternoon if she started dreaming up the various fates that could have befallen the missing fifty quid.

'I'll ring you back, Mam.'

I phoned Chris at work. He'd left before the post had arrived. Then I rang Billy.

'I hope you're not running up the phone bill, Sadie. What do you want?'

'Did a letter come for me this morning?'

'Aye, I put it on top of the record turntable before I left for my work. Is that all you're ringing for?'

There was no sign of the bloody letter. Maybe it was amongst the junk mail I'd swept off the lid earlier. I pulled the cabinet out and looked down the back of it, praying that the letter containing fifty beautiful smackers was there. It was.

Hallelujah! I danced around the room, unable to believe my luck. God bless the Inland Revenue and my wonderful mother! I rang her back.

'Sex ett dabble tu.' She always answered the phone by giving the number out in her telephone voice.

'I've got it, Mam.'

'Thank Christ for that. I was sweating cobs there worrying in case it had gone missing.'

'Thanks for cashing it in for me.'

'I signed the back of the cheque for you. Do you think they'll find out that I forged your signature? They used to boil forgers alive in Elizabethan times, you know, and poisoners.'

'Stop worrying,' I said, itching to get off the phone so I could run downstairs and buy twenty cigs and something to eat. 'I'd better go, Mum, they don't like me using the phone in the day as it's so expensive.'

'Quite right as well, the price of it. I'm off to the library. Make sure you pay your maintenance before you go squandering all that money, you don't want to end up in nick. Behave yourself. Ta-ra.'

Billy was full of praise when he got home to find a clean flat and two weeks' rent waiting for him on the table. Chris had met an old squeeze and brought him home, a former male model slightly the worse for drink, and staggering up the stairs he stumbled, ripping a couple of posters down as he made a grab for the wall to steady himself. While Billy was helping Chris get him into the bedroom I seized my chance.

Running into the kitchen I salvaged what was left of *The Women*, brushed the cat litter off it and took it down to where the carnage lay, pinning it back on the wall.

'Chris'll be livid when he's seen what he's done,' Billy sighed, leaning over the banister to take a look. 'Those posters have had it. Oh well, serves him right. Put them in the bin, Sadie, and let's have a cup of tea.'

CHAPTER 5

The Abattoir

I MANAGED TO LAND A JOB IN A PUB IN COVENT GARDEN, WHICH was still a working market back then in the early seventies. It was a market traders' pub and one of the biggest drawbacks was the hours. I had to start at 5am, which meant getting up at four, an unholy hour of the day to have to get up for work as far as I was, and still am, concerned. The memory of my first and only morning in that place is vague to say the least. I can recollect tobacco smoke thick as a peasouper hanging low in the air and circling a sea of male faces across the bar, all clamouring to be served: 'Come on, Scouse, move yourself, we 'aven't got all bleedin' day.' Jesus, they could drink. Confused at not knowing where anything was or, if I did manage to find it, how much it cost, I tear-arsed around in the confined space behind the bar, wild-eyed and demented, pulling pints, serving food and mixing some sort of hot toddy that the porters liked to drink. Come late midday when my shift thankfully came to an end I fell out of the door, dazed, knackered and with my ears still buzzing from the sheer volume of noise inside. Even though I badly needed a job I quit there and then, the landlord begrudgingly handing over my four pounds' wages for the eight hours of torture I'd just put in, vowing to myself that wild horses wouldn't get me back into that madhouse no matter how dire the predicament I might find myself in in the future.

Taking myself off to the Brook Street Bureau, an employment agency with branches all over London to see if they had anything exciting on their books, I ended up working for them as one of their 'jobfinders'. After a short induction course on how to sell jobs to unwitting secretaries and office clerks in search of a change of career, I found myself sat behind a desk in the Fleet Street branch, painfully aware that I was totally out of my depth. It was all about selling and meeting quotas, and it was obvious that I was the worst salesperson ever to flip through a card index as I declared unconvincingly to the hapless victim before me that 'I might have the perfect position for you.' I quit before they unmasked me as the inept fraud that I was, taking with me the details of a job in a pub on the river. I was better off behind a bar than a desk, that I was sure of.

The Samuel Pepys was a pub restaurant in what is now a building called Globe Wharf. The customers were mainly City types, it was a pleasant atmosphere to work in and the guv'nor was a decent chap. In the end I stayed there for over three months, even managing to get a promotion from barman to wine waiter in the restaurant. It didn't matter that I hadn't a clue about wines apart from those Yates's had sold as the Pepys could hardly be accused of having an extensive wine list, and if asked by a diner to recommend a wine I'd suggest the ones that I could pronounce.

There was a girl called Tawny working as a waitress and we quickly became mates. Forthright and inquisitive, a brilliant photographer and artist with a quirky sense of humour, she was small, wore wire-rimmed glasses and had soft curly hair. Before opening time every morning we cleaned the bar and the restaurant together, singing along to the radio. She taught me the words to Pirate Jenny's song from Brecht's *Threepenny Opera* (she was that type of girl) and we'd belt it out with real meaning as we wiped down tables and washed the floors.

I thought she was 'frightfully posh' as she 'spoke nice' and lived in a beautiful old house in Hampton Court with her lovely family. I couldn't help wondering what the hell an extremely intelligent, articulate, brilliant girl with so much potential was doing wasting time waiting tables.

'I'm treading water, just biding my time,' she explained, waving a Camel about in the air. (The ciggy, not the animal.) 'Just waiting for the boyfriend to whisk me off to Seville and marry me.'

I rechristened her Fudge, God knows why. The name just seemed to suit her and anyway she was delighted with it.

Fudge drove me up to Birkenhead for a few days in her little car. She was desperate to photograph Liverpool's waterfront and explore the art galleries and museums, while I was desperate to get away from Chris and Billy, who seemed to think that even though I was paying a fiver a week rent they were entitled to use me as their very own domestic servant. Admittedly I was allergic to the household chores but their constant demands were worthy of Cinderella's stepsisters and I had frequent rows and spats with them, Billy in particular.

At night as I lay on the living-room floor in my makeshift bed I'd harbour dark thoughts, fantasizing about the great day when I would eventually snap and wring his bloody neck.

Poor Billy, having an untidy teenager around who played records at full volume, was late with his rent and never stopped talking was no holiday for him either and I'm surprised he didn't throw me out.

As soon as we got to Birkenhead I realized that I wanted to stay. Fudge was having none of it and tried to reason with me.

'Look at what you have in London and then look at what you have up here.'

I did and decided that up here was the better option. The bitter realization was this: nothing was going to happen for me in London, it would be a life of bar jobs and sleeping on people's floors. I was kidding myself if I ever thought I'd make a decent living down there and as for saving enough money to rent my own flat, well, dream on, kid. Plus, if I was really honest with myself I was lonely in London. I only knew a handful of people there, yet up here in Birkenhead and Liverpool I had my family and loads of mates. No, best quit while you're ahead, I told myself, and come home. Now all I had to do was get round my ma.

Since I'd left home my mother had discovered a new lease of life. She'd joined St Joseph's Union of Catholic Mothers, made a whole new circle of friends she went on outings and coach trips with to the various shrines that the Virgin Mary had reputedly appeared at, spent her weekends with her grandchildren and, although she still mourned my father, as she explained to Tawny she was slowly discovering that life as a single gal was not without its advantages.

'I'm not at anyone's beck and call, can come and go as I please and I don't have the worry of lying in bed waiting for this big article to get home from a night tomcatting it over in Liverpool till all hours. Now would you like another little sandwich, Tony?' she asked, getting up from the sofa.

'It's Tawny actually, Mrs O'Grady.'

'Oh is it? That's a very unusual name. Did your mother like owls then, love?'

We drove back to London on the Wednesday morning, and while I put up what I considered a good pretence of looking forward to getting back, inside I was screaming, 'Turn the car round, I want to go home.' We arrived in London and pulled up outside Formosa Street around four thirty in the afternoon: good timing as it meant Chris and Billy wouldn't be home from work yet. Perfect. I'd just enough time to get in the flat and grab what few items of clothing I'd left without any nasty confrontation. There was a little matter of two weeks' rent being overdue, not that I had it. I had just about enough for a single ticket on the coach. Be easier to leave a note and send the rent on when I found myself in funds again – whenever that might be.

'Are you OK, Paul?' Fudge asked, leaving the engine running as she waited for me to get out of the car. 'You've seemed very distracted the entire journey.'

'I'm going back to Birkenhead,' I blurted out. 'I've made up my mind, I can't stay here.'

'You mean you've driven all the way down with me only to turn round and go straight back up again? You're crazy, certifiably insane,' she said, turning the ignition off and folding her arms.

'Yup,' I replied, feeling like the biggest fool in Christendom.

'Unpredictable as the weather, but then I suppose that's all part of your charm and one of the many reasons I adore you,' she said, stroking the back of my head. 'I shall miss you, but if you insist on going back home to the frozen north then I'm damned if I'm going back to that God-awful pub without you. I'd shrivel up and die of boredom. I'm going to become a recluse and lie on my bed listening to Eric Satie and smoking copious packets of Camels.'

We sat in the car in silence, uncomfortable in each other's company after my sudden and drastic change of heart.

'Well, I suppose that's that then,' she sighed, breaking the silence and turning the ignition back on. 'If I can't get you to change your mind I'd be grateful if you'd hop it before I start blubbing.'

Standing on the pavement watching her pull out from the kerb I felt a hard ball of misery forming in the back of my throat, making it impossible to swallow without producing strange gulping noises. I was never much of a hero when it came to saying goodbye.

'Turn again, Whittington, three times Lord Mayor of London!' she shouted out through the open car window as she sped round the corner and out of my life. I never saw her again. She married her Spaniard and went to live in Seville, we exchanged letters for a while and then as so often happens we simply lost touch. So if you read this, Fudge, give us a call.

It was a grim morning at Liverpool Coach Station, the sky overcast and in the distance the sound of thunder rumbling, probably somewhere in the vicinity of Holly Grove and my fulminating ma. I viewed the storm clouds as a prophetic warning and needed to think things out before getting the underground back to Birkenhead and the inevitable Spanish Inquisition. Sat in the Punch and Judy Café on Lime Street I considered the situation, and after a second cup of frothy coffee and a piece of toast I thought it might be wiser to lie low for a few days rather than going straight home. After all, I'd only just left my mother the day before and I could imagine the line of enquiry when I burst through the back door unannounced. Maybe a friend of mine, Ron, could put me up. I rang him at work from the station.

'Course I can, my pearwents are away for the west of the week on holiday. Tell you what, pop down to the office and I'll give you my keys.'

Ron was rhotacistic (couldn't pronounce his 'R's) and worked for a theatrical agency. He was very theatrical himself, tall with matinee idol good looks and known somewhat incongruously to his close chums as Trixie Delight. I dutifully popped down, my numerous carrier bags bursting at the seams, and gratefully collected his house keys.

Ron lived in an area that was unexplored territory up till then and I asked the bus conductor if he would mind giving me a shout when it came to my stop. You could still do things like that then. Nowadays, if such an obsolete curio as a bus conductor could still be found, your request would probably be met with a stony silence or a curt 'dunno'.

'So c'mon, what's happened? Tell your aunty Twixie all about it,' Ron said through mouthfuls of beans on toast as we sat at the kitchen table eating our tea. 'I had Chris on the phone this afternoon wanting to know if I'd heard from you. He said you'd just packed up and gone. You're not in any twouble, are you?'

'Jesus, Ron, you sound like my mother. No I'm not in any trouble apart from being skint, jobless and homeless. I don't know what to do.' We sat in silence, listening to Bob Greaves on *Granada Reports* talking about the birth of a baby llama at Knowsley Safari Park from the telly in the front room.

'Well, you do know that if I lived on my own you'd be welcome to stay for as long as you like,' Ron generously offered, 'but the pearwents are back at the weekend and then, well . . .' His voice trailed off as he daintily picked up a bean that had strayed on to the table, putting it on the side of his plate.

'I know, I know,' I chipped in to save him any embarrassment. 'I didn't expect to stay any longer than a couple of days. You've been a real mate for putting me up in the first place. I'll ring Nina, maybe I can stay there for a while.'

'I've got an idea,' Ron said, clearing the plates away. 'Why don't you go down to the employment agencies in town, see if there's anything going, get a job, any job for the time being. You can then tell your mum the weason you came home was because you were offered a job. Pwoblem solved.' He was right. 'Now get yourself changed, I've got a friend coming wound from my theatre gwoup who I'm absolutely dying for you to meet. She's divine. She wants to be an actwess.'

He was making her sound like Sally Bowles. The friend in question turned out to be a well-spoken young girl named Angela Walsh. She was a year younger than me and startlingly pretty with soft reddish-brown hair and pale translucent skin. She was wearing a 1920s black velvet evening coat with a matching beret and reminded me of a picture I'd seen in a film book of a young Greta Garbo. We hit it off right away. As Ron had explained, Angela went to the Unity Youth Theatre with him.

'They're always looking for new people who are interested in acting,' Angela told me. 'Why don't you come down? We're reading a new play next week.'

'Do you get to perform in public?' I asked, the not-so-dormant showbiz bug rearing its head again.

'Oh yes,' she replied, skipping around the kitchen, 'we put on shows at the Everyman. Shame you weren't here for the *Marat / Sade*. I played a lunatic, it was wonderful.'

I wanted to play a lunatic and be in a show with Angela Walsh, but first I had to get a job. The next day I took the bus into town and perused the vacancies on the board in the Job Centre. Even without being too particular I could see that jobs I was suitable for were thin on the ground, besides which the take-home pay was, as usual, laughable. One caught my eye: clerk in a meat business, a position that I had no interest in whatsoever but seeing as it was based in Birkenhead and the money wasn't bad I presented myself at the desk with the job number. It turned out to be FMC Meats, the abattoir on the old Chester Road, and reluctantly I made the trip over the water for an interview, praying that I didn't bump into anyone or, in particular, my ma. The job came with perks, my prospective boss informed me. Half-price meat, you finished for the day at three thirty and it was only a ten-minute walk from Holly Grove. Besides the mind-numbing banality of the work (adding up figures all day, great choice of career for a numerical dyslexic) and the fact that I was surrounded by animals being slaughtered, the only major fly in the ointment as far as I could see was the start time. I had to be in for 6.45am. I chose to ignore these drawbacks and gratefully accepted the job, promising to be in first thing Monday morning.

'An abattoir? You mean that dirty, filthy lairage down the hill?' My mother was incredulous. 'You're telling me that you came back from your precious London to work in a bloody abattoir? An abattoir? Well, I've heard it all now.'

'I get half-price meat each week, think of that,' I added feebly, throwing this nugget of information in as compensation.

'I don't give a shite if they send you home with a live cow each night,' she squawked. 'I'd like to know the real reason you've come back here with your tail between your

85

legs. You'd better not be in trouble with the police again, my lad.' She ranted on as she stomped from kitchen to front room. 'And you needn't think I'm getting you up every morning at half six. I should be taking it easy, not running around after you, cleaning and cooking all day. Jesus, wait till I tell our Annie that you're back.'

All things considered, the return of the prodigal went down better than I'd anticipated. I was a veritable paragon of virtue for the next few days, getting home at a reasonable hour, keeping the house clean, doing the shopping without complaint, all of which did nothing to allay my ma's suspicious nature. Meanwhile, life at the abattoir was everything I'd predicted and more. I shared a tiny office with three other people. Dora, a rotund little woman who was in the Salvation Army, went around humming snippets of hymns under her breath all day. She'd been with FMC Meats since the Stone Age when it had been based at Woodside Ferry, as had the elderly man who sat facing a wall and hardly ever spoke a word. The final member of the team was Tony, only a couple of years older than me, who took his job very seriously, which was just as well since I didn't have a clue what I was doing. The ever-patient Tony was forever correcting the piles of figures that I'd totted up on the antiquated adding machine even though he had enough of his own work to do.

Our depressing little time warp of an office overlooked the slaughterhouse. I very rarely went down there unless I had some meat to condemn, a process that involved filling in a lot of forms in triplicate and stamping the dead creatures' flanks with a large rubber stamp that proclaimed 'Condemned Meat'. The sight and smell of the slaughterhouse made me feel physically sick. I was forever talking through my nose so I didn't have to inhale the smell of raw meat and blood, and the slaughtermen must've thought I had either adenoids or a permanent cold.

Occasionally a sheep or cow would escape, briefly enlivening the boredom, and make a bid for freedom up the old Chester Road with everyone in hot pursuit. Once a pig ran out of the gates and jumped on to a Crossville bus that had conveniently just pulled up at the bus stop outside. Somehow it managed to climb the stairs and get up on to the top deck, knocking an old woman over. Poor things must've been terrified, the pig and the pensioner.

A story that sickens me to this day was told to me by one of the slaughtermen. He was a big beefy bullet-headed hunk of a man, stripped to the waist, his magnificent chest and thighs covered by a blood-splattered black leather apron, a massive turn-on, I suppose, for some gay men and heterosexual women but one that did nothing for me. He had huge hands and swollen fingers with blood ingrained dark red and deep around each fingernail. Standing outside one afternoon having a fag and absently watching a small bonfire at the end of the yard, I wondered what it was they were burning. It certainly stank. 'Spontaneous abortion,' a slaughterman told me. 'If a cow comes in pregnant then we abort it and burn it along with the condemned meat. If the abortion comes out a decent size then we sell it on as veal.' I'm not sure if that story was true but it was enough to put me off meat for over a year, and even today I'm still slightly nauseous at the sight of a well-stocked butcher's window.

The Unity Youth Theatre got me through the boredom of the daily grind at the abattoir. I'd been cast in a strange play called *Punch and Judy!* and we rehearsed in a building in an alley off Church Street. We were a mixed bag. There was Florence, small and plump with apple-dumpling cheeks who appeared to be very intense until you got to know her and made her laugh, then her eyes twinkled and her solemn little face lit up in a smile. Flom, as we came to call her, could play the piano and had been cast as the Proprieter of the Punch and Judy Show. Christina, a delightful redhead who came (according to gossip) from a very good family, played a jolly-hockey-sticks-type doctor. A lad named Dave made an excellent Mr Punch. I'm not implying that his nose met his chin or that he had a hump on his back; no, he was an energetic and inventive performer who threw himself into this peculiar role as if he were playing Lear's Fool at the National. Angela was his Judy.

'Not much of a part really,' she said airily, in the manner of a seasoned actress who had done the rounds, over a half of cider in the pub after rehearsals. 'Couple of lines and then I get hit over the head with a stick. I think I'm going to play her Irish, she sounds Irish with a name like Judy, don't you think?' I could only bring to mind the Judys Garland, Holliday and Carne (this last Judy from *Rowan & Martin's Laugh-in*) and none of those seemed remotely Irish to me but I caught Angela's drift and nodded in agreement like an old pro. In addition to Judy she was also playing Lola, Joey the Clown's assistant. I was never off the stage, playing the roles of both Joey and the Hangman as well as appearing as chorus in a couple of numbers. I was in seventh heaven and if Ron, who'd introduced me to Unity in the first place, was a little put out that he had only been given the part of the Illustrious Gentleman, which he wasn't very keen on, then he was big enough not to show it.

The part of the policeman went to a lugubrious chap with a face like Deputy Dawg whose name I can't remember, and then there was Christine. Christine was understudying the women's parts and also appeared as the Ghost. She was tall and wan, slightly old-fashioned and prim in appearance with her cardigans and pale pink lipstick, and we were surprised to hear that on the nights this shy creature wasn't rehearsing for *Punch and Judy!* she was a hostess at the Vernon Johnson School of Dance in Bold Street, substituting as a dancing partner for those lonely souls who'd arrived at the studio unaccompanied.

Christine was an excellent ballroom dancer who completely transformed herself when she entered the doors of Vernon Johnson's. With her sensible little hairdo teased into a coif of mightier dimensions and her shimmering ballgown with yards and yards of peach tulle underskirt to make it stick out, Christine was a knockout. She had a fabulous figure and was a real marvel when it came to dealing with her shy and clumsy protégés, who looked upon her as a goddess. She encouraged me and Angela to join up. We did, and for ten bob a lesson we learned how to samba, tango and do the American jive.

Our director at the Unity was an excitable and slightly hysterical fellow with a bright orange tongue that flicked in and out of the side of his mouth like a nervous lizard with a tic. However, he allowed us to improvise and include songs and sketches in this otherwise dreary production. Christine and Flom wrote a song called 'Did Somebody Call For A Doctor' and, surprise, surprise, I managed to get something from *Gypsy* in – 'May We Entertain You' as an opening number for Joey the Clown and Lola. We were in our element.

To prepare us for this epic the cast were treated to a private viewing of a real Punch and Judy show by the maestro himself, Professor Codman, a showman whose family had been presenting Punch and Judy shows on Merseyside since the late 1800s. I remember his booth outside St George's Hall and no, before you start, it wasn't in the 1800s, it was the late sixties. Punch and Judy fascinated me when I was a little kid and I'd have hung around the booth in the gardens of the Floral Pavilion Theatre, New Brighton, all day if I'd been allowed. In the end my dad made me my own miniature booth, complete with puppets. He even fashioned a link of sausages out of one of my ma's old stockings stuffed with cotton wool and tied up with pink wool at regular intervals to form the links, and I performed shows for my mate Steve Davies, who lived at the top of the Grove.

Most of the costumes for *Punch and Judy!* were borrowed from Unity's wardrobe store. Angela and I wore tatty old Pierrot and Pierrette costumes for the clowns, which she tarted up with a bit of sequin trim she'd bought in Blackler's, but for the Hangman I had other ideas. A guy I was having a fling with made leather trousers for a shop in Church Street and he gave me a brown leather pair with matching waist-coat. They were a bit on the large size and what with me not having much in the way of a bum they hung in folds behind me like a pair of Odeon curtains, but I didn't care. I thought I was the dog's bollocks up there on that stage, head to toe in saggy brown leather, my chin smeared with black greasepaint to represent stubble, a veritable testosterone-fuelled killing machine.

In the Policeman's number, three of us acted as chorus, dressed as coppers in ill-fitting uniforms poncing up and down behind Deputy Dawg, who was executing (literally) a shambolic dance routine while he tried to remember the words to 'A Policeman's Lot Is Not A Happy One'. I had a flash of what I considered comedy genius, fleshing out my part by doing it in drag. Just before I went on I quickly shoved one of the doctor's coats down my tunic as a makeshift bosom, gave my already enormous barnet a quick backcomb, rolled my trousers up and smeared my gob with red carmine, not subtle but surprisingly effective. I drew on the dancer I'd seen playing a wonderfully deadpan tart in Lindsay Kemp's *Flowers* for inspiration and went for it.

'It wasn't what we wehearsed,' Ron sniffed, purse-lipped when I fell into the dressing room after the number had finished. 'It's not vewy pwofessional behaviour, y'know.' I didn't care, I was high as a kite on the laughter from what few punters were out front.

Despite all the hard work and effort we'd put into this ill-fated production – Angela and I had nearly been arrested illegally fly-posting homemade posters all over the city centre – *Punch and Judy!* wasn't a hit. The odds were against us from the start as we didn't go on until 10pm, after a play called *Female Transport*, about a gang of women who were being transported to Australia. This was a time when most sensible theatre-goers were on the bus home or in the pub, and hardly anybody came to see it. Of course it could have been a crap show but in our youthful optimism we could see nothing wrong with it, preferring to view *Punch and Judy!* through heavily rose-tinted spectacles.

'That's showbiz, kid,' Ron said philosophically in his best Liza Minnelli manner as we retired to Sadie's for a cider and the after-show post-mortem.

CHAPTER 6

The Conny Home

'THERE'S A JOB IN THE *BIRKENHEAD NEWS* I WOULDN'T MIND applying for,' I said to my mother as she sat on the sofa knitting away like a dervish.

'What's that for then, village idiot?' she replied without missing a beat. She was what you'd call 'on one' that day. Best not to rile her.

'Actually it's for a housefather in a kids' home in West Kirby.'

'If you want to look after kids then you've got one of your own over in Bootle,' she sniffed, looking up briefly from her knitting to give me the evil eye before setting off on a bout of head-shaking and tut-tutting, 'or have you conveniently forgotten about that?'

I hadn't forgotten, far from it. I thought about Sharon every day. I was going over to visit regularly but still couldn't raise any of the paternal instincts I'd hoped might have been lying dormant inside me. No such luck. To be honest, the baby still scared me. No, she terrified the life out of me and I looked upon my daughter, sweet little thing though she undoubtedly was, as if she were somebody else's child, nearly always coming away from a visit hating myself for harbouring what I considered unnatural emotions. After all, didn't I come from a warm, loving family? So why then couldn't I express the same love and affection for this child? Jesus, for an eighteen-year-old I was carrying a lot of guilt around.

Diane and I would get on fine for a while, spend a lot of time together, go for nights out, usually to Sadie's or the Bear's Paw, but it would inevitably end in bitter recriminations and ultimately tears. In retrospect I can now see that ours had turned into a destructive relationship, riddled with mistrust, jealousy and failed responsibility, but for some reason we always went back for more. I liked Diane very much when she wasn't playing what I saw as the martyr, a role for which she could have won an Academy Award, but try as I might I just couldn't live up to the expectations, real or imaginary, that I felt she had of me. Quite simply I was still too immature, an airhead and a flibbertigibbet unable to come to terms with the cold hard truth that I was a father. Consequently I felt trapped, compromised and as if I was being forced into a corner that said 'Daddy and Partner'. I buried my head in the sand, hoping that somehow the problems would resolve themselves and go away.

Despite my ma's misgivings, I applied for the job of housefather. A few days later I received a reply inviting me to attend an interview the following week with someone called M. Dickie, Ass Mat.

The Children's Convalescent Home and School was a large, unremarkable Victorian red-brick building, nothing at all like the grim, imposing orphanages of Dickensian lore that I'd expected. Situated on Meols Drive, West Kirby, a pretty town that we considered posh with its elegant mansions, smart apartment blocks along the promenade, yachting marina and beach with its spectacular views across the River Dee to North Wales. Neither did Mrs Dickie, the remarkable woman cursed with being in charge of the childcare staff, resemble the archetypal orphanage keeper. She was small and tidy, brisk and efficient, somebody I was prepared to like immediately as physically she reminded me of my aunty Annie. Little did I realize that underneath the soft grey perm, fly-away spectacles and neat little twinset lay a strict disciplinarian with a fixed set of values who ruled her staff with a rod of iron. The home was run by a mainly matriarchal hierarchy starting with Matron Evans at the top, followed by Mrs Dickie, an assortment of nursing sisters then chief childcare officers and, at the bottom of the barrel, the housemothers and fathers. I was shown into a sitting room and told to wait. The room had a beautiful set of Royal Doulton tiles around the fireplace depicting highly romanticized scenes of pastoral life and featuring children and animals. After a while a small child with a forehead the size of a cliff face stuck his head around the door. He stared at me for a while before enquiring, 'Are you in trouble?'

For once I wasn't and I answered him in the negative.

'Then why are you sitting in 'ere?'

I told him that I was waiting to see Mrs Dickie.

He stared at me for a while without making any comment before announcing proudly, 'I've got hydrocephalus.'

'Have you now?' I smiled cheerfully, not having a clue what hydrocephalus was. A Greek island perhaps? 'I'm sure it'll get better very soon,' I added patronizingly.

He raised his eyes skywards and exhaled loudly. 'You're fucking stupid, you are' was his parting shot as he slammed the door behind him. Charming.

I sat staring at the Doulton tiles, wondering how much they

were worth and thinking what a waste they were hidden away in a room that looked like it was hardly used, when Mrs Dickie appeared. She led me into her office and on the way I attempted to make medical small talk with the information I'd just gleaned from my encounter with the brat.

'I've just been talking to a child with hydrosyphilis,' I said casually, hoping to impress her.

If she found my faux pas amusing she certainly didn't show it.

'The correct term is hydrocephalus, Mr O'Grady,' she said briskly, directing me to a chair that stood before an ornate and colossal desk. 'Water on the brain in layman's terms. Now kindly take a seat and you can tell me what experience you've had with children.'

After half an hour's grilling and much to my surprise, she offered me the job. 'The hours are seven thirty in the morning till nine thirty in the evening, five days a week. You will be given an hour off in the afternoon and fifteen minutes in the morning and evening for coffee break and evening meal. You will be expected to sleep in once or twice a month. The salary is £1,410.00 per annum, live in or out optional. We would like you to start when term begins on 6 January and I will be writing to you presently with your Contract of Employment. Good day.' And so for a seventy hour week I would earn £27.11p before tax. I considered myself in the money.

'They're letting you loose with a gang of handicapped kids?' My mother's tone was sceptical but she also sounded more than a little impressed. 'Well I never, it might be the making of you.' My poor ma, always hoping that each new employment venture would be the 'making of me'.

'Wait though before you start handing in your notice, don't

go leaving that abattoir before Christmas,' she warned, hand on hip. 'You don't want to lose out on the free turkey and a nice piece of beef, do you, it'd be a crying shame.'

It was customary for FMC Meats to give their employees a turkey and a joint of meat at Christmas. My mother had been looking forward to it since I started working there.

'Have you seen what they want for a turkey these days?' she said, her voice rising in sheer disbelief. 'And as for the price of meat, well, don't talk to me about that. I bought a piece of liver last week from that robbing sod on Church Road, this big it was.' She demonstrated the size of the offending offal using her thumb and forefinger. 'The price of it! I told him, I only want it for a casserole, not a bloody transplant. Now what d'ya want for your tea? There's a nice bit of yellow fish in the fridge I can throw in the pan.'

My ma never did get the turkey or the beef. The afternoon that I left the abattoir I met some friends at the Woodside Hotel for a leaving drink and ended up getting so plastered that I left both turkey and beef on the number 60 bus. They're probably still there, going round and round on the top deck.

At first I opted to 'live in' rather than get up at some ungodly hour to make the journey to West Kirby in time for work at half seven, even though it meant paying a sizeable chunk out of my weekly wage for the pleasure. Mrs Dickie was a stickler for punctuality and had been known to lock the door a minute after half-past seven so that any latecomers would have to ring the bell to get in and face one of her eloquent retributions. I was frequently on the mat in Dickie's office over the years for bad timekeeping as well as other misdemeanours. The living-in quarters were like monks' cells, tiny grey cubicles containing a bed and a sink. There was a communal sitting room, equally grim, with a television that had the worst reception on the Wirral. I hated it and lasted a month, running home to Mamma with a bag full of dirty washing to be greeted with 'Not again! Will I ever bloody well get rid of you?'

My memory of the first day at the Convalescent Home (or Conny Home as we all called it) is a frenzied blur of wheel-chairs, suitcases and children arriving back after their Christmas holidays. The children never called us by our Christian names, I was always Mr O'Grady, which I thought an unnecessary formality and one I never really got used to. The noise was incessant as they chattered away excitedly about the time they'd had at home and the presents, both real and fictional, that they'd received for Christmas. Suitcases had to be unpacked, clothes sent down to the laundry to be washed and then put away, heads deloused, school uniforms sorted, beds allocated, medication given – it was chaos.

Apart from a few odd lectures from the nursing sisters after I'd been there three years, I received no formal training at all. I was simply thrown in at the deep end and left to get on with it, gleaning information about the children and their dis-abilities as I went along. It was undoubtedly a baptism of fire, but I left the home with a valuable education in caring for children with disabilities that would stand me in good stead in the years to come.

There were over a hundred and forty boys and girls of all ages and disabilities in the Conny Home, separated into units with names like Truth, Courage and Prudence. I was put in charge of Courage and by God I needed it. Courage housed fifteen boys ranging from eleven to thirteen. They totally ignored me at first, sensing and then taking advantage of my total ineptitude and lack of experience. These kids had been at the home for a few years and by now were old lags, so they weren't about to let a gormless novice rule the roost. After a fourteen-hour shift I'd stagger upstairs to my cell of a room, completely exhausted and feeling totally inadequate, wondering if childcare had been the right choice of profession.

After a term on Courage and just when I'd begun to get to know this surly bunch, and more importantly had become fairly adept at keeping them in some semblance of order, I was moved to another unit, Truth 2. These boys were a lot younger, their ages ranging from seven to nine, and surprisingly I found caring for them a lot easier even though they required far more attention. Out of the eleven in my care, there was an older boy with muscular dystrophy, three asthmatics, two boys with colostomy bags, a diabetic, assorted skin diseases including a lad covered from head to toe in psoriasis, a spina bifida, and a couple with what was then known as 'social debility', a euphemism for neglected, unloved and abused. The kid with hydrocephalus who I'd met the day of my interview was also on my unit. His name was Alan and he was a troublesome but hilarious little monster, an arrogant, precocious peacock of a child who barely reached my kneecaps and who I swear was the inspiration for the devil baby Stevie in the animated sitcom *Family Guy*. From the minute he opened his sly little eyes in the morning he chattered away incessantly until by teatime every member of the staff could be found hiding in the sluice, driven there by this child's unabating confabulation. Undaunted, Alan would then shift his attention to his imaginary friend (who no doubt had a pig's head, fiery red eyes and was known in his locality as Beelzebub) and proceed to turn his ear into a piece of well-chewed liver.

To the uninitiated Alan looked as if butter wouldn't melt in his mouth, yet he possessed a vicious temper and was prone to violent outbursts if provoked. For an eight-year-old he had a remarkably extensive vocabulary of profanities, cursing like a docker who'd just lost his pay packet and lashing out with his tiny fists and feet at his unfortunate antagonist. Even his imaginary friend kept a low profile on days like this. The other boys loathed him and tended to keep him at arm's length, wary of his unpredictable temper and over-fondness for snitching on them. As it happened, snitching was Alan's favourite pastime. Forever trying to curry favour with Mrs Dickie, if at any time he couldn't be found he was more than likely to be in her office, spinning a yarn about either a member of staff or one of the boys. He was an inveterate tale-teller and a shocking liar who told outrageous stories about his wonderful home life to compensate for the sad lack of one and, despite all his shortcomings, I was very fond of the little horror.

My favourite boy – not that we were supposed to have any favourites – was Stephen, a lad of twelve who had muscular dystrophy. There is as yet no cure for this terrible muscle-wasting disease and sufferers rarely make it into their middle teens. Stephen was dependent on his carer for everything, paralysed from the neck down apart from a slight movement in his right arm and hand which enabled him to operate the 'joy-stick' on his electric wheelchair. His neck muscles were beginning to atrophy and his head shook like a bobble toy as he slowly steered his massive girth in his electric chariot down the corridor, barking instructions to any children in his path to 'Move your arse, spaz.'

The kids could be terribly cruel to each other and highly inventive with their abusive insults. Stephen's arch enemy was Andy, another wheelchair-bound boy with spina bifida, and together they would enjoy long sessions of verbal spats.

'Blob, you can't even wipe your own bum,' Andy would shout at Stephen, which was a bit rich since Andy couldn't either.

'Crab's legs,' Stephen would retort, referring to Andy's withered limbs. 'You should be in a bucket on the beach.'

'Fat bastard!'

'Hunchback!'

'Mong!'

'Sir?' (This coming from little Alan, who could sniff out a good row at ten miles and enjoyed nothing more than muscling in and adding fuel to the fire.)

'What is it, Alan?'

'Can you tell these two spackers to stop calling each other names, please. They're giving me a fucking headache.'

To spare you endless pages of Life at the Conny Home, why don't I describe a typical day?

6am

The alarm goes off. I ignore it completely and roll over. Mother's voice from next door shouts at me to 'Get up or your head will go flat and why should I be persecuted at my time of life with the thankless task of trying to raise a lazy swine out of his pit?' Quick swill in the bathroom sink, what my aunty Chris calls a prostitute's wash – face, neck, hands and armpits. There's no such thing as a shower in Holly Grove and it would have taken too long to heat the water for a bath and my ma would have ended up in hospital after the murderous expense of using the immersion heater and all the fifty pences that would have been eaten up by the electricity meter. ('Who do you think I am? One of the Rothschilds?')

Quick cup of tea and a fag ('They'll kill you, those bloody

things, stinking the house out') and then leg it down the hill to Green Lane Station to catch the train to Hamilton Square and change for the West Kirby line. Nina la Roche enjoyed taking the train to West Kirby with me, on the odd occasion I had to pay a trip to my bank on my day off, transforming the half-hour journey into a trip on the Orient Express. Manor Road was revamped into Rue du Manoir while Hoylake became Hoylaken, an exclusive spa town some-where in the Dolomites.

My solitary journey into work was less exotic and I'd usually arrive at the Conny Home in time for a quick cup of scalding milky coffee from the tea urn in the staff room before running upstairs to wake the kids. If the train timings had not gone according to plan or if I'd overslept, a late arrival meant finding the front door locked and the wrath of Mrs Dickie waiting inside.

7.30am

Wake the boys and send them off into the bathroom to get washed. Strip whatever beds have been peed on in the night, and then make and change eleven beds. The able-bodied boys were supposed to do this themselves, but they made such a pig's ear of it that their attempts would never pass muster with Mrs Dickie so it was easier to do it myself.

Tell the boys to get dressed while I get Stephen out of bed and into his wheelchair (not an easy task with a twelve-stone boy). Take Stephen into the bathroom and get him on to the toilet. Run back on to the unit to separate Alan and Colin, who are tearing each other's hair out. Get Stephen off the loo, give him a good all-over wash applying cream and powder to his pressure points, get him into his tracksuit. Have a look at the eczema and psoriasis boys to make sure their condition hasn't worsened in the night and then ask if Tommy has changed his colostomy bag. He assures me as always that he has.

8.15am
Check the boys' uniforms to make sure that they'll pass Dickie's eagle-eyed inspection and get them all down for breakfast. Any kid with a button missing or a hole in his sweater is sent back upstairs by this good woman to change. Supervise breakfast, the smell of the hard-boiled eggs over-powering, added to which is the stench of Tommy's overflowing colostomy bag. This has just fallen off due to its weight and slapped on to the floor, spraying liquid shit all over my jeans and most of the dining-room floor. He'd lied as usual and hadn't changed his bag at all. 'Serves you right for not checking,' Mrs Dickie admonishes me in front of every-one. Take Tommy upstairs, clean us both up and fix a new colostomy bag to him. This was a complicated routine back then, involving rubber flanges, belts and tapes and a foul-smelling solution called Zoff which was intended to keep the bag smelling sweet. Return to breakfast room, collect boys, take them back upstairs to gather their school things, comb their hair, wipe egg off their faces, take them to the toilet and then line them up and traipse back downstairs to deliver them into the hands of their respective teachers.

9am
Return to unit and commence cleaning the bathroom, toilets and sluice. The first time I undertook this task I was hauled back by an outraged Dickie, who demanded to know why I hadn't polished the taps.

'Polished the taps, Mrs Dickie?' I laughed, thinking she

was joking. Surely nobody polished taps? Boy, did I have it wrong.

'Indeed we do polish taps, Mr O'Grady.' She raised her eyebrows and pursed her lips tightly to indicate that such wanton slovenliness was inexcusable. 'We also scour and clean every inch of this bathroom, not forgetting the sluice and the toilet area, thoroughly. The spina bifida children are prone to urinary infections and we can't risk any of the children catching anything from unhygienic surroundings, can we? Now have I made myself clear, Mr O'Grady?'

'Crystal, Mrs Dickie.'

'I beg your pardon?'

'Yes, Mrs Dickie.'

I am dragged back on to the unit from scouring urinals and made to pull a bed away from the wall. Mrs Dickie proceeds to run her finger along the waterpipes and bed rails then holds it under my nose for inspection.

'And what is this, Mr O'Grady?'

'It looks like dust, Mrs Dickie.'

'Correct. And you have children in your care who suffer from severe asthma. Dust such as this could bring on an attack. Get it cleaned if you will, please.'

'But isn't it the cleaner's fault there are dusty pipes?'

'No. The children are in your care, not hers.'

'Yes, Mrs Dickie.'

I hated myself for rolling over and being so subservient but it was easier than confrontation as Mrs Dickie was never wrong.

Clean unit and finally go down for coffee and fag break with fellow workers, bemoaning our lot in life, until Dickie puts her little grey head around the door and asks us if we've any intention of returning to work.

10.30am
Break time from school. The teachers don't supervise the kids during playtime, that task is left to us. They retire to the cosy staff room for coffee and biscuits while we try to keep our charges in order. Change any colostomy bags, apply creams, supervise medications, etc.

11.00am
Return kids to school. Check the boys' lockers. Tommy's has two used and very full colostomy bags hidden at the back. Check and sort the linen cupboard, repair holes and replace buttons on any clothes that need it, which seems to be most of them. Up till then I'd never so much as threaded a needle, now here I am stitching away like the brave little tailor.

12 noon
Collect boys and take them into the dining hall for dinner. We sit and eat with the children and it is my least favourite part of the day. I try and teach them some table manners, to no avail, so I slope off and have a sly fag with Janet, one of the housemothers. Get caught having sly fag by 'she who must be obeyed' and verbally cleaned to within an inch of our lives. Return to dining room, supervise playtime, making sure that any of the kids who need changing or medication are sorted out. Take Stephen to the loo. Return kids to school.

2pm
One hour's break so sit in the staff room drinking tea and smoking as leaving the building is not encouraged.

3pm
Return reluctantly to the unit. Sit on a bed with Roma,

another housemother, swinging our legs and chatting until Dickie arrives unexpectedly and enquires if we have nothing better to do and if we knew that beds are not for sitting on. Clean downstairs showers and toilets.

4pm
Kids arrive back from school and line up hungrily in what was probably once a gym for a piece of cake and a glass of milk off a tea trolley.

5–7pm
A period known as Activities. This involves traipsing round West Kirby pushing a wheelchair with a gang of kids hanging off it or sitting in a ridiculously small room known as the telly room trying to keep them entertained for two hours. The telly is a tiny black and white portable of dubious age that sits on a high shelf in the corner and has the same lousy reception as the antique in the live-in staff's sitting room upstairs. The more able-bodied boys go off to play sports or do something with a Christian group called the Crusaders.

7pm
Supper. Those of us who have been on the dreaded Activities are given fifteen minutes to go and have something to eat ourselves, usually rubbery luncheon meat and cold mashed potatoes or my bête noire, cheese pie.

7.30pm
Get the boys washed and ready for bed, check that they have clean shoes and school uniforms for the morning. Bathe the boys with skin conditions in an oatmeal bath and then plaster them with various creams. Betnovate for the eczemas and

something foul-smelling and sticky for the boy with psoriasis. Get Stephen ready for bed, which always takes quite some time as understandably it requires a lot of different positioning in the bed until he is comfortable. Read the boys a story, tuck them in before lights out at eight thirty-ish. Clean bathroom, toilets and sluice, write up notes and if all is quiet on the Western Front leave at 9.30, arrive home if I am lucky at 10.45. Sit eating cheese on toast and watching a bit of telly until the white dot appears and the continuity announcer cheerily reminds me to make sure I've turned the television set off. He's followed closely by a slightly louder reminder from my mother upstairs, who has a phobia about all things electric, to make sure I've pulled all the plugs out and turned everything off. In bed by midnight. Up again at six to start the whole bloody circus anew.

Most of the regular children went home at the end of each term. Only a handful of kids remained behind, including Stephen and Andy and some of the more severely disabled children who had nowhere else to go. To make sure that the staff didn't idle the time away we were ordered to clean the place from top to bottom, scrubbing floors, washing walls down, scraping off the wax that had steadily accumulated on the wheelchairs' wheels and perform endless other tasks. Add to this a number of disabled children who came to stay for a month as convalescents and you're talking hard graft.

I had a real affection for the Down's syndrome children. I loved them and still do. One in particular, a Welsh girl named Moya who must've weighed in at fifteen stone and could probably fell a brewery dray horse with a single blow, was one of my favourites. She was indiscriminate as to where and to whom she would drop her drawers and reveal her bare backside. She got us banned from the newsagent's by the station. Sensing that the owner wasn't very keen on having gangs of kids from the Conny Home in his shop she consequently dropped the voluminous bloomers and bent over, offering the rather proper proprietor a bird's-eye view of her ample buttocks. To give this action a bit more clout she'd shout her name at the top of her voice and slap her bum repeatedly in a manner reminiscent of a tribal war dance. It was quite a sight and caused pandemonium among the more genteel members of West Kirby society. I personally laughed until I got a stitch in my side every time she did it. Not very professional behaviour, I know, but I just couldn't help myself nor could I bring myself to tell off this otherwise enchanting girl.

One of the nursing sisters, a grisly little Irish woman, said to me one day in the dispensary, 'They're not human, you know, Down's children.'

'How d'ya mean, Sister?' That statement sounded a little too Third Reich for my liking.

'I don't mean this in any nasty way, I just mean that they are so very special, untainted by worldly worries, that I really do believe they are related to the faery folk.'

I knew exactly what she meant. Down's children are indeed very special and we can learn a lot from them. Unsullied, they see the world and those who inhabit it with a different eye and are a joy to be with.

One good thing about the holidays was that we got to take the children to the cinema. There was a really old-fashioned local picture house that didn't mind us bringing a gang of kids in on a Saturday morning. In fact they went out of their way to accommodate us by opening fire doors so the kids in wheelchairs had easier access, and even gave them free drinks and ice cream. There was quite a steep rake in this cinema, and I'd park my two wheelchairs in the aisle next to my seat where I could keep an eye on them, Andy next to me with Stephen close behind him. Halfway through the film I heard Andy cry out, 'Sir, Stephen has taken my brake ahhfffffff . . .' just before he rolled down the aisle and into the orchestra pit. With his severely limited mobility it had taken Stephen the best part of forty minutes to lean forward and surreptitiously remove the brake on Andy's wheely.

Thankfully Andy lay unhurt but squawking like a parrot upside down in his chair, trapped in the folds of the velvet curtain that ran around what was once the orchestra pit, while his nemesis Stephen sat shaking in his chair, what bits he could still shake, tears of laughter running down his cheeks. What could I say to him? I was roaring with laughter myself and besides, it did your heart good to see him having fun even if it was at Andy's expense.

Stephen was a brave lad who accepted the curse of muscular dystrophy without complaint. After I'd been at the home nearly three years I came in one morning to find his mattress rolled up and his locker cleared out. I didn't have to ask where he was, I knew what had happened by the red eyes and trembling lips of the other housemothers and fathers. It was Shelagh, a housemother unsurpassed at caring for children, who took me into the sluice and gently told me that he'd died in the night. I was devastated.

'Where have all his pictures gone from around his bed,' was all I could think of saying, 'and the little radio I bought him?'

'Mrs Dickie took them all down earlier. She wants us to take his mattress downstairs to be fumigated and—'

Before she could finish the sentence I was off in a blind rage and down to Dickie's office, barging in without even bothering to knock. How could she be so clinical and unfeeling towards a boy who she knew we were all so fond of?

Dickie was sat behind her desk, Stephen's pictures of the Bay City Rollers spread out in front of her. She gave me a sad little look that silenced me in my tracks. 'Yes I know, dear,' she said calmly and quietly, 'I'm so very sorry as I realize how close you were to him, we all were, but you must remember that we still have other children in our care. Their welfare comes first and foremost and we must remain professional at all times, regardless of any heartbreak. Life must go on as normal for the children's sake. Now go and get yourself a cup of coffee and gather your wits.'

It was at that moment I realized just what a supreme nurse Mrs Dickie was. All the bullying and cajoling to motivate us, the obsession with cleanliness and high standards, it was all for the sake of the children. If hospitals today had the likes of a Mrs Dickie at the helm then I dare say there would be no such things as MRSA or E. coli; no self-respecting germ would dare put its slimy foot near any of Mrs Dickie's wards. I've seen her sit up all night nursing a child who was having a severe asthma attack when she should have been off-duty, and watched her roll her sleeves up and get stuck in when we were short-staffed. The woman was a bloody legend.

I was three years working at the Conny Home, the longest I'd ever stayed in any of my jobs so far, and it was during this period that I first met Vera. Aficionados of Lily Savage will know that Vera was Lily's sister, but how many realize that Vera actually exists? Diane and I were in one of our 'getting on like a house on fire' periods; we'd even spent Sharon's first Christmas together, although if I recall rightly we were at each other's throats come the Queen's Speech. However, during this relatively halcyon phase we thought we'd enter a fancy dress competition at the Bear's Paw. Sharon was a toddler now and no longer screamed like a banshee if she was left alone in a room with me. These days she preferred to glower at me mistrustfully from her high chair, her bottom lip the size of a Suri tribeswoman's and wobbling dangerously.

I'm not very impressed with tiny babies. Their sole purpose in life, as far as I can see, is to eat, sleep, shit and scream and turn perfectly sane and amiable adults, who once had lives of their own, into complete baby-obsessive bores ('I'm sure she smiled at me today' . . . 'Who drank nearly a whole bottle this morning then?' . . . 'She slept all through the night, didn't you? Yes you did, who's a good little girl for her mummy?' . . . 'Would you like to hold her?' etc.) and indeed I do like to hold them as long as I can give 'em back but I much prefer them as toddlers, when they're far more interesting. Now that Sharon was nearly two I was beginning to get over my earlier fears and even secretly finding her very appealing.

The three of us, Diane, myself and the baby, went over to a fancy dress hire shop that we'd heard of in New Brighton to see if we could find anything suitable for the Bear's Paw's fancy dress do. I felt quite proud pushing Sharon along the prom in her buggy, trying to pretend that Diane wasn't with me as she trailed behind, her nose running in the biting wind, shuffling along in unsuitable footwear like an old Chinese concubine with bound feet, moaning, 'Hang on, will you? I can't walk very fast in these shoes.' Why pay a small fortune for a pair of shoes that don't fit you, are crippling to wear and are impossible to walk a couple of yards in without screaming in silent agony just because you think those killer heels will make you the envy of every other woman on the street? I know, I know, it's a woman's thing . . . an unfathomable mystery to most men unless you happen to be a tranny or a drag queen and something I didn't understand myself until I started forcing my size nine and a halfs into a pair of size seven mules from Huddersfield market. My feet look like quavers today, a legacy of twenty-five years of Lily bloody Savage – even though eventually, when I was earning a few bob, I started having Lily's shoes handmade by Mr Savva of Chiltern Street and oh, the bliss of that, handmade stilettos crafted out of soft kid leather.

Our trip turned out to be a bit of a wasted journey as there wasn't much of a selection in this drab little shop which, not surprisingly, is now long gone. There was just the usual grimy tat and dusty Am-Dram cast-offs for which you'd need a tetanus jab before you'd dare put one on. In the end we made the best of a bad job and hired two ballet dancers' outfits, but only after Diane assured me that she'd have these two louse-ridden costumes with their greasy seams and dubious stains dry-cleaned before we wore them on the big night. I was going as Margot Fonteyn and Diane as Rudolf Nureyev, not my ideal choice, but given the circumstances and our highly limited finances there was no other choice. We sat in a café and had fish and chips before making the trek back to the flat in Bootle. The waitress made a huge fuss of Sharon, remarking to Diane while looking at me, 'She's the ringer of her dad, isn't she?' I wanted the ground to swallow me whole. To be mistaken for part of a cosy domestic scene terrified me.

Later that afternoon, when we made it back to Diane's, she found that she had unexpected company.

'Hiya, girl, yer downstairs neighbour opened the front door

for us and since your flat door was open we thought we'd come up and wait for yer, hope you don't mind.'

It was Penny. Penny was one of the first 'real' queens I'd come across after a guy I'd met took me to the Lisbon, a Liverpool gay pub. I'd been a little wary of Penny at first, not being impressed in those not-so-distant days with men who acted like women and called themselves by female names. However, exposure to the gay scene had made me a lot more liberal-minded and less uptight, and besides, who was I to throw stones at glass houses seeing as I was now renowned in certain circles as 'Lil'. Penny was a real character, hard as nails and always on the mooch, and if you were short of funds then you could always count on Penny to find a 'mush' to buy you a half of cider. Diane's make-up was spread all over the kitchen table and Penny was carefully smearing foundation on a younger queen's face.

'This is me mate, Alisssssssse.' Penny drew his 'S's out like the snake in *The Jungle Book*. I recognized this Alice as someone I'd once refused to serve when I was working as a barman in the Bear's Paw. He'd come in one night just before closing time absolutely out of his mind and stood swaying at the bar like an Indian fakir's cobra, his watery eyes starting to meet in the middle behind a pair of round John Lennon specs tinted orange. He was incapable of coherent speech and clutched on to the bar top for dear life as he tried to steady himself and order a drink before a combination of booze and gravity got the better of him and he finally hit the floor with a loud slap and a low moan. I can visualize him now being helped to a bench by a couple of customers: slightly smaller than me, as thin as a lath (he made Olive Oyl look clinically obese), shoulder-length blond hair parted down the middle, the specs with lenses as thick as milk-bottle bottoms sliding down his nose. His ensemble consisted of a Snow White and the Seven Dwarfs T-shirt, skin-tight denim loons, torn and frayed at the hem, a ratty old fur coat and flip-flops. 'Bloody drugged-up hippy,' I sniffed, giving him a filthy look my ma and my aunty Chris would've been proud of.

I looked at him now, sat in Diane's kitchen with a full face of badly applied make-up and squirming uncomfortably on a kitchen chair. Penny stood back, sucking on a tail comb, and proudly admired his handiwork.

'I've always been good with make-up,' he boasted without a hint of irony in his voice. 'She'd easily pass as a real woman, don't ya think? Look at her, she's as camp as Christmas, aren't you, queen?'

Penny spoke to Alice in the same way Hylda Baker spoke to Cynthia and it was very hard not to laugh. Alice brought a new meaning to the word 'camp' and at first glance it was hard to tell whether he was a girl or a boy. He peered myopically at me through blind eyes before frantically rummaging among the make-up on the table for his glasses. His face fell when he recognized me and you could see him flushing a deep shade of crimson even under the inch-thick make-up.

'Hiya,' he muttered, mortified with shame.

'Hiya,' I answered back, trying not to laugh. Little did I know that this Alice and I were to become lifelong friends (give or take a couple of years when we fell out).

'I'll go and wash this off and get changed,' he mumbled, making his way to the bathroom. It was only then that Diane realized what he was wearing.

'Get my halter top off, please,' she shouted after him as he skulked out of sight. 'And my earrings if you don't mind. Honestly, bloody queens.'

Alice was to undergo many changes of name over the years – Blanche, Miriam, Mrs McGoo – before finally arriving at the moniker by which almost everyone knows him today, Vera Cheeseman. Confused? You will be. In the thirty-five years that I've known him I've never called him by his real name, which happens to be Alan. Neither has he ever called me Paul. I've always been Lily or, as he pronounces it when he's had a drink, Lully. He adopts a 'half-crown' voice when he's pissed that very few people can comprehend. Fortunately, after years of experience, I can now speak and understand 'Veranese' fluently and over the decades have been called upon on many an occasion to translate for bemused strangers.

'Wot turm uz a, Lully?' translates into 'What time is it, Lily?'

Anyway, Diane had a bottle of wine which I convinced her to crack open and after a few glasses we all became quite matey and jolly, eventually convincing Vera (the artist formerly known as Alice) to come to the fancy dress with us. 'I've never dressed up as a woman before,' he protested. Bloody hell, you haven't got far to go, I thought

Vera, confident after a couple of glasses of Blue Nun, confessed that he'd never liked me and had always referred to me as 'that long snotty streak of piss who always swept into Sadie's, nose in the air, with those two other long streaks of piss trailing behind'. By the two other streaks of piss I assumed Vera meant Nina and Ron. We buried our past loathing for each other and proceeded to get on like long-lost brothers, or should I say sisters?

We came from totally different backgrounds. He'd been born in a tenement block in the Chinatown district of Liverpool, the second youngest of a large family, and as a boy to earn a few coppers he'd minded the car of a Chinese prostitute called Miss Wong while she visited one of the Chinese gambling dens. He was very bright and extremely funny and worked at a place called the Rod Mill, making pillowcases on an industrial sewing machine and then stuffing them with feathers. What really sealed our friendship was the discovery that we shared a mutual obsession in life – going out clubbing, preferably seven nights a week and, in Vera's case, seven afternoons as well. Yep, you've got to hand it to Vera. No, I mean it, you really do have to hand it to him, he's as blind as a bat and would drop the glass otherwise.

Diane rooted out one of her sixties monstrosities for Vera to wear for the fancy dress and so, clad in a hideous full-length floral dress and straw hat complete with umbrella, he went as Mary Poppins and came second, the bastard. Diane and I were flaming, after all the effort we'd gone to we'd come nowhere. I knew from the start that we shouldn't have gone as a couple especially in these nasty costumes – me in my cheap sateen leotard with sagging net tutu dotted with fag burns slung around my waist, wrinkled tights and scuffed ballet slippers, a child's plastic tiara that I'd bought in Woolies pinned to an ash-blond ball of frizz that I had the nerve to call a wig; Diane in her brown and orange velvet tunic with a Coke bottle that I'd shoved down the leg of her tights, despite her many protestations, as a crude representation of Rudolf's masculinity. During the course of the evening the Coke bottle slowly slid down her leg, finally settling at her ankle, causing people to think she had a peculiar deformity. Vera won five quid for coming second and promptly spent it all across the bar. Say what you like about Vera, he's always first up to the bar when it comes to getting the bevvies in, providing he's in funds.

We went out on the town more or less every night of the week whether or not we had any money. There was always a 'mush', to quote Penny, who would see you right for a couple of halves of lager. The phone would ring.

'Are you there, Lily? What you doing tonight?'

'I wouldn't mind going out.'

'I've got no money though.'

'Well, I've got about a pound. That will get us into Sadie's, buy us a few drinks and a packet of fags. Can't you borrow a couple of bob off your mam?'

'I can't, I still owe her money from last week.'

'Go on.'

'Oh all right, I'll see what I can do.'

'Meet you outside James Street Station at half eight, we'll have one in Kingston House first.'

'Bollocks, me jeans are wet, I'll have to iron them dry. Oh, there's the pips, see ya later.'

Kingston House was a sailors' club on the corner of James Street, supposedly for the use of merchant sailors only, but if you cracked on that you'd just docked and wrote down the name of your ship when you signed in the doorman would turn a blind eye, even though Vera and I were the most unlikely pair of sailors ever to set foot inside the door. The club was subsidized so the booze was extremely cheap, ideal for two queens with only £1.75 between them. Invariably once inside we'd find Josie, a world-weary sea queen, perched on a bar stool nursing a pint of lager. Josie had worked for the Blue Funnel Line as a steward since the days when Odysseus had set out from the Trojan Wars on his ten-year voyage home to Ithaca. There wasn't a port in the world that Josie hadn't docked in over the years. He was a solitary figure, thin as a whippet and always dressed in the same ensemble of skin-tight jeans and black leather jacket, his bony fingers adorned with a startling collection of gold rings and an enormous pear-shaped gold earring hanging from his right earlobe. Considering he'd spent so much time at sea he was a gentle soul, softly spoken and rather delicate. I was envious of what I considered was a fabulous lifestyle and wished that I could sail into Hong Kong Harbour instead of Woodside Ferry or the Pier Head.

If there were no sailors in the bar interested in buying a couple of chirpy scrubbers a drink we'd move on quickly to Paco's Bar in Stanley Street or the Lisbon before hitting Sadie's Bar Royale in Wood Street, providing Sadie, the fearsome chatelaine of this establishment, would let Vera in. Sadie hated Vera as he had got it into his head that Vera had once tried to make a pass at the boyfriend of one of his trusted cronies in the gents' lav. It was obvious that Vera had done no such thing because picking men up in lavs wasn't his forte and the boyfriend was a grubby piece of pier-head rent with a mean face and the sallow complexion of an undernourished maggot who Vera, even in the most advanced state of intoxication, wouldn't have touched with surgical gloves and a gas mask on. Once you'd rung the bell on Sadie's door you'd have to wait for him to stick his head out of the second-floor window to see if you were suitable enough to enter the premises.

'Hiya, Tony,' (for this was Sadie's real name) I'd shout up feebly, my voice trailing off into the night at the sight of Sadie's gimlet eyes scrutinizing us in the manner of a carrion crow eyeing up roadkill. The window would slam down in disgust and the testy old troll would make his slow descent down the long flight of stairs that Vera had tumbled down once or twice in the past before flinging the door open with a cheery greeting.

'Is she pissed again?' mine host would bark, glaring at Vera.

'No I'm not, honest to God, on me life,' Vera would splutter, swaying slightly.

'She's not pissed, we've just come straight from work,' I'd plead. 'We haven't had a drink yet, honestly . . .'

'Get in then,' Sadie would snap at us grudgingly, holding his hand out for the admission fee, the princely sum of twenty pence each which we thought was daylight robbery.

'And if I catch you anywhere near that cottage with Bertha Bucket's affair you'll be down these stairs and out that fuckin' door before you can fart, d'ya hear me?'

I'd try and make polite conversation as we followed Sadie up the stairs.

'Is the club busy?'

'Well, you'll be able to find out for yourself in a minute when you get in there, won't you?'

Small talk with the clientele was not Sadie's finest quality.

Midweek, Sadie's could be a bit grim. A dimly lit bar with only a handful of the usual suspects dotted around the place staring into their drinks, glancing up momentarily at each sound of the doorbell in the vain hope that it might herald the arrival of a customer who could just turn out to be 'the one', or at least a quick grapple for the night. The overpowering stench of Jeyes Fluid emanating from the gents' toilets caught in the back of your throat and you secretly wondered why you bothered making the effort as you drank your warm bottle of cider and stared at the lone drunk dancing with himself to the New Seekers' 'You Won't Find Another Fool Like Me' on the tiny dance floor. Vera and I made the best of it. We were out on the lash and that was all that mattered. We never went out with the intention of 'pulling', we much preferred to get hammered and go in search of the elusive 'good time'. If a lift home or a promise of a tumble in the sack came along, so much the better, but it certainly wasn't at the top of our list of priorities.

At weekends Sadie's was packed to the rafters and full of characters. Big Carol, the ten-foot tranny, dressed head to toe in mini skirt and polo neck courtesy of Littlewoods' catalogue, would sip a pint of bitter as if it were a cut-glass schooner of sherry. A male nurse, known affectionately as the Queen Mum, who stood at the end of the bar with a rabbit-fur cape draped around his shoulders and a cheap diamanté tiara wedged in his hair, would wave regally at passing customers as he knocked back the Babycham. He committed suicide by jumping out of a window and through the glass roof of the ear, nose and throat hospital, or so we were led to believe until he turned up years later in a Blackpool disco very much alive and well.

The local comic, Pete Price, former compère of the famous Shakespeare Club until it burned down, would sweep in with a retinue of followers. Talk about the circus arriving in town. Pete was quite a sight – not in the least bit camp – three-inch platform shoes peeping out from under the turn-ups of a pair of Persil-white flares, a vivid pink paisley-patterned shirt unbuttoned to the waist to reveal a deeply tanned chest and an assortment of gold chains nestling among the hair. A diamond ring that would've knocked the breath out of Elizabeth Taylor flashed on his little finger and an enormous pair of designer sunglasses sat on top of his peroxide-yellow head. To complete this eye-catching wardrobe a full-length wolf-fur coat hung casually from his shoulders. He could've been the love child of Dick Emery and Cruella de Vil and made Liberace look like a member of the Amish. I was terrified of him at first until I got to know him and found that underneath this flash exterior lay hidden a compassionate man.

Penny could be found in a corner draped across some hapless 'mush' that he'd managed to lure into his net. Flushed with success (and large gins), he'd tip Vera and me a sly wink and beckon us over as we mooched past on our way to the dance floor for a jive.

'This is John,' he'd say proudly through pursed lips, introducing us to the elderly drunk he was hanging off. 'He's just going to the bar, aren't ya?' John nodded vaguely in our direction while Penny mimed the words 'Fuckin' loaded' at us behind his back. 'Get them a drink, John,' Penny said grandly as he forcefully assisted his hapless prey to his feet. 'And while you're up there get us a large gin and tonic and twenty Number Ten, will ya.'

Sadie's was a melting pot of good girls and slappers, butch dykes and screaming queens, students and sailors, gangsters and rent boys, sad old drunks and imperious trannies, with the odd respectable queen who'd come over for the night from Knutsford and wondered just what had hit him thrown in for good measure. By the time Sadie threw us all out at closing time ('C'mon, you shower, I've had your money now sling yer 'ook and gerr off 'ome') and I got home, it would be gone two thirty. I had to be up for work at the Conny Home by six but even after only three hours' sleep I'd nearly always manage to drag myself in to face a fourteen-hour shift. If after the alarm clock went off I rolled over and went back to sleep, as I was very much inclined to do, I could always rely on my ma to give me a wake-up call from her bedroom next door.

It was purgatory to get out of my nice warm bed as it was always freezing in that house. Even in the summer there was a distinct chill in the air. I'd charge downstairs and crouch, shivering in front of the gas fire, waiting for the bloody thing to warm up before I could even contemplate facing the Siberian draughts of the back kitchen to put the kettle on. There was never any time for breakfast, just a swallow of tea, a quick swill in the sink, dressed and out of the door and down the hill to catch the train. Once there, the smell of wet beds, leaking colostomy bags and fourteen little boys crammed together in one room would've brought tears to the eyes of a sewage worker. I used to spend the first few minutes dry-retching, particularly if I was a little hung over, but I got used to the early morning smell after a time and could rinse lumps of shit from a soiled sheet in the sluice without even flinching. Fourteen hours a day looking after a gang of handicapped kids would have Mary Poppins reaching for a stimulant, but fortunately for me I had more energy than I needed.

Occasionally once I'd got the boys off to school and could feel my eyes burning from lack of sleep I'd try and sneak a quick kip on one of their beds, not so comfortable when you're over six foot tall and the bed you're attempting to have a sly zizz on wouldn't look out of place in a production of *Snow White and the Seven Dwarfs*. I'd wait until Mrs Dickie was on her coffee break before I'd attempt an illicit snooze but invariably I'd oversleep, only to be woken up out of my coma by a sharp prod in the ribs. Mrs Dickie would want to know exactly what I thought I was doing and if it wasn't too much trouble would I care to come down to the office and explain my behaviour? Eventually the penny dropped that I couldn't burn the candle at both ends and for a while I only went clubbing when I knew I had the next day off, even though it was torture for me to have an early night when I knew that over the water Sadie's and the Bear's Paw were jumping, and somewhere in the crowd was a millionaire who would take me away from a world of nagging women and shitty sheets.

CHAPTER 7

London Calling

'BARKENHEAD SEX IT DABBLE TU.' AS ALWAYS, MY MUM PUT on her Mayfair voice when she answered the phone. 'Heng orn and arl get him for you, Tony.' She put her hand over the mouthpiece and hissed, 'Paul! It's Tony on the blower for you. Get a move on, will you, he's ringing from London and this must be costing him a bloody fortune . . . Heng orn, Tony, he's jist caming.'

Tony was still living in Southend-on-Sea, working for the Customs and Excise, hating every minute of it but sticking it out so he could get his promotion. He was ringing because he wanted me to go down to London as one of his wealthy 'gentleman friends' had given him the keys to his pied-à-terre in Mount Street, Mayfair, for the weekend. Tony attracted wealthy men of a certain age like moths to a flame; he should've been living in the lap of luxury under the patronage of these old geezers instead of rotting in a crummy bedsit in Southend but he was hopeless at playing the whore. Instead it was Tony who spoiled them with gifts of expensive wine and opera tickets out of his paltry civil service wages. The idea of being a kept man was anathema to him. A few meals in fancy restaurants or a weekend on the country estate in Yorkshire was one thing but to actually accept a cash handout was out of the question. I despaired of him.

I jumped at the chance of a couple of lairy days in London. It was my weekend off and I'd just been paid so I arranged to meet him on Saturday morning at the address he gave me.

'We'll have a ball,' he promised and I didn't doubt him.

The pied-à-terre turned out to be a four-storey mansion stuffed full of priceless artworks and antiques, and there was even a self-contained flat for the staff just off the vast kitchen. My room, which had a real air of tranquillity about it, was beautifully decorated with a vast antique bed, an Aubusson rug on the parquet floor, oil paintings on the walls and a vase full of fresh flowers on the highly polished dressing table. The real selling point for me though was the white marble en-suite bathroom complete with a shower in which I spent the best part of the morning.

Showers were a novelty to me. A bath in Holly Grove meant sitting in three inches of tepid water dispensed from the smallest, most miserly immersion heater on Merseyside. You sat hunched up with your knees under your chin, clutching a grainy bar of Lifebuoy soap in one hand and an ancient flannel with the texture of woodchip wallpaper in the other, dodging the icy droplets of water that fell repeatedly from the pulley of wet washing hanging over the bath. It wasn't a particularly joyful experience.

On the bedroom wall over the dressing table hung a small pencil drawing of a woman's head. It wasn't even properly framed. 'What's this bit of old tat?' I asked Tony, highly unimpressed. 'All the other paintings are lovely but this thing spoils the look of the room.'

'That,' he replied, 'is a Leonardo da Vinci etching. Now

stop tapping it, you'll crack the parchment. Come downstairs and we'll have a glass of champagne.'

We sat in the immaculate drawing room drinking Dom Perignon, which Tony assured me was the only bubbly that Dietrich ever drank. I would've been quite happy to drink bleach for breakfast if it meant staying in somewhere like this beautiful house for the entire weekend without once having to venture outside the door, but Tony was having none of it.

'Get your backside into gear, we're going to the Salisbury,' he said.

The Salisbury was a gay pub on St Martin's Lane, full of etched glass, ornate mirrors and polished wood. It was very cruisy and hardly anyone spoke to anyone, preferring instead to communicate via furtive glances and knowing looks. The predominantly Irish bar staff were dismissive to the point of rudeness and one got the feeling that they were more than a little homophobic. Despite the pub's beautiful interior it wasn't one of my favourite places to go for a drink, thanks to the naff bar staff and cruisy old queens, although this was years ago and the staff and pub owners have now changed. The clientele is no longer gay these days; they sensibly moved on long ago to a boozer that appreciates their custom.

I sat down while Tony got the drinks in and as he was waiting to be served he started to chat to a podgy little guy who was wearing a bespoke suit that in its heyday had obviously been extremely smart but was now grubby and shiny with age. Tony, being Tony, bought him a drink and then brought him over to our table.

'This is Robin,' he said, smiling slyly as he presented me to this scruffy little hobbit.

Robin shook my hand effusively and sat down, blowing his

nose on a piece of ragged toilet paper before necking three-quarters of his pint without drawing breath.

'Ah, that's better,' he gasped in his plummy public-school accent, wiping his mouth with the back of his hand. 'I've literally just flown in from Nice, had a quick spot of lunch at La Colombe d'Or before jumping on the plane. Do you know the Colombe d'Or by any chance? No? Oh it's fabulous, up in the hills on the outskirts of Saint-Paul de Vence. Wonderful roast lamb and an incredible cellar, I must take you both for dinner one night.'

Yeah, sure, I thought, watching him greedily demolish the remainder of his pint. He didn't look as if he could run to egg, chips and beans at the New Piccadilly Caff, never mind fancy restaurants in Nice.

Tony, however, seemed impressed and nodded knowingly at the mention of the wine cellar. Being a bit of a connoisseur himself, there was nothing he loved more than a chance to show off his impressive knowledge, but before he could speak Robin had wiped his mouth on the back of his hand again and was carrying on the conversation from where he'd left off.

'Yes, absolutely glorious cellar. May I have a cigarette? I seem to have run out,' he said, smiling, helping himself to one of my Cadets. He inhaled deeply and threw his head back, blowing the smoke towards the ceiling and scrunching his face up as if he were in agony.

'My God, these are strong, aren't they? What are they called?' He examined the cigarette as if he'd never seen one before. 'Are they Turkish?'

'No, they're Cadets,' I snapped, 'and if you don't like them then I suggest you buy a packet of something that's more to your taste. There's a fag machine at the bottom of the stairs, bloody ponce.'

'I would if I had any money, my dear, but I'm afraid all I've got on me are francs at the moment. I haven't had a chance to change them into sterling yet. You couldn't let me have a few quid until we get back to the hotel, could you?'

'What hotel would that be? The Sally Army?' He was getting on my nerves.

'No, I'm staying at the Hilton for the time being and I'd be delighted if you would both join me for dinner tonight,' he said, ignoring my jibe and smiling disarmingly. 'Now are we having another drink?'

Gullible as I was, I didn't believe for one minute that he'd just flown in from Le Column or whatever it was called with its fancy wine cellar *et al.* He looked to me suspiciously like he'd spent the night sleeping rough, unshaven and unwashed as he was with his dirty fingernails and creased suit, and the closest he'd get to a meal at the Hilton would be whatever he'd fished out of the bins round the back. He was all my arse, I thought, a conman, the type who could charm a maggot off a corpse. He'd certainly captivated the normally sagacious Tony, for here he was gaily handing over a tenner so that the bum could 'get a quick round in before we go off and eat'. Robin? Robbin' bastard more like, I muttered as I stomped off to the lav.

We took a taxi to the Hilton, which Tony paid for amid apologies and promises of immediate reimbursement from Robin.

'Let's dump him and go back to the house, I don't believe that he's . . .' The words died on my lips as the doorman opening the cab door tipped his hat and greeted Robin with a 'Good evening, Lord Robin.' Tony winked, delighted with himself and his catch. He liked collecting men with titles, his address book read like *Burke's Peerage*.

'Are you a real lord then?' Out it came before I could stop myself. 'Are you a real lord then?'

Tony snorted and I cringed with embarrassment as I became painfully aware that my voice sounded higher than usual and my already broad Scouse accent more pronounced. Most annoying of all was that my tone suggested I was impressed by this news when in fact I'd intended to sound disbelieving.

Looking at Robin again, it started to make sense. Didn't my ma and Aunty Annie and Chrissie say that 'real gentry' always looked like they 'didn't have a pot to piss in or a window to chuck it out of'? Well, wasn't Milord Robin living proof of that rather direct but nevertheless well-founded theory? Unshaven and tousled, looking like he'd slept in a skip and sounding like Lord Haw-Haw? He certainly appeared to have the right qualifications.

'Nobs never carry cash on them,' I remembered my aunty Chrissie saying. 'They put everything down on account. They haven't got any ready cash anyway, all their wealth is tied up in property and land and then there's the crippling taxes. They haven't got an arse in their trousers.'

'Yes, awful, isn't it?' Lord Robin said over his shoulder as we followed him into the hotel lobby. 'But please don't even think of addressing me as "Lord". I'm plain old Robin to my friends.'

'No danger of that,' I wanted to say, but left it unexpressed as suddenly the night looked like it was beginning to show some potential. Robin breezed up to the reception talking loudly and flapping his hands about, and people were staring. My brown leather bomber jacket and skin-tight jeans felt out of place in the lobby of the Hilton Hotel among the immaculately dressed staff and flashy Yanks.

'Yes, good evening, can I have my key please?' he said, sounding suddenly vague and flustered, exactly like the toffs and eccentrics in *The Avengers*. 'And can you tell me, has my luggage arrived yet?'

'Not yet, Lord Robin, but as soon as it does I'll have it sent directly up to your suite. Is there anything else I can do for you, sir?'

Suite? Suite? Maybe I've got this all wrong.

'Could you cash a cheque for, say, five hundred pounds and, erm . . . send some cigarettes up. A couple of packs of Winston for me and, er, what are those fags you smoke called, Paul?'

Please don't say I smoke Cadets. Cadets were one of the less expensive brands, down there with Sovereign and No. 10. Common as muck. Not the done thing to be seen smoking in the hallowed corridors of the Hilton. A sophisticated Sobranie, yes, or even one of those awful French things that Scottish Billy smoked. Galoshes? Galouise? Ghastly. But most definitely not a humble Cadet.

'Cadets! That was it,' he shouted triumphantly, his voice carrying across the lobby.

Oh Lord.

'I'm afraid we don't stock Cadets, Lord Robin.'

Sweet Jesus, just let the earth open up and take me now.

'However, I can send a member of staff up to the garage to get you some. How many packs?'

'Oh, a couple of cartons,' Robin said absently, ambling off towards the lifts, 'and send some champagne up as well. Oh, and make a reservation for eight o'clock at Trader Vic's, will you?'

His suite was impressive, brown suede sofas and modern art – very *Jason King* – and we sat glugging champagne and looking out of the window at the view across Park Lane to Hyde Park while Robin took a shower. He appeared from the bedroom definitely looking cleaner but still wearing the same clothes. Peeling a few twenties off the five-hundred-quid wad from his recently cashed cheque, he offered to pay back his debt to Tony. It seemed a more than generous interest rate on a loan of ten pounds, give or take the one pound twenty for the taxi, but as I expected Tony refused it. Wouldn't hear of it, he said, please put it back in your wallet. Robin insisted, Tony resisted. In the end Robin turned to me.

'Make him take it, will you plea—?' It was out of his hand and in my pocket before he could finish his sentence. Gift horses and mouths? Not me.

Dinner was very lively. We drank nearly every cocktail that was on the menu, followed by wine and then more champagne and became very animated and loud. I lost all inhibition and did the court jester bit and when the cigarette girl with her tray appeared at the table (they still had 'em then) Robin insisted I took at least a dozen packs. By the end of the evening I had enough to stock a small tobacconist's shop. Oh, a good time was had by all. The other diners must have hated us and even today I'm squirming a little bit as I recall it. Robin in his matter-of-fact way told us wild and highly improbable tales about his titled friends and family and the many adventures and interesting people he'd en- countered on his extensive travels. An outrageous fantasist or not, there was no doubting he was great company and I started to warm to him, my affections no doubt fuelled by that inner glow you get from slugging enough booze to make you feel affable towards all mankind.

He insisted that we came back up to his suite, which suited me fine as I'd never have got back to Mount Street in my condition without having my collar felt. Imagine it: Scouse, blind drunk, weaving up Park Lane with two hundred fags under his coat. I wouldn't have stood a chance, would I? Six months, O'Grady, stand down.

Robin passed out on one of the sofas as soon as we got in. Tony and I collapsed on the bed, too drunk to even raid the minibar. We discussed Lord Robin quietly in the dark, trying to work him out, and in the end came to the unanimous decision that he was indeed a lord, albeit a little eccentric, but obviously very wealthy. I must remember to take the shampoos and soap out of the bathroom before we go was the last thing I remember thinking before I sank into a deep sleep.

The phone was ringing. I came to with a start and half opened my eyes. Where the hell was I and why won't somebody answer that phone? I moaned like a cow in labour as the pain of the hangover started to kick in and put my hands over my ears. The phone eventually stopped ringing and from another room I could hear a voice talking to the inconsiderate swine on the other end of the line. Who would be so persistent as to ring and ring at this godforsaken hour of the morning? A pox on 'em whoever they are, I rambled to myself, rolling over and trying to go back to sleep. As I lay there, the night's events slowly came back to me in sporadic flashes. I nudged Tony.

'Jesus,' he groaned.

Robin knocked on the door before breezing into the room. There was something pathetic about him in his crumpled suit, trying unsuccesfully to disguise the anxiety in his voice as he explained, 'I just have to pop downstairs to the main desk, there's a bit of a problem to sort out. Bloody American Express. Order yourselves something to eat, I shan't be long.'

133

'What time is it?'

'Good heavens, it's one thirty. What a night, eh? Got a fag on you, anybody?'

'Help yourself, there's thousands of 'em on the bedroom floor,' Tony croaked, slowly pulling himself up in the bed. As soon as Robin left to attend to his 'bit of a problem' Tony was out of the bed and hastily pulling his clothes on.

'Get up now and get dressed,' he demanded. 'We've got to get out of here.'

'Why?' I could do with another hour in bed.

'American Express, that's why. Didn't you hear him? He said there's a problem with his card which means it's probably nicked, so get dressed unless you want to be seen as an accomplice.'

Not again. Not the police. My mother would kill me.

I was out of bed like a whippet on cocaine and we were both dressed and out of the door within minutes, taking the lift to the mezzanine instead of all the way to the ground floor so we could watch the front desk from the balcony, un-observed. There was a bit of a commotion going on. The manager was there and a couple of members of security. Two coppers were talking to Robin, who was running his hands through his hair and shouting that there had been a terrible misunderstanding. The police eventually took him off.

'Told you,' Tony said. 'That card wasn't his and you were right all along, he was a fraud, no more a lord than you or me. Still, it was a bit of fun. Now let's make a discreet exit. Side door, I think?'

Before I caught the train back to Liverpool and Tony to Southend on the Sunday evening we went for a drink. I can't remember which pub it was but I do remember a guy at the bar telling me that he was an 'out' gay football referee and also a lord. It seemed that London's streets were not paved with gold but with peers of the bloody realm. He asked me for my phone number so I gave him Diane's address and told him to drop me a line there, not wanting my mother to come across any fruity correspondence as she was 'tidying up'. Hopefully Diane wouldn't mind me using her address as a PO box providing I read her the contents of the letter. Either way I'd had my bellyful of lords, even fairly handsome ones like this specimen. The ball's in his court, I thought, and if he wants to get in touch then fine and dandy. If not, well, I really couldn't care less.

CHAPTER 8

Littlehampton

NORMAN DID WRITE, AND I WROTE BACK, WHICH eventually led to regular conversations on the phone. On my twenty-first birthday he sent me a hundred pounds and a promise of a trip on the Orient Express. He also asked me to go and live with him, in Littlehampton. I hardly knew the man but the head was well and truly turned. The movie *Murder on the Orient Express*, featuring Albert Finney and a galaxy of stars, had recently been released. I must have seen it at least three times and would've done just about anything to ride on that beautiful train from Istanbul to Paris. I loved trains, still do, although it would be years before I fulfilled my ambition to travel on the Orient Express.

My twenty-first birthday party took place in Sadie's. Back then, after a few drinks I became, to put it mildly, boisterous and mischievous, although in retrospect I think yobbish would describe my drunken behaviour more accurately. Once I pushed Vera down a six-foot hole in the road on our way up Church Street from the Bear's Paw to Sadie's. His cries brought the workmen out of their hut, exclaiming, 'Don't worry, lad, we'll get your girlfriend out,' as they mistook the tears of laughter running down my face for those of grief and concern.

At my twenty-first I really excelled myself, flinging my birthday cake across the club and scoring a direct hit on Vera's face, and dragging Diane around the floor by her ankle until she had carpet burns on her back and one of her contact lenses fell out. Not surprisingly, come closing time no one was speaking to me. This darker side of me, the unsuspecting Norman knew nothing about. When I was 'lively with drink' I made mild-mannered Clark Kent look like Attila the Hun.

I'd been at the Conny Home three years now and typically I was bored. In my last year the nursing sisters gave us a few tutorials to prepare us for a written exam. If you passed you got a certificate that meant absolutely nothing as it was not a recognized qualification. I did very well, thanks to the *Reader's Digest Medical Dictionary*, and can still remember today how to do an Acetest for ketones in a diabetic's urine and how to change a colostomy bag.

The winds of change blew through the Conny Home. A new childcare superintendent had been appointed and he was supposed to be a bit of a mover and shaker, a wonder boy with innovative methods who was going to transform the place. Let's call him Greg Tate. He wore a cravat and had a goatee and I hated him from the minute he first swanned into the building with a lion cub in tow, encouraging the children to stroke it while reassuring a surprisingly captivated Mrs Dickie that the animal was perfectly safe around children. The cub seemed to grow into a hefty beast literally overnight. I remember sitting in the staff room trying to pretend I was invisible as it prowled menacingly around the tables, looking for something or someone to eat. Greg Tate liked to drive around West Kirby with this cub on the back seat of his car, hanging out of the window like a dog, until one day the sensible creature leaped on him from behind and badly mauled his face. He ended up in hospital and the cub went to Chester Zoo.

In my three years at the home I'd never once hit any of the children, wouldn't dream of it as belting kids just wasn't and isn't in my nature. No matter how near to the brink of insanity I was driven, I'm proud to say I never resorted to violence. Hitting a child was quite rightly a sackable offence and so I was more than a little bemused to find myself on two occasions in Greg Tate's office, wrongly accused of hitting two of the boys. Curiously he refused to name the boys I'd supposedly given a good hiding to, claiming he'd witnessed me in action and that was all the evidence he needed. He was a liar and he knew it, but it was his word against mine and Mrs Dickie took Greg Tate's side. 'One more warning,' she said angrily, 'and you will be instantly dismissed. Now get on with your work.' Oh for a union for underpaid, overworked houseparents, I moaned for the umpteenth time, for if there were such an organization the staff at the Conny Home certainly didn't know about it.

Tate definitely had it in for me and wanted me out, and since it was impossible to keep secrets in the home all the staff and most of the children knew of my alleged crimes. Tate's pet houseparents had been told to keep a close eye on me and what authority I had with some of the boys went out the window. Tell them to clean their teeth and they'd threaten to go downstairs to Tate and whine that I'd hit them. One night as I was reading the boys a story, Tate marched through the unit. I used to act out the tale I was reading and the lads loved it. Tate caught the tail end of the evil fairy's speech to the prince she had chained up in her dungeon: 'You'll never escape from here,' I cackled over one of the boys, who was squealing with mock terror in his bed. 'You're trapped in here for ever!' Ten minutes later Tate's main henchwoman, a surly cow who had more or less ignored me for the last three years, took great delight in telling me that she'd take over my unit for now as I was wanted in the office.

When I arrived Tate flew at me like a maniac, his face purple with rage.

'What right have you to tell a boy that he will remain in here for the rest of his life? How dare you bully these boys like that.'

I tried to explain but he refused to listen, instead ranting some textbook shit at me about building a child's confidence. I told him in no uncertain terms where he could get off and after giving the matter some thought handed in my notice to Mrs Dickie a few days later.

She busied herself at her desk with a bunch of papers, muttering angrily as she shuffled them around.

'This really is most inconvenient, Mr O'Grady,' she snapped. 'Won't you please reconsider? Apologize to Mr Tate for swearing at him and we'll try and forget about it.'

I was flattered but above all surprised that she wanted me to stay and for a brief moment considered changing my mind. However, wild horses couldn't have got me to apologize to the loathsome Tate and besides, Littlehampton beckoned.

'What will you do?' she asked.

I thought for a moment before confidently announcing, 'I'm going on the stage.'

She couldn't have been more surprised if I'd hit her in the face with a large, fresh trout.

'Well really!' was all she could say, as if I'd said a dirty word.

The staff had a whip-round and bought me a silver nugget on a chain and we had a leaving do that ended in the usual drunken carnage. Some of my boys cried when I left, waving at me forlornly from the window with red eyes and wobbling lower lips as I walked away up Meols Drive, holding back the tears myself. I started to panic, indecisive as always, wondering if I'd made the right decision. What the hell was I going to do in Littlehampton with someone I wasn't even sure I liked? It had been hard work at the Conny Home but I was fond of the kids and there was great camaraderie among the staff. I was going to miss those Saturday nights when, rather than go home and then have to come in again at the crack of dawn the next morning, I'd stay with Eileen and Janet or Jane and Ged in their rented flats nearby and spend the night talking. We did a lot of talking through the night and when it was our turn to sleep in at the home we'd sit up most of the night in the staff room, smoking like chimneys and drinking endless cups of tea, chewing the cud until the night sister came along and asked us if we knew what beds were for.

Just before I left the home, a summer fête was held in the gardens at the back of the building. There was the usual tat – hoop-la, guess how many sweets in a jar, a lucky dip – and when asked by Mrs Dickie if I would like to do something theatrical to help raise funds I volunteered my services as a fortune-teller and offered to read the tarot cards. I could no more read the tarot than I could hieroglyphics but it beat making a fool of myself singing 'What Are We Going To Do With Uncle Arthur?' Besides, I'd have to be pissed before I'd do that in public.

'We'll erect a tent,' Mrs Dickie said, 'and charge fifty pence a reading, or is that too excessive? I wonder if you need a licence to tell fortunes? I don't suppose anyone will mind providing you don't predict anything too alarming. You won't, will you?'

On the day of the fête I did roaring business, sat in my tent behind a little card table dressed in my brand new cream double-breasted suit, made for me out of Norman's birthday money by a tailor who had a tiny shop across the road from the Magistrates' Courts, and an elaborate scarf borrowed from Angela wrapped around my head and held at the back with a nappy pin as a makeshift turban.

I had quite a queue and surprisingly my readings seemed to make sense to a lot of my gullible customers. Perhaps I have the gift, I seriously wondered, seeing a career as a fortune-teller in Blackpool beckoning until Angela brought me down to earth by telling me that desperate people will believe anything. My bubble burst, I took her for a tour around the home and she was shocked and saddened by what she saw, finding it impersonal and sterile.

It was interesting to see the home through an outsider's eyes. In my three years there I had become as institutionalized as the children and had learned to accept the rigid routine and stark surroundings without questioning. It's a different story these days. I believe the children now have their own rooms and live in an informal and happy environment. Some of the old staff are still working there. Give those girls a medal!

One of the customers in my fortune-telling tent was Tate. He had contempt stamped all over the face that probably he told himself was devilishly handsome every day in the mirror.

'Have you seen what you look like?' he scoffed. 'Go on then, Gypsy Rose, seeing as it's for a good cause. I don't approve of fortune-tellers, particularly blatantly fraudulent ones like you, but I'll show willing and go along with it.'

'Fifty pence please.' I held my hand out.

'Well, what do you see in the cards then?'

Oh, I wanted to take the cards and shove them up his arse,

but I resisted the temptation. Instead I studied the spread I'd laid out in front of me intently, with what I hoped was a professional air.

'Well, come on then, tell me what they say,' he mocked.

'You have no future left. It's all used up,' I said solemnly, handing him back his fifty pence and quoting a line from Orson Welles's *Touch of Evil*: 'Now please leave.' I had the satisfaction of seeing him slightly unnerved by this and, as time would tell, my prediction proved to be more than accurate.

In 1997/98 a number of people alleged that they had been sexually abused while living at the home as children. Four male members of staff were put on trial and given lengthy prison sentences: an 81-year-old man, two members of the Christian group the Crusaders, and Greg Tate. Jane, one of the housemothers I was friendly with during my time at the home, rang to tell me.

My initial reaction was sheer disbelief followed by guilt. How could I not have known that the sexual molestation of children was taking place on a daily basis under my very nose? Why didn't the children tell me? I felt that I'd let them all down.

Jane felt very much the same but offered an explanation. 'Did you know anything about paedophiles?'

'No.' I'd never heard the word in the seventies. I knew about dirty old men, I'd had dealings with one when I was a paper boy flogging the *Liverpool Echo* around St Catherine's Hospital. A male nurse had attempted a feeble grope, for which he received a kick in the balls.

'Did any of the senior staff ever tell you to keep your eyes out for sexual abuse?'

'No.'

'Were you trained to spot it?'

'Not at all, it was never mentioned and anyway at that time I would've refused to believe that any adult was capable of molesting a small child, let alone a disabled one.'

It was an unthinkable act and I put my ignorance down to lack of training and youthful naivety, not being much older than some of the boys myself. To abuse a vulnerable child in your care is one of the most heinous of crimes. To abuse a mentally and physically handicapped child is incomprehensible and unforgivable. I hope the other cons in prison are giving them a rough ride.

On 12 July Norman came up to Liverpool to bring me down to Littlehampton. The Orange Lodge was marching through town and Vera and I, fuelled by a few scoops in the Lisbon, stood on the edge of the pavement in Moorfields watching the parade go past. We couldn't help getting stirred up by the rousing pipe and drum bands and clapped and cheered like mad things.

'Thank Christ me mother's not here to see me,' Vera said. 'This would put her in hospital.'

'Thank God mine isn't here to see me either,' I replied wryly, 'as I'd be the one in hospital.'

I went and met Norman at the St George's Hotel. Although I was going off into the sunset to live with him in a couple of days I couldn't wait to get away from him and go back out with Vera, so I told him a cock-and-bull story about having to visit the family to say goodbye and made my excuses and a hollow promise to return later on. I never did. Liverpool was buzzing that night, lots of ships in dock meant lots of activity and we hooked up with a gang of Greek sailors in

144

Paco's, got very drunk and went on to a restaurant with them. Vera vanished into the night; I don't know what happened to him, nor for that matter does he. I can vividly recall waking up the next morning in a cabin on a German tanker with a second engineer called Vulcan but how I got there is anyone's guess.

The next evening Norman took me, Vera, Angela and another friend called David (known as 'Ruth' because he was proper and Ruth seemed a proper name) for dinner at the swankiest eatery in town, the Tower, now the home of a radio station. It was very chic with a revolving restaurant that afforded the lucky diner a panoramic view of Merseyside and beyond. It really was a truly magnificent outlook, unless of course you suffered from vertigo as Norman did. Then you'd just throw up, which Norman also did. Vera found it a bit confusing when he staggered out of the toilet in the central column only to find that our table had vanished. This was his first posh restaurant. He was shy and clumsy until he'd had a few drinks, and was beside himself with shame when he mistook his fingerbowl for a clear soup and drank it.

Why was I going to live in a place called Littlehampton with someone I hardly knew who optimistically believed we'd enjoy a life of domestic harmony? Poor Norman, he was not only barking up the wrong tree, he was in the wrong bloody forest.

Despite my misgivings, the following afternoon I was on the train bound for Euston with eight carrier bags of LPs and a suitcase full of books, clothes and the new suit. In the middle of a cheese and chutney sandwich, Norman gave me a ring: a sapphire and diamond girly engagement ring that made my skin crawl as he slipped it on. What the hell was I thinking of? I wanted to throw it in his face, pull the communication cord and leg it back to Liverpool.

*

If Madame Arcati had ridden up Littlehampton high street on her bike or Miss Marple were to be found buying stamps in the post office I wouldn't've been the least surprised. To my eyes Littlehampton was akin to a graveyard in the sun. My heart sank as I was shown into my new home, a modest ground-floor flat with a tiny garden, not exactly the smart beachside Riviera-style apartment that I'd been led to believe I'd be living in. Nor was Norman a genuine lord, he'd bought the title. Oh dear, all that glitters . . . He also ran ice-cream kiosks on the seafront which thankfully meant he was out for most of the day.

I mooched about the town window-shopping, although the contents of the wool shop and Burton's hardly set my pulse racing. To help pass the time I wrote letters to friends and family every day which Norman would offer to post, though not before he read them himself. I only found this out months later when I wondered why Vera's address and then everyone else's were in his handwriting on the envelopes. His phone was on a party line, which meant his closest friend could listen in on any of my calls and then report back to Norman anything interesting she might have picked up.

I had nothing in common with his friends, a dull group of middle-aged married couples who adored Norman and viewed me with suspicion. Oh, the torture of those pretentious little dinner parties that they held and the mindless small talk that had me inwardly screaming behind my fixed grin.

Norman was a political animal. In the early sixties he'd been the leader of the Littlehampton branch of the Hunt Saboteurs Association and had been arrested for feeding the hounds to distract them and bound over to keep the peace for two years. The HSA wrote to him forbidding him to get involved in any further activity, insisting that he kept to the terms of his sentence. This annoyed Norman and, feeling slighted, he changed tack and became pro-hunting overnight out of spite. He rode with a hunt, giving the press ample ammunition to ridicule the HSA, Norman himself declaring from his mount that they were nothing more than 'incompetent amateurs' until his horse, sensible creature, threw him into a thorn bush.

As a professional referee he'd bravely 'come out' to the FA and despite the homophobic slant was secretly delighted with the coverage that he received in the Sunday rags. It was a big deal to publicly come out back then, to stick your hand up and say, 'Yes, I'm a gay man and proud of it.' The macho world of football was not an arena generally known for its tolerance towards gays. Norman rose above the hate mail and dog turds through his letterbox and ignored the sick chants and abuse from the moronic fans on the terraces and lived his life, and for that he was a hero.

The Littlehampton branch of the CHE (Campaign for Homosexual Equality) met once a month in Norman's flat. I mistakenly thought that it was going to be an excuse for a party, even an orgy, but apart from a couple of good-looking ones with a twinkle in their eye they were an intense lot on the whole and it seemed to me that all they did was sit around drinking tea and moaning.

One afternoon when I was feeling particularly low in the self-worth department after a futile session job hunting around town (I'd quickly realized that being 'kept' wasn't all it was cracked up to be), I wandered into a performance of 'Old Tyme Music Hall' on the marina to escape a sudden shower. It was pretty dire as they often are but the mainly elderly audience lapped it up, singing along lustily to 'My Old Man'. One of the turns sang 'I'm Only A Bird In A Gilded Cage' and despite hearing my aunty Chrissie's voice mocking that she'd seen 'better turns in an eye' I could relate to the corny old lyrics. They suited my melancholic mood and seemed to sum up my situation. Here I was, homesick and alone, broken-winged, just like the tragic heroine of the song that was being crucified on stage by the fat lady with the parasol and floppy hat (to show she was meant to be Victorian) in a quavering soprano voice that shook the fillings in your teeth and scared the seagulls off the roof.

Returning to the flat, I told Norman that I wanted to go home because I was bored to tears with having no job, no friends and nothing to do. His response was to send for the cavalry in the form of Vera and to throw a big party. A padded envelope containing the train fare to Liverpool was sent up to Vera, who ironed his jeans dry immediately and caught the next train down.

Vera's arrival in the peaceful little town coincided with a parade of bands and floats down the high street. I don't know what the occasion was but we pretended it was in Vera's honour and after a swift half in the pub marched along with the band as they played 'Before The Parade Passes By'. Oh, it was good to see Vera again. Norman was also delighted to see Vera, for he believed whatever made me happy made him happy; however, he wouldn't be feeling quite so benevolent towards him after his forthcoming 1920s-themed party. With someone of my own age and interests to hang around with, Littlehampton became a different place. Suddenly life was a holiday.

Norman gave us twenty quid to spend at the funfair. There was a ride called the Mad Mouse, a decrepit old wooden roller coaster that I half expected to collapse as the tiny little car containing Vera and me zigzagged violently around the extremely narrow track, darting backwards and forwards. This made Vera jerk his head back hard into my nose, and my screams of pain and Vera's squawks from the blows to the back of his neck from me could be heard all over Sussex. When we took a high-powered speedboat ride out to sea, I sat up front. Vera sat at the back, quite contented until a gigantic wave hit him straight in the face knocking his glasses off. 'Look at that poor girl at the back,' said the woman next to me. 'She's soaked right through to the bone.'

Predictably the 1920s party resulted in drunken carnage. The guest list was mainly made up of elderly ladies in home-made flapper outfits acting in what they considered a decadent manner (cigarettes in holders and a couple of shaky Charleston moves while twirling beads) and their geriatric beaus, self-conscious in rented tuxedos or fancy-dress-shop military uniforms. The flat was beginning to look like the court of Vulgaria in *Chitty Chitty Bang Bang*. Norman, as Fred Astaire, was dressed in top hat and tails whilst I'd come as the Depression in collarless shirt, baggy pants and braces with a cloth cap and dirty face. Vera came as himself, his only concession to the twenties a sequined headband with a battered turquoise feather stuck haphazardly in the side.

The evening started pleasantly enough, but soon degenerated into a free-for-all. Through the glass panels of the bathroom door I could see the silhouettes of two people, one of whom I recognized as Vera. Forcing the door (no Herculean display of strength as it was only secured by a little catch), I caught Vera, roaring drunk, with a member of the CHE in flagrante delicto. There was a bit of a commotion, resulting in an outraged Vera fleeing the bathroom but not before seizing the chance to push me over a Calor gas heater and down a flight of stairs into the cellar. Once the bluebirds had stopped flying repeatedly around my head and the tweeting was over, I gave chase with one aim in mind – to kill Vera. We charged through the party, scattering the glitterati of Littlehampton in our wake until I finally cornered him in the tiny garden by jumping on him. I also brought down two genteel matrons dressed as Andrews Sisters and all the fairy lights in the tree above. Remarkably, even though he'd done a double somersault over two collapsible chairs, Vera never spilt a single drop of the large vodka tonic that he was clutching.

Later, in the early hours of the morning after the guests had finally gone home, I wandered into the bedroom to find Vera and Norman both blind drunk, having a little fumble on the bed.

'Oh, you're so soft,' Norman moaned in the dark, caressing Vera.

'Aye, she must be to be giving you a nosh,' I scoffed and went to sleep on the sofa. I wasn't bothered in the slightest, in fact I was secretly delighted as it meant that I now had something on Norman. I fell asleep relishing the prospect of playing Norman at his own game and giving him a taste of the injured martyr act.

I was woken in the morning by a contrite and very hung-over Vera bearing a cup of tea as a peace offering and proposing to put my favourite album, *Shirley MacLaine Live At The Palace*, on the record player. Norman had got up early and gone to work and when he came home later in the day I gave him the deeply wronged and injured treatment, which he totally disregarded, going about his business as if nothing had happened. Regretfully Vera went home the next day and, at Norman's suggestion, I started work in one of his ice-cream huts on the seafront. It was an undemanding and fairly pleasant job that I shared with a number of different young women. My favourite was a feisty student who took me back to her parents' house one afternoon to show me their microwave oven as I'd never seen one before and was desperate to witness this miracle in action. After watching it scramble eggs we ended up in bed together. Me and the girl, not the microwave.

'I'm living with a fellah and I'm supposed to be gay yet I'm in bed with you, so what does that make me?' I asked her later.

'A very confused young man,' she replied, taking a pull on her ciggy.

Things went from bad to worse between Norman and me. I'd got to the stage where I couldn't bear to be in the same room as him, let alone the same bed, and the highly implausible excuses I invented to avoid any physical contact with him grew increasingly wild with each telling. I should've done the decent thing and gone home. For the gold-digging tramp I was reputed to be (I'd overheard one of his friends calling me that at the party) I was certainly mining a barren seam. Ever since I'd taken up my new career in the frozen dessert business I'd been contributing towards the food and rent. So much for being kept. Whatever happened to happy ever after, living in the lap of luxury in a villa on the beach? I was flogging ice cream eight hours a day for a pittance, sleeping on the couch in a basement flat in a one-horse town with a control freak who was far too old for me.

Being with Norman dampened my spirits. His idea of a good time was to sit in the flat of an evening, holding hands on the sofa and watching the telly, the prospect of which was anathema to me. Instead I'd carry on behind his back in the sand dunes with a member of the CHE and go up to London once a week to visit what Barbara Cartland would delicately refer to as a lover. Poor Norman, our relationship hadn't lived up to his lofty expectations and his 'bit of rough' (something else I'd been described as at a party) was most certainly not the person he'd originally envisioned spending the rest of his life with. Getting through the week was hard enough, never mind a lifetime.

In the end it was Norman who decided my fate. Angela came to stay for the weekend and I insisted that she shared the bed with me while Norman took the couch. Bit of a bloody cheek really, throwing the man out of his own bed, and we ended up having a huge argument that nearly came to blows. Angela tried to act as mediator, even offering to go to a bed and breakfast, but I was adamant that I was not sleeping with Norman. I got my way in the end but it was a pyrrhic victory, and typically and not unjustifiably Norman sulked, morose and alone on his sofa, drinking brandy and listening to Leonard Cohen and Timi Yuro records until finally he passed out.

He got up early the next morning and left for work, leaving me a note to say that it would be better for all concerned if he didn't find me there when he got home. Next to the note was a letter addressed to me that had been opened. It was from the London lover telling me that he didn't want to see me again. It seemed as I mulled over both my Dear Johns that I'd not only killed two birds with one stone, I'd flattened the whole bloody aviary. And so, packing up the LPs again, I took the train with Angela, who was a little miffed at having her seaside holiday cut short, to London.

By the time we'd pulled into Victoria Station, Norman and Littlehampton were ancient history. I had over fifty quid in my post office savings book and two weeks' wages in my pocket and for the first time since I'd half-heartedly believed that I could make a go of it with a complete stranger in a quiet little seaside town I felt liberated. It was a beautiful summer's day and I splashed out on a taxi to take us to where we were staying with a friend of Angela's from the drama school. Angela's sister Kate got wind that we were in town and, desperate to get a look at Angela's 'boyfriend', demanded that we paid her a visit.

Kate was an aspiring actress who had only recently left drama school. She shared a tiny flat in Camden Town with an occupational therapist called Louisa, a willowy blonde, tall and slender, who I thought to be the height of sophistication. Louisa – or Lozzy as she was to become known – was well travelled and smart as a whip with a rather vague and dis-interested air about her that masked her extremely practical side and zest for life. She had fine baby-blonde hair which she tried to keep in check with an assortment of diamanté clips and hairpins adorned with feathers and she painstakingly attached individual false eyelashes to her eyelids with the aid of a pair of tweezers and a little tube of black glue. After a while they went haywire and either fell off altogether or stuck out at odd angles like the hairs on an old paintbrush.

Kate was small and voluptuous with long brown hair swept up in a Wilma Flintstone-style hairdo that gave her that just got-up look, which she probably had. With her heart-shaped face and big eyes she came across as sexy yet vulnerable, a working-class Liz Taylor, except Miss Taylor probably didn't wear her keys and lighter slung around her neck on a bit of string.

Both Kate and Louisa had a penchant for causing a stir when they went out on the town. They were full of enthusiasm, dressed outrageously and always the first up on the dance floor. Kate's terpsichorean skills involved hurtling around demonstrating a vigorous interpretive dance routine while Lozzy dreamily floated about on tiptoe in her pink leotard and tutu, trailing a moth-eaten feather boa and assorted bits of chiffon and tinsel behind her like a discarded Christmas tree hanging out of the back of a bin wagon. Angela was no slouch herself when it came to partying and would join in with gusto. They'd flirt and cavort and dance and drink like three wild women, yet at the end of the night they always kept their knickers on and went home together, unsullied, like the well-brought-up Maid of Kent and the two Liverpool Irish Catholic gals that they were.

For some reason I bought two cheap wigs from a shop in Camden Town, a curly brown Afro which I immediately plonked on my head, firmly believing it was undetectable as a teaser, and a violent red wavy creation that Angela teamed with an emerald-green velvet frock and high heels that made her look like a 1950s Irish barmaid. We went busking in Camden Town, or rather she did, playing an ancient squeeze box and singing Irish songs while I stood by, slightly self-conscious but putting a brave face on, holding out a cap and greeting passers-by with an optimistic 'Thank you'. It felt like begging to me and I was hesitant to give it the hard sell . . . that is, until people started dropping coins in the cap, which prompted me to have a quick change of heart and turn into the most enthusiastic spieler on Camden Lock. 'There's money in this lark,' I said to Angela later as we spent some of her earnings on ice cream at Marine Ices in Chalk Farm.

We slept late, ate in cafés, visited everyone Angela knew and seemingly went to a party every night. It was a halcyon time and I discovered that this was a London I liked. After my many previous abortive attempts to settle here, I began to feel at ease with the place, less of an alien, and decided on the spur of the moment to give it another go. Angela would be returning to drama school after the summer and would be looking for somewhere to live and someone to share the rent with her. I could be that someone.

Lozzy came up trumps with a job idea for me, saying that she'd have a word in the physiotherapy department of the hospital where she worked to see if there were any vacancies for physiotherapists' aides. There was. One of the aides would be leaving to go to college and there would be a vacancy in a couple of months. Perfect. Even though I had no idea what a physio's aide was or did, it sounded glamorous enough and I duly went along to the Royal Northern Hospital for an interview with Miss Peggy Handley, Senior Physiotherapist, full of enthusiasm. My eagerness must have won that lady over because she gave me the job.

I was thrilled that I was going to work in a hospital and had visions of myself in a starched white coat, mopping the brow of a dying patient ('Quickly, nurse, more morphine'), willing him back to life ('No one dies on my watch'), or teaching a child, supposedly paralysed for life, to make those first few tentative steps before bravely rushing into the arms of his mother, her face wet with tears of gratitude. Oh yes, I was going to become indispensable to the physiotherapy department of the Royal Northern Hospital, beloved by patients and staff alike and the trusted right-hand man of Miss Peggy Handley, Senior Physiotherapist.

CHAPTER 9

Crouch End

'PHYSIOTHERAPIST'S AIDE?' MY MOTHER'S VOICE WENT UP A few octaves and she looked at me as if I'd just declared that I was taking up a career in the armed forces. 'Physiotherapist's aide?' She kept repeating it to herself as she pulled at the tight ball of hard, unnatural curls that she used to call hair before the hairdresser on Church Road had got her hands on it.

'Look at me bloody hair,' she moaned, poking it with her index finger and watching in the mirror on the front-room wall. 'It's like a Brillo Pad. I don't know why I go to her, I really don't.'

I did. It was half-price on a Wednesday for pensioners, not that you would dare to refer to my ma as a pensioner. The word was anathema to her. 'I told her,' she ranted on, 'I clearly said I wanted it loose. A loose perm. Does this look loose to you? It's like a pan of winkles, and she's scalded the gob off me under those bloody dryers. She leaves you under them for far too long, y'know. There's no need, half of those pensioners have hardly got any hair on their head in the first place, just a couple of strands teased up around their face. I

157

don't know what we must look like, a gang of old women sat like battery hens in plastic capes reading the *Woman's Own* having the 'eads roasted off us for an hour.'

'It's nice,' I lied, trying not to laugh at the red welts across her forehead and down the sides of her heat-blotched face where she'd had the 'ead roasted off her. The smell of setting lotion was so overpowering she could've been used as a general anaesthetic.

'And I've had a rinse as well,' she went on, ignoring me. 'Supposed to be Burnished Copper. Burnished Copper my arse, look at it! I look like Elvis!'

I gave her my letter of acceptance from the hospital to read. 'I don't know how you go from selling cornets one day to working in a London hospital the next,' she said examining the letter sceptically, turning it over in her hands to see if she could find any signs of fakery. 'When are you finally going to settle down and get a proper job?'

'This is a proper job,' I protested.

'They've all been proper jobs, son,' she sighed, handing me back the letter. 'And what's come out of them, eh? You've either ended up in court or back here on the bones of your bare backside. Anyway, what are you going to do up till then? It says there that you don't start until September. You needn't think you're hanging around here, I can't afford to support you.'

The post office savings had long gone. The ring that Norman had bought me along with a couple of others I'd acquired on the way had been pawned by Vera in a pawn shop in Liverpool. I was too ashamed to go in but Vera, no stranger to the pawn shop, had no such qualms, even haggling to get me a better price for my paltry bits of jewellery.

So I got a job as a barman in the Plaza Bingo Hall on

Borough Road where surprisingly the women were extremely generous, particularly if they'd had a win, and I earned more in tips than wages. Aunty Chris was a regular at the Plaza, sweeping into her usual seat in her good camel coat, her face a mask of concentration as she checked nine books, fag in one hand, felt tip in the other, scanning the numbers up and down, ready to pounce.

Out on the town one dull Monday night with Vera, we met a couple of fellahs who were strangers in town. One was a huge Dutchman who looked like he had his enormous head on upside down, with his bald pate and 'old Dutch beard', the type that flared outward in width at the bottom. He bore a striking resemblence to Bluto, Popeye the Sailor's arch enemy, and found his Olive Oyl in an unresponsive and reluctant Vera, who he wooed relentlessly but unsuccessfully. His mate was called Ryan, a good-looking lairy Jack-the-lad Scouser, fresh from working in the Far East and now running his own business. We had quite a fling. He took me to Amsterdam for a weekend, the first time I'd ever been 'properly' abroad, and it was certainly a bit of an eye-opener. On the way home we were detained by Customs. Ryan had lots of stamps in his passport from the Far East and since we were on our way back from Amsterdam the Customs officers assumed we were international drug smugglers. Taken into a separate room and questioned, I was unclear what they meant when they asked, 'Are you sure that you haven't even brought a little bit back for yourself?' A bit of what?

'You do realize that you'll go down for a long time if you're caught smuggling marijuana?'

Marijuana?! I'd never smoked a joint in my life, let alone shoved a couple of pounds of the stuff up my bum and high-tailed it through Customs. And as for coke, that was something you either drank or burned. My heart sank as a thought crossed my mind: maybe Ryan really was a drug smuggler and was at this very moment trying to explain why he had bags of white powder hidden in the false bottom of his suitcase. Perhaps he'd hidden some in my case? My mouth was as dry as a bone from fear and I couldn't answer the officer rifling through my case when he asked what I was doing with a half-empty tub of margarine in among the T-shirts.

I'd brought it back because of the name, Bona, which was Polari for 'good'. I'd thought it was funny at the time but I wasn't laughing now. He was threatening to strip-search me.

Oh God, get me out of this one and I'll never be bad again.

How would I explain this to my mother?

'Sorry, Ma, I won't be home for my tea for at least ten years . . .'

'That's all right, son, at least I'll know where you are of a night.'

In the end they let us go. Ryan wasn't an international drug smuggler after all and I'd been spared the rubber-gloved finger. I was never so glad to get out of anywhere in my life.

When the time came round for me to go back to London I typically didn't want to leave. Life was good at the moment so why change it? The summer seemed endless, the hottest on record the papers screamed, but then they always do, don't they? A hosepipe ban had been introduced so my mother took to watering her tiny front garden in the dead of night, admitting that she'd rather deprive herself of water than see her precious flowers go thirsty. The warm night air was heady with the scent of nicotiana, night-scented stocks and evening primrose, mostly grown from cuttings she'd acquired on coach trips to the gardens of the stately homes of the north.

'Come and have a sniff out here, Paul,' she hissed from the

front step in a voice she believed was inaudible to the neighbours yet could probably be heard in Rock Ferry. 'You've never smelt anything like it.'

I stood among the flowers in my bare feet and inhaled deeply. She was right, I had never smelt anything like it and seeing her garden illuminated by moonlight, it seemed almost magical. Time seemed to momentarily stand still and I controlled my breathing so as not to disturb the silence, staring across the Mersey, as still as a mill pond, at the lights of Liverpool in the distance. Why would I want to leave all this?

'Mind where you're standing,' my mother roared in her stage whisper, emerging from the house with her secateurs, 'you don't want to be standing in cat shit. Now shift yourself while I dead-head that rose.' I was going to miss moments such as these, gardening at two in the morning.

I was also going to miss Ryan. Our relationship had grown pretty intense. He was keen and didn't want me to go to London. But I had to go, I'd promised Angela and didn't want to let her down, her or Lozzy, who'd gone to the trouble of finding me a job in the first place. Besides, I tried to convince myself, I couldn't spend the rest of my life working behind the bar in a bingo hall, surely I had more going for me than that?

Life was certainly a worry and on that note I went indoors and back to bed.

It was raining as I stepped out of the tube station at Camden Town. No, not raining, more like an Indian monsoon. Camden High Street was flooded and I dodged the mini tidal waves caused by passing buses as they coursed down the street like liners, dragging my case and sodden carrier bags of LPs towards Jamestown Road and Kate and Lozzy's flat. I was staying there temporarily until Angela and I found a flat of our own, which meant that four adults, two cats and a cat-litter tray with a life force all of its own would be sharing a tiny two-room-and-kitchen flat.

I wouldn't be impolite or out of line if I was to describe the flat as a dump, for that's what it was, but it was a cosy dump and Jamestown Road wasn't the smart little series of bijou des reses that it is today. It was run-down and seedy and most of the properties housed sweatshops, where women were busy on sewing machines day and night. Around the corner in Arlington Road was a flophouse or, to use its correct term, a working men's hostel where Brendan Behan had once stayed and where the drunks shouted abuse as you passed on your way to the café in Inverness Street. All in all it wasn't the most salubrious of addresses but it was in a great location, plenty of shops, near a tube station and a stone's throw from Regent's Park. There was even a gay pub, the Black Cap, the self-styled 'Palladium of Drag'.

I was in love with Camden Town. It had everything going for it as far as I was concerned and I felt totally at home there. Each morning hordes of hungover Irish navvies congregated outside the tube station, hoping to be picked for a job. There was a pet shop on Parkway that was like a zoo, selling every creature from monkeys to white mice. I can remember the window being piled high with tortoises, with a great blue and scarlet macaw keeping watch over them. Inverness Street was (and still is) a thriving fruit and veg market. It was also home to our favourite greasy spoon café, which we'd pile into every Saturday for pint mugs of steaming tea and beans on toast.

Today Camden High Street is populated by shops that sell mainly boots, jeans and leather jackets. Back then there were bakers and fishmongers, butchers and stationers, lots of independently owned shops that sold almost everything. My favourite shop was on the corner of Jamestown Road, an art deco dealers that had a film star's dressing table made of mirrored glass and chrome in the window that I coveted more than anything else. Further up towards the bridge was a barber and a tiny little shop that sold gay porn and was presided over by a large geriatric queen and his young side-kick. Dingwalls market wasn't the conglomerate it is in present times. It was just a yard that sold second-hand clothes, with a stall by the entrance where you could buy a sausage served in wholemeal pitta bread.

The nursing staff at the Royal Northern Hospital were mainly Irish. Nearly all of them (the women that is) sported the Purdey bob made popular by Joanna Lumley in *The New Avengers*. The trend for this pudding-basin hairstyle swept through the hospital like dysentery in a prisoner-of-war camp and while it may have suited the lovely features of Miss Lumley it didn't have quite the same effect on a twenty-stone nurse with a face like a full moon. Still it was manageable and, more importantly, tidy so it met with the approval of the tyrannical sisters who ran the wards. Sister Woods ran the men's surgical ward with an iron fist. Mean and wiry with a face like a plucked boiling fowl, Woody allowed no crease ever to sully a counterpane on her ward. A broken thermometer was a hanging offence and God help the poor unfortunate fool who wandered off or on to her ward without permission. She treated the patients' visitors as a necessary evil, one that was not to be indulged for a minute extra after she'd rung the bell to indicate that visiting hours were over. She'd clear the ward quicker than a tear-gas attack simply by standing there and glowering at them.

163

If she barely tolerated the physiotherapists then the likes of me, a lowly physio aide, she looked upon with the same regard she did the residue of a soiled bedpan. One of my duties every morning was to evacuate the congested lungs of those who had just had surgery, usually elderly men confined to their beds. I'd pat them on the chest repeatedly with cupped palms, encouraging them to cough the contents of their stagnant lungs into a sputum cup. Half the time they'd miss, hitting my hand instead, their phlegm hanging like webbing between my fingers, the very same fingers that ten minutes earlier had been holding a bacon butty. I'd retch my guts up on the spot, giving Sister Woods a valid excuse to lecture me on ward etiquette in front of everyone before showing me the door.

I had my wisdom teeth out at the Northern and was under a general anaesthetic as they were impacted, and after the operation I was put in a side room on Sister Woods's ward to recover. Anaesthetic, apart from making me ill for months afterwards, has a very strange effect on me and, like alcohol, it makes me lose all inhibitions and do and say things that even I in my worst moments wouldn't normally dream of. Consequently, as soon as the porter's back was turned, I escaped, running first on to the ward and exposing myself to Sister Woods before legging it down the Holloway Road, my bare backside hanging out of my hospital gown, with a couple of hysterical nurses in hot pursuit.

My worst job, apart from post-op evacuation that is, was manipulating the freshly hewn stumps of the amputees, raw and bloodied and resembling for all the world a nice joint of marbled sirloin. What I found most disturbing at first was the way the amputees would implore me to scratch imaginary itches on a foot that was no longer there.

My favourite job was in the electromedical department, a latter-day torture chamber, or so it seemed to me, complete with boiling wax to dip the arthritic claws of elderly ladies in and a traction machine to serve as a contemporary version of the rack. Fortunately for the hapless patients, I wasn't allowed to go near it in case I inadvertently snapped a vertebra in my enthusiam. Joss, a good-natured and very pretty little New Zealander, ran this department, and after we'd set our patients up under the microwave machines we'd retire to the staff room for a cup of tea while the deep heat revived bad backs or swollen knees.

'You OK in there, Mrs Moore?' I shouted behind the screens to my favourite patient, surgical stocking rolled down to her ankle to reveal her mottled leg propped up on a stool to allow her 'bad knee' half an hour of microwave treatment.

'Yesh thanksh,' she'd reply gummily, her false teeth temporarily wrapped in a clean hanky and sat on her lap to 'give her poor gums a rest'.

A lot of male patients with sports injuries came into this department. Joss would do anything to avoid having to give ultrasound for a hernia as this involved rubbing a torch-like instrument soaked in oil round and round in a slow circular motion in the groin area. Occasionally, some of these virile young men lying spread-eagled and naked from the waist down on a bed with an appealing young woman's hand centimetres away from their tackle couldn't control their emotions and would find themselves with an involuntary erection.

Joss, although mortified to the core, was ever the professional. Pointedly ignoring the swaying monster bobbing dangerously near her wrist, she would stare at the ceiling and chat about the weather. She'd say later, after her embarrassed

165

patient had fled the building, that if she'd wanted to give relief massages then she wouldn't have bothered studying for all those years and that in future I was to do any ultrasounds to gentlemen's groins. Funny, none of them ever got a hard-on with me.

Two of the male physiotherapists, Dennis and John, were partially sighted, one of them to the point of near blindness. Their hands, in particular their fingertips, were a remarkably accurate substitute for any ocular deficiencies. Dennis claimed that he could 'see' through his fingertips into the very tissue, sinew and muscle that lay under the flesh. Watching the Master at work on a patient stricken with a crippling and debilitating back injury as he probed, manipulated and applied just the right amount of pressure to certain areas until his patient, finally released from the misery of constant pain, could walk out of the hospital unaided, I could well believe it. Dennis was a real inspiration, curing a bout of painful sinusitis that I was suffering from by gently manipulating the vertebrae at the top of my spine, causing me to consider physiotherapy as a career even though I was hopelessly unqualified.

Dennis was called up to the private wards one morning as a female patient recovering from knee surgery was requiring treatment. This woman was from Holloway Prison, a stone's throw away from the Royal Northern. The ice machine on 'privates' was broken and so I was sent up with a bowl of ice, Miss Handley quietly informing me as I waited for the lift that the woman I was about to meet was high security and I wasn't to engage in conversation with her or even look at her.

'Who is she?'

'I can't say, but I'll tell you this: the woman is evil personified.'

Two coppers standing guard outside the woman's door grudgingly allowed me to pass, but only after I'd provided them with a lengthy explanation as to who I was. I didn't know what to expect – a shaven-headed Amazon, nostrils flaring and crazed blood-red eyes popping out of a tattooed head as she tried to struggle free from the straitjacket that held her? Consequently I felt short-changed at the sight of a dark-haired middle-aged woman chatting affably to two women prison guards, swigging tea and swinging her legs as she sat on the end of the bed.

'Hello,' she sang out cheerily, fixing me with dead eyes that belied her tone. 'Have you come to look at my knee as well then?'

I started to explain, forgetting Miss Handley's instructions outside the lift, but was silenced abruptly by Sister Brogan, a terrifying specimen of womanhood with the raw-boned features and jutting masculine jawline of a Russian peasant.

'Shut up and get out,' she barked, grabbing the ice off me and manoeuvring me out of the door and back into the hall. 'There's no need for you to be here now we've got the ice to bring down the inflammation, thank you very much.'

Who the hell was this woman I wasn't allowed to speak to, I asked one of the officers on guard outside the door.

'If I tell you, will you promise to keep your mouth shut about it?' he said.

'I won't say a word,' I lied.

'It's Myra Hindley.'

So that was who she was, none other than the bloody moors murderer herself, unrecognizable as the subject of the familiar mugshot of a bleached blonde child killer with dark circles under her eyes. I was glad I had been thrown out. I might have said something.

*

Searching for decent accommodation in London when you're trying to exist on a limited to virtually non-existent budget is without doubt, as anyone who has experienced it can testify, one of the most soul-destroying ways to pass a winter's evening. Each miserable night after work, Angela and I would tramp the streets of the less salubrious parts of north London to view the various flats to let from the ads at the back of the *Evening Standard*.

I recall a hovel in Highgate: they were all hovels, but this one was as welcoming as the back bedroom of 10 Rillington Place. We stood in the middle of this grim little room and listened to our prospective landlord reassure us that if Angela happened to fall pregnant he'd be more than happy to perform an abortion on the premises, a service that I assumed wasn't included in the rent.

Our search for a home was made doubly difficult by our different sexes. Two males, fine. Two females? No problem. A male and a female? 'Sorry, the flat's been let.' Landlords seemed to be under the misapprehension that as soon as a couple moved into one of their grubby rented rooms they'd start breeding like rabbits, dropping babies with the alacrity of Queen Victoria. These Rachmanesque landlords existed solely to cheat the desperate and the vulnerable like Angela and me and we'd begun to give up hope of ever finding somewhere to live. Again, it was Lozzy who came to our aid, pointing me in the direction of a supposedly reputable letting agency near Archway. I rang up first to make an appointment.

'And how many of you are there looking for accommodation?' an officious voice asked on the other end of the phone. I couldn't make out if it was male or female.

168

Left: The proud father, aged eighteen. Sharon seems unimpressed by both the shirt and its wearer.

Below: Mum enjoying a day out on the beach.

Bottom: 'It's no good rubbing her head, she still won't come out of her shell and play.' My brother-in-law, Peter, and mum.

Above: In the garden at Holly Grove with my mum, 1979.

Above: The Children's Convalescent Home, West Kirby.

Below: The infamous Yates's Wine Lodge, Moorfield, now sadly closed down.

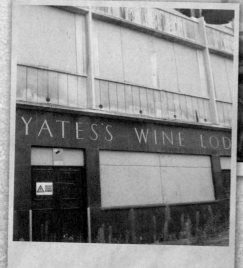

Above: Pram race at Scratby Caravan Park, Great Yarmouth.

Right: Vera took these photos on a day out round London. We popped into a few pubs on the way, so they're a bit out of focus.

Clockwise from above left: Smoking in Poland; butter wouldn't melt – passport photos for Amsterdam; working for Camden; the ginger moustache.

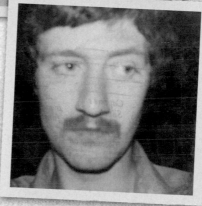

Above: Flanked by the Polish landlady and the princess.

Right: The Polish leopard-print polo neck.

Above left: The best man and bride.

Above: The groom.

Left: Bridesmaid, groom and guest.

Below left: Chrissie and Vera, the Executive Club, Liverpool, 1975.

Below right: The Showplace Club, 1978, Theresa on right.

Right: Vera and Angela at the Showplace.

Below right: Lozzy and Kate (on left and right).

Below left: Another blurred photo taken by Vera, 1979, in the front room at Crouch End.

Bottom: The Zipper float, Gay Pride, 1979. Me in the middle, next to Reg and Vera (with Joyce behind).

Phil and Alistair, the fabulous Harlequeens.

*For Phil
with much love
x x x*

Right: The Moth leaves the stage at the Black Cap, 1979.

Below: The sweetest girl in the convent. Ladies and gentlemen, may I present the embryonic Lily Savage . . .

'Two,' I replied.

'I must warn you that it is not our policy to rent out to couples. We prefer single men.'

Do you now?

'Can I take you and your friend's names please?'

'Paul O'Grady and Ang—erm, Andrew Walsh.'

I was granted an interview for the following evening but first I had to find an Andrew Walsh to take along to the interview with the owner of the androgynous voice. I had no male friends in London, they were all up in Merseyside, but Angela produced a boy named David from her class at drama school who was willing to play the role.

The gender of the voice on the end of the phone turned out to be male, and if I were a casting director looking for someone to play the part of Rumpelstiltskin then Lionel Crawley would've got the job without question. He hopped about the room like a rook on hot coals, wearing one of those red nylon overalls that are meant to look like jackets and are usually found on barmen in social clubs. To make up for his lack of stature he wore boots with platforms at least three inches high and a wig that stuck out on top, a vain attempt, I assumed, at realism but it only made him look ridiculous. In addition, the back of this dusty old teaser had a tendency to curl up like a threadbare doormat peeking over the end of a tenement landing, flapping open each time he waved his hands excitedly about and putting me in mind of the gills of a fish gasping for air.

Much as I disliked him on sight, he obviously took a shine to 'Andrew' and me, mistakenly assuming that we were a nice young gay couple deeply in love and looking for a cosy bolt-hole to nest in. Lionel was only too happy to play mother, ushering us into the back of his tiny car and whisking us off to the wilds of north London to view a 'superior' property that had only recently come on to his books in a place called Crouch End. I'd vaguely heard of Crouch End but had always assumed that it was a mythical place, a bit of a send-up like Futtocks End, but no, as we drove over Hornsey Rise and down towards Crouch End Hill here it was in all its 1950s suburban misery.

The superior property turned out to be a two-room/kitchen and bathroom ground-floor flat in an old Victorian house situated on a leafy, tree-lined road near the library. It was a big flat, with high ceilings and large windows, a bugger to heat, I heard myself thinking, echoing my mother. Whoever had designed the decor of this flat was either blind or had dropped a tab of a powerful hallucinogen and gone on a rampage in a shop specializing in hideous furniture and psychedelic paint and wallpapers. It was a homage to bad taste that made your eyes bleed if you stared too long.

The floor of the living room was covered in battered and scuffed turquoise lino (did you know that they made turquoise lino?) and an orange rug in the centre had paisley whirls in brown, mustard and green woven into it. The three-piece suite had a six-seater sofa, wonderful if it hadn't been covered in the most disgusting red and gold velour fabric and then adorned with fringing and tassels. If there was a giantess knocking about Crouch End who fancied becoming a burlesque stripper then here was her brassiere.

'This came from one of our properties in Golders Green,' Lionel said, stroking the arm of the monster lovingly. 'Pure quality, this beautiful sofa, like everything else in this flat.' The purple velvet curtains adorned with a pattern of fading cabbage roses clashed beautifully with the orange, brown and yellow circle design of the shock sixties wallpaper.

The bedroom was sedate in comparison, except that you couldn't move for the four wardrobes, two beds and seven mattresses that cluttered up the space, whilst the miserable bathroom was familiar territory, shades of Holly Grove – hardly any hot water and freezing. It was going to be fun in the winter.

Despite the generous dimensions of the rooms I didn't take to this flat at all, in fact I hated it. The rent was more than we could afford at ninety pounds a month, nothing by today's standards but a sizeable chunk out of your income when your take-home pay was around thirty quid a week, plus Crouch End seemed miles away from anywhere. It would mean more to pay out on bus fares, and disappointingly it also seemed pretty dull compared to the raucous rough-and-ready nature of Camden Town. I came to the sorry conclusion that if it was excitement I was looking for then I wasn't going to find it in sleepy Crouch End, a hamlet that looked like it shut down at teatime.

Nevertheless I was desperate, and besides I was sick of having to trawl unfamiliar streets each night looking at slums to rent, and so, despite my reservations, I agreed to take it. Lionel was delighted that he'd be providing shelter for two 'lovely boys' and it was agreed that pending suitable references and more importantly a month's rent in advance I'd be able to take possession in a week's time.

'It'll do until we find something better,' I said to Angela in the pub later, not realizing that I was to stay there three years.

Lozzy and Peggy Handley provided the references and the deposit of eighty pounds came out of my first month's wages. Angela made sure to tell everyone to address her mail to a sexless A. Walsh, just in case Lionel saw the post in the hall and rumbled that he had, horror of horrors, a female living

171

on the premises. For the first few months, to avoid detection, she crept in and out of the flat like a member of the French Resistance in war-torn Paris.

Before Crouch End became gentrified in the 1980s and long before the hedge funders and media types moved in with their skinny lattes and pavement cafés, the area was predominantly bedsit land. The only eateries I can recall were a couple of caffs, a Kentucky Fried Chicken and a kebab shop. Our life-line out of the place was the 41 bus, an unreliable and intermittent service. I believed it was the stuff of legend, a vehicle that only appeared when the moon was full and a mist lay low on the ground, to be driven wildly through the streets of Crouch End by a headless driver.

I spent hours stood at that bloody bus stop on Crouch End Hill, silently willing a 41 to suddenly appear from around the corner. When the damn thing eventually did creep up the hill it was impossible to lose your temper with the clippie. She was one of the old brigade who wouldn't have put up with any lip anyway, one that my aunty Chris would've approved of: in her sixties, immaculately made up and smartly dressed in a neatly pressed uniform with a gossamer-fine hairnet dotted with tiny beads covering her neatly waved blue hair.

After my initial prejudice towards Crouch End wore off I found that I quite liked the place. It had a village atmosphere; in fact Kate used to say when she came to see us that it was like visiting relatives in the country. One of the first things I did on moving into the flat was to join the library. They had a pretty good local history section, which was handy as I've always had a passion for local history. Fuelled by what I'd read, every Sunday Angela and I would explore nearby

Alexandra Palace, Waterlow Park and my favourite, Highgate Cemetery.

One book that I'd read was about the Highgate Vampire and I was very taken by the tale of supposed sightings of a vampire in the west part of the cemetery. The story caused quite a fuss when it broke in the early seventies. Huge crowds gathered in Swains Lane after ITV televised a live interview with Eamonn Andrews, of all people, and a couple of vampire hunters.

I could well believe that vampires existed among the vandalized headstones and overgrown crypts. The decaying angels and the marble faces that embellished the ornately carved tombs, taking their final bows before the all-suffocating ivy finally enveloped them for eternity, certainly fired my imagination. The entrance to the magnificent Egyptian Avenue is pure D. W. Griffith, the perfect setting for a scene out of his 1914 silent film *Judith of Bethulia*.

One of the most disturbing aspects of Highgate Cemetery was the lengths that vandals and would-be 'worshippers of the occult' had gone to and the desecration that they'd inflicted. The Victorians buried their dead with some very nice pieces of jewellery, worth a fortune or so the legend went. Consequently the tombs were smashed and the coffins inside forced open, their mummified contents ransacked and left hanging over the side, grinning obscenely at us. Hammer Horror couldn't compete. I took these images home with me, we both did, and we became so obsessed by the Highgate Vampire and the fear that he might just pay us a nocturnal visit that we pushed the beds together and sprinkled a circle of salt around them to protect us.

Vera and Ryan had come down from Liverpool for the weekend. I hadn't seen Ryan for a while and now felt uncomfortable in his presence, rejecting any amorous advances and treating him as if he were a plague of cockroaches. I'd moved on, or so I thought, and Ryan was history. Vera, on the other hand, I'd missed and I encouraged him to make the move and come and live with us.

Angela and I seemed to go to a lot of parties. There was always someone in her drama school having a 'do' and Lozzy's friend over in south London was forever throwing parties in her flat in Victoria Mansions. Apart from the partying we lived a fairly frugal lifestyle. We had to, we were permanently skint. Angela was barely getting by on her student grant and I found it impossible to live on what I earned at the hospital, so I looked for a part-time bar job. After all I was well qualified.

I got a job in a gay club on Westbourne Grove called the Showplace. It was owned by Mr Stavros, who seemed to spend most of his time playing cards with his cronies in a local gambling den, leaving the running of the club to Peter the manager, a tough little Irishman, and Alana, his much younger and very attractive 'business partner'. Alana's job was to stand guard at the till, slowing the process up by taking the money from us and putting it in the till herself just in case we were tempted to fiddle or undercharge our mates for drinks.

Trusting no one, least of all the bar staff, she treated and spoke to us as if she were a Chinese empress dealing with the eunuchs of the Forbidden City and the only way to get into this petulant female's good books was by flattery. While some of the staff crawled to her on their bellies like reptiles I'd have much rather kicked the supercilious woman in the arse than kissed it, but needs must when the devil drives and if occasionally buttering her up meant getting her off your back, then so be it.

'Your hair looks lovely, Alana.'

'Does it?' (Mock surprise as she preened in the mirror behind the bar.)

'Yeah, especially that big long one growing out of your nose and the tufts hanging out of your armpits.'

I didn't dare say it, but I thought it.

At the time I thought the Showplace was very smart but looking back I see a long room with two dimly lit bars, one with a dining area, and a DJ console in the style of a ship's prow complete with figurehead overlooking the dance floor. Typical 1970s nightclub decor.

If you have any knowledge of London then you'll appreciate that Westbourne Grove is a hell of a way from Crouch End, especially at two thirty in the morning, but undeterred and to save on cab fares I'd walk some of the way home after work, trying to get as far as Edgware Road tube before finally giving in and flagging a cab down. Out of the four quid a night I earned for five hours' work, two of it went on a taxi home and the rest on bus fares and dinner money the following day. I stuck it out because it got me out of the flat and allowed me to 'go clubbin'' and get paid for it, and as I hardly knew anybody in London this was a good way to meet like-minded people, i.e. gays. However, I didn't expect that I'd meet my future wife.

On the gay club scene in Liverpool there was very little antagonism between the lesbians and gay men and apart from inbred misogynists like Sadie who didn't want his club 'overrun with fucking fish' we all got along just fine. As far as Vera and I were concerned, we were all in the same boat. A lot of our women friends were lesbians. One in particular, Renee, a fat peroxide blonde with a turn in her eye, was a prostitute and would turn up with her sombre Chinese pimp

175

and tough little girlfriend in tow and buy us all drinks. We liked the dykes and thought a club patronized solely by men unnatural.

It was a different story at the Showplace, where there was a noticeable segregation of the sexes. The men gathered around the top bar, the women the bottom and very rarely did the twain meet, seemingly having nothing in common apart from the love of their own sex. I tried to keep out of the way of a middle-aged woman called Jake, who if she had a psychotic condition, which she undoubtedly did, then you could bet it would be hard to pronounce. She was a vicious bully, proud of her reputation for being barred for life from the women-only club the Gateways, and existed solely to terrorize those weaker than herself, which meant 99 per cent of the Showplace lived in perpetual fear whenever she was in. Tall and rangy with a teddy boy quiff, her hard masculine face set in a permanent scowl, she stalked the club, an anachronism among the trendy young lesbians, in search of trouble.

'Large dark rum,' she snapped at me, elbowing her way to the front of the bar one busy night. I ignored her, pretending that I hadn't heard.

'Are you fucking deaf?' she shouted. 'I said I wanted a large rum.'

Reluctantly I stopped what I was doing and slammed a large rum into a glass from the optic. She snatched the drink out of my hand and threw the money in my face. Before I had time to respond, Theresa the Portuguese barmaid stepped in.

'Get out, bitch,' she growled at a disbelieving Jake. 'I said get out. Who do you think you are, throwing money in his face? Now leave before I kill you.' Jake, who nobody had ever stood up to before, leaned across the bar and tried to grab her.

'Touch me and you're dead,' Theresa said, calmly meeting Jake's furious gaze. 'I'll cut your throat.'

Jake threw her drink over Theresa and in a flash the normally placid Theresa went for her. All hell broke loose, Jake tried to jump over the bar but was grabbed by Bill the bouncer, Peter the manager and a couple of strong-armed women, and dragged cursing out of the club.

'Crazy bitch,' Theresa said, laughing, wiping her denim shirt down with a dishcloth. 'But I had to do something before she killed you.'

I'd liked the good-natured Theresa from the moment I first met her. She was über-cool and laid-back and was a big hit with the women customers, who all fancied her David Cassidy good looks. She was working in a local hotel as a chambermaid by day, supplementing her income behind the bar of the Showplace by night. Originally from Lisbon, Theresa was under tremendous pressure from her devout Catholic family to find herself a husband. Little did we realize as we swigged our Bacardi and cokes that she was soon to become the future Mrs O'Grady . . .

One night I turned up for work at the Showplace to find the place locked up. The lease had expired and the owners weren't renewing it, or so I was told as I gathered outside on the pavement with the rest of the staff.

'Don't worry,' Peter the manager said. 'As soon as we've found new premises we'll all be back in business.'

Theresa's work permit was about to expire and she was dreading having to return to Portugal and face the numerous suitors that her mother, unaware of her daughter's true sexuality, had lined up as possible husband material. I listened to her woes as we sat drinking in the restaurant on Westbourne Grove that we frequented after work because they sold booze after hours, and on a whim I offered to marry her.

People assume my motives were venal. They weren't. I married her simply because I liked her and wanted to help her out of a tricky situation and for no other reason. And so we set a date for May.

CHAPTER 10

Wedding Bells

O N APRIL FOOL'S DAY 1977, VERA ARRIVED FOR ANOTHER
weekend but this time stayed three years. Since he didn't
have a job he needed to sign on and so I duly went round
to W. H. Smith to buy a rent book which I then gave the
'treatment', enabling Vera to claim rent. I was an expert at
ageing rent books, fancying myself as a master forger, the
John Myatt of rent books.

My technique was simple but effective. I'd start by rubbing
both sides of the cover with a used tea bag until it had
reached the right depth of sepia to pass, even under the closest
of scrutiny by the most officious of social security employees,
as a document of suitable maturity. A little fag ash rubbed on
to parts of the cover for depth, the corners dilapidated with a
few dog ears and then, as a finishing touch to this masterly
piece of fakery, my signature mark – a casually placed ring
from a coffee cup on the cover and a couple of doodles and
phone numbers scribbled hastily on the back. Inside I'd
laboriously fill in the dates and the amounts supposedly paid
over the months, using a selection of different biros and

adding a little extra of course to the amount Vera would actually be shelling out in the way of rent as a way of making the entire enterprise financially viable. I could put years on a brand new rent book in under an hour, and by the time I'd finished with Vera's it could've passed for the one that Mary and Joseph had used to pay the rent on that stable.

As it happened, after all that work Vera didn't bother using it. He got himself a job in a pub in Islington called the Sportsman instead.

The Royal Northern was downsizing and both the physiotherapy and the occupational therapy departments were told to shed a few staff. As it was a case of last in first out I was one of the first to go. Privately I'd often felt that I was superfluous to requirements anyway, often finding myself on a quiet day with nothing to do, and wasn't particularly surprised when I was given my marching orders. The blow was softened by the two months' wages and three weeks' holiday pay that came with it.

First thing I did was pay off the Access card that I'd allowed to build up when I'd overused my 'flexible friend' to pay for Christmas presents and clothes, and then I rented a black and white telly from DER. There was no aerial on the roof of the house so we had to make do with an indoor one that proved to be absolutely useless. The reception was – and still is, I'm reliably told – crap in Crouch End and it wasn't until Vera replaced DER's standard *My Favorite Martian* aerial with a bent wire coat hanger that we made contact with Weatherfield and were able to enjoy *Coronation Street*, providing you didn't mind watching the newly married Len and Rita interacting in what looked like a dense fog and intermittent lightning storms.

The Showplace re-opened on the Finchley Road. It was tiny in comparison to the original and became popular with a predominantly lesbian crowd, and on most nights Vera would be the only male customer in the place. Theresa and I went back behind the bar with the ever-watchful Alana in attendance, hovering over the till as usual as if she was guarding it as Gollum did his precious ring. She'd sacked the cleaner after only two weeks, suspecting that she'd been helping herself to the booze, her suspicions confirmed when she turned up one night to find the club still filthy from the night before and the cleaner passed out, stinking of Pernod, in the middle of the dance floor. I must have been panicking as my funds, what little I had, were running low and I offered my services as a temporary solution until they found a replacement. It was a rotten job. Before I could even begin to wield a mop in the direction of the lavs there were hundreds of dirty glasses to be washed and then dried with a succession of soggy and undoubtedly germ-laden tea towels, a time-consuming and laborious waste of an hour thanks to the parsimonious Stavros's refusal to buy a machine that did it for you.

Although I'd worked there for some time now and had proven myself to be honest and reliable I still wasn't trusted enough to be given a spare set of keys to open up, but instead had to wait outside the club for Stavros to arrive and let me in. He was never on time, often over an hour late, and sometimes if he was having a run of good luck in a card game he'd forget about me completely and I'd be left standing like a fool in the street cursing him for a fat, balding, inconsiderate little creep as the early evening turned to night and the street lamps came on.

*

It was a curious assortment of people who gathered on the steps of the register office on Harrow Road that Saturday morning, 27 May. Big Phil, the jovial Irish lesbian, a woman built like a Royal Marine who made Charles Bronson seem rather fey in comparison; Stella, lesbian of the old school in her early fifties, always the perfect gentleman in both manner and appearance, neat and dapper in a three-piece suit, shirt and tie, her steel-grey hair cropped close to her head and slicked back with brilliantine, giving her the appearance of a wartime spiv. Both these women had a capacity for booze that would make a gang of slappers on a shag-fest in Malaga appear teetotal.

Vera, resplendent in a mint-green double-breasted suit, and Theresa's latest girlfriend, a beautiful Swede called Inga, acted as witnesses, with Kate and Angela in matching blue dresses and flowers in their hair in attendance as bridesmaids. The bride wore a white trouser suit whilst the groom was in his old faithful – the cream suit bought with Norman's birthday money. The star of the show was undoubtedly Lozzy acting in loco parentis as the groom's mother (the real model having been wisely left out of the equation for obvious reasons). She wore a picture hat the size of a cartwheel with a couple of fox furs draped nonchalantly over her arm, and stopped the traffic. At the end of the ceremony, after the immortal words 'I now pronounce you man and wife' had been uttered, the registrar turned to me and said, 'C'mon, you know what to do now, don't you?'

'Pay the fee?' I replied.

'No, dear, kiss the bride.'

To a chorus of wolf whistles and cheers from the congregation I leaned forward and planted a chaste kiss on the cheek of my blushing bride. I was a married man.

We repaired to the pub next door for a few jars, and suitably refreshed Big Phil rounded up a fleet of taxis and we headed off to Crouch End for the official Wedding Breakfast. I'd gone to a lot of trouble over this, having spent most of the night cleaning the flat (no small task considering that we were all slobs), and the best part of the morning making sandwiches and putting cheese and pineapple on sticks. I'd even managed to get a wedding cake, half price because nobody wanted it, from Dunns Bakery on The Broadway. By the time we got back to the flat my carefully prepared sandwiches had dried rock hard and curled up at the edges in the heat, not that anyone particularly noticed. We were all too bladdered to care. Wedding day or not, Theresa and I had still to go in to work at the club that night, pleasantly drunk and a little exhausted from the day's events but I'd also decided to fortify myself with a couple of 'Blueys', little blue pills that kept you going all night. They were amphetamines, cheap speed at five for a pound that turned your lips blue and made you gnash your teeth but gave you bags of energy. I was reluctant to try them at first until I discovered that they also made a long Saturday night serving booze to rowdy lesbians seem to fly by and, as an added bonus, had the ability to sweeten the mood and make me feel extremely affable even towards Alana.

The Showplace was my sole source of income and the fact that if someone asked me what I did for a living I'd have no choice but to reply 'scrubbing toilets and serving drinks' was something I found depressing. I'd applied for other jobs with not much success and was beginning to feel despondent at the frightening prospect that I might be trapped as a lowly paid skivvy in a shitty north London lesbian club for life. There seemed to be no way to escape from my present circumstances and I was the most lachrymose cleaner in London. As I mopped the dancefloor, I reflected bitterly that this latest bite from the London bug was fast turning septic.

The flat was becoming a place of refuge for other hopeful Scousers in exile. As well as Vera, Angela and myself we now had David, known to us as Ruth, and a couple of young hair-dressers, Alma and Anne. These two girls changed the colour and style of their hair on a daily basis. Anne, who in a dark wig was a dead ringer for Shirley Bassey, would leave for work in the morning a peroxide blonde and return that evening bright orange. Between them they went through every colour in the Koleston Tint range. The habit proved to be infectious and soon Vera was sporting a bubble perm, tighter than anything my mother had ever come home with on a Wednesday afternoon, whilst I was what Alma described as a 'dazzling shade of strawberry blond', which in the cold light of day turned out to be ginger. To complement my new look I grew a beard, which to my surprise came out bright red. I tried to dye it to match my hair but only succeeded in inten-sifying the red tones until it glowed an even fierier ginger than the barnet. Angela suggested toning the colour down with a coat of mascara but after coming to the reluctant conclusion that it only made matters worse I regretfully shaved it off.

Anne and Alma had their own unique styles. Devotees of punk, they had a pretty inventive and original wardrobe of clothes between them and they spent hours getting dressed and applying their make-up, chattering away like a couple of budgies as they applied coat after coat of technicolour cosmetics.

Mornings in the flat were bedlam as those who had jobs or college to go to vied to get into the bathroom. Ruth, who was very particular about his toilette, would lock himself in until Angela, growing more anxious by the minute that she'd be late for class, threatened to kick the door in. Ruth never had a hair out of place. He'd lay his clothes out for work, neatly pressed, the night before and polish his shoes. Previously he'd lived in a very nice flat in Birkenhead and was used to the order and routine that come from living alone and which become precious. The chaos we existed in must have been a shock to his system and in an attempt to gain some privacy he built a sort of Berlin Wall out of the four wardrobes, lining them up in order of height across the bedroom floor and sleeping behind them. I'd watch him from my bed as he scuttled from the bathroom in his silk dressing gown and vanished like the white rabbit behind the wardrobe wall, marvelling when he finally reappeared at how anyone could look so perfectly groomed and immaculately turned out at such an ungodly hour of the morning. He seemed content in his cosy billet behind the wardrobes until the night I came home from the Black Cap slightly the worse for drink with the devil inside me and pushed all the suitcases, which were piled high on top of the wardrobes, over on to his sleeping form below. Not surprisingly he was nervous after that and must have been relieved when he moved to an equally small living space in a house off Baker Street run by a ferocious landlady.

It was just as well we had seven mattresses in the flat, for as well as present company we had frequent overnight visitors. The young Holly Johnson, a friend of Anne's, spent a couple of nights on the floor, as did the French actor Lambert Wilson, who was studying with Angela, and his father the actor/director Georges Wilson. Lionel would've had a heart attack if he'd found out exactly how many people were passing through the doors of his 'superior property'.

He'd taken to coming round unexpectedly and had discovered Vera rabbiting on the pay phone in the hall one
morning, dressed in Angela's kimono and a pair of high heels.
Lionel, in the manner of an outraged school matron discovering an intruder in the girls' dorm, wanted to know who
he was and what he thought he was doing on the premises.

Vera, not one to mince his words, especially when suffering
from a crippling hangover, told him in no uncertain terms
where to go, and swishing back into the flat slammed the
door in his outraged face. Lionel happened to be a dyed in
the wool, Bible-thumping, fully paid-up member of a more
extreme branch of Christian fundamentalism. He also
happened to be firmly entrenched in the back of the closet, his
sexuality conflicting with his religious beliefs, making him,
amongst other things, a troubled man constantly at odds with
himself. He hated on sight what he saw as a foul-mouthed,
mincing troublemaker flouncing about in women's clothing in
his hall. He marked Vera down as an evil influence over me
and a drunken sodomite (his words), doomed to burn for ever
in the eternal flames of Hell. I, on the other hand, was a
paragon of virtue, one who was always polite and paid his
rent on time, with the saintly qualities of a young Francis of
Assisi. This infuriated Vera.

'It's not fair,' he moaned. 'He hates me and thinks the sun
shines out of your arse because you put on the holier-than-
thou act whenever he comes round. Just as well he doesn't
know what you're really like.'

Just as well indeed. A mental image of the paragon banging the head of a gobby youth on the bonnet of a parked car
outside the Showplace flashed before my mind. My growing
concern over whether I would end my days in the service of
Stavros and Alana had been alleviated the previous Saturday

night when two lads swaggered into the bar, a pair of morons who should never have been allowed into a gay club. Predictably, after they'd gained a little Dutch courage from a few drinks, they started to verbally abuse the other customers, Vera in particular. Now Vera had been the victim of mindless queer-bashing so many times it was turning into a career. Not so long ago he'd returned from a trip to Liverpool unrecognizable from the injuries sustained after three big brave men had used him for a spot of impromptu football practice outside a club, and I could see him growing understandably anxious feeling threatened in the face of further homophobia.

With the help of Theresa's latest girlfriend, a tough but glamorous Essex gal, we threw these two goons out of the club but they lay in wait for us to finish work and then pounced on Vera as we left. That's how I came to be banging a head on the bonnet of a car in the middle of the Finchley Road, not caring that passing cars were missing me by inches, deaf to the sound of their horns blaring, hearing only the sweet music that a cretin's skull makes when bounced repeatedly on the bonnet of a Triumph Dolomite. Far from being supportive, Stavros, Alana and Peter blamed us entirely for the trouble and accused us of over-reacting, Peter even going as far as to slap Theresa's girlfriend across the face when she confronted him.

Theresa and I never went back to work at the club after that night, and apart from running into her in a west London pub a few years later I never saw her again. We were married for twenty-eight years, one of the longest and happiest marriages in showbiz, until I finally got divorced in 2005.

The worry of now having no visible means of support was worth it for the sheer relief of being able to finally tell Stavros and Alana by means of the most mellifluous and inventive invective exactly what they could do with their job.

Considering I was allergic to all forms of housework I can only imagine that it was desperation that drove me to respond to an ad in the back of *Time Out* magazine proclaiming 'Students! Earn fast cash cleaning private houses! Phone London Domestics . . .' I went round for an interview with a young woman named Pat, who agreed to put me on the books for a trial period until I proved satisfactory. I was embarrassed to admit that I was an unemployed no-hoper so I concocted a cock and bull story about how I was a student studying to be a children's illustrator. It was an interesting fantasy life that I conjured up for the benefit of Pat and the clients who bothered to speak to me, and one that was infinitely preferable to my current mundane existence. For the grand sum of a pound an hour plus tube fares, I got to clean the homes of the most pernickety and demanding women in London.

Mrs Taylor expected me to scrub every nook and cranny of her three-storey, six-bedroomed mansion in Golders Green in four hours with a five-minute break for a quick cup of tea. 'Cleaner, elevenses,' she'd shout up the stairs in the kind of rich plummy voice one imagined was reserved for garden parties on the manicured lawns of the homes on The Bishops Avenue, bestowing upon me a cup of tea as if it were the Order of the Garter. Mrs Goldfingel was an Orthodox Jewish woman who wore a shiny nylon wig pulled so low on her forehead it looked as if it was growing out of her eyebrows, and expected me to clean the grouting between every tile of her expansive bathroom with an old toothbrush and a tablespoon of Vim she'd parsimoniously doled out on to a saucer. These women and many others like them certainly expected their pound of flesh for a quid an hour but in time I grew cunning, only hoovering and dusting what you could see, and relying on little tricks such as a good squirt of Pledge in the mouthpiece of the phone to lead them to believe when they smelled it that they had a veritable 'treasure' in their employ, so thorough he even cleaned the phone.

I polished the piano on which Duke Ellington composed 'The Single Petal Of A Rose' in a smart little apartment off Park Lane, the home of Mrs Renee Diamond; carefully dusted the many artefacts belonging to John Auden, the explorer brother of W. H. Auden, and ran a mop over the lino in Dame Margot Fonteyn's kitchen. One of my favourite clients was an indefatigable old lady, paralysed from the waist down and confined to a wheelchair, who lived in a chaotic two-roomed flat with a roll-topped bath in the kitchen, surrounded by hundreds of back copies of the *Guardian* and assorted musty dried twigs, flowers and mummified fruits arranged in a mis-shapen hand-thrown bowl she called *Still Life*. She liked me to spend my four hours taking her out shopping, and since she lived on the sixth floor of a block that had no lift it meant a terrifying descent, bouncing her cautiously in her wheel-chair down each step, digging my heels in, terrified that I'd lose my grip and let her go. She was a heavy lady and getting her back up the stairs with a laden basket on her lap was near impossible. How I held on to her was nothing short of a miracle and I used to shake with both exhaustion and relief when we eventually reached the top in one piece. She'd been an artist in her youth, studying in Paris and Vienna, leading a bohemian lifestyle with a string of lovers. In the sixties she'd been involved in a motoring accident and in her own words 'drove into the back of a stationary bus at great speed on the King's Road, darling, and broke my spine.' She still cruised up and down the King's Road only this time in a wheelchair, reeking of 4711 cologne to mask the ever-present whiff of pee and living way beyond her means by spending her state pension on what she referred to as 'little extravagances essential to life' such as quail and oysters. Sometimes there was nothing left to pay me with and on occasions I'd even find myself having to lend her money.

In a nursing home in Regent's Park I'd wash dishes in a scullery kitchen unaltered since the thirties. There was even a servants' hall or 'pugs' parlour', complete with a dark green chenille tablecloth covering the table and a bowl of waxed fruit in the middle. I half expected Rose to appear down the back stairs carrying a breakfast tray and announce to Mrs Bridges that Lady Marjorie would be out for lunch. There was a Rose but she was a much put-upon Irish woman, unable to relax even when eating, sitting on the very end of her chair ready to sprint into action at the command of Miss Carroll, the old curmudgeon who ran the home along the same lines as Captain Bligh did the *Bounty*. Despite her fearsome tongue I could never take Miss Carroll seriously due to her uncanny resemblance to Hylda Baker, forever heaving her bosom and patting the corkscrews of her wiry tangerine hair, which were always escaping their moorings of steel grips and sticking out in the way of springs in an old horsehair sofa.

As well as washing dishes I had to help the foul-tempered old chef (aren't they all?) who had a gammy leg and couldn't lift anything heavy, but without doubt the job I hated the most was cleaning the front steps. My face would burn with mortification whenever a smartly dressed young man of my own age passed by on his way to what I presumed was a wonderful job, convinced that they viewed me with pity as I scrubbed the steps on my hands and knees, my head bowed to hide my shame. On the upside you got a full half-hour break and a three-course lunch at the end of your shift, which was more than you got anywhere else, so I frequently volunteered to work the nursing home.

'You ever waited on?' Pat asked me one morning as I was collecting that week's wages. I answered in the affirmative, neglecting to add that I was possibly the most inept waiter ever to spill food in a diner's lap since Manuel in *Fawlty Towers*.

'Well, there's a chap here looking for a waiter to serve drinks at a private party in The Bishops Avenue. Do you think you could manage it?'

'Pat,' I replied indignantly, 'you're looking at someone who is Silver Spoon trained!'

'I think you mean Silver Service,' she said, smiling, rustling through some papers on her desk until she found a slip of paper with an address and phone number written on it. 'He wants to speak first to whoever we send, so give him a ring but for God's sake don't mention the silver spoon.'

I rushed out of the office to the phone box over the road, had a quick fag while I prepared my speech, and rang the number.

'Yes, this is Mr Adelman,' the voice at the other end informed me in a thick middle-European accent, launching me into my self-promotional spiel.

'Good, good,' he said, after listening to this highly fictional CV. 'But I must ask you. Are you a tolerant young man?'

I assured him that tolerance was my middle name.

'Discreet?'

As a priest hearing confession. You wouldn't get a peep out o' me. There was nothing on this earth that could faze me.

'Good, good,' he said again, in a voice less anxious than previously. 'In that case we'll see you at six sharp.'

Chez Adelman turned out to be a Gothic mansion with a drive so long it should've had its own bus route. The door was answered by a dowdy middle-aged woman wearing a cheap striped dress and ill-fitting cardigan with a headscarf tied at the back of her head peasant-style who I assumed must be the maid.

'Good evening. I'm your waiter,' I said in a voice that I'd been practising and which I hoped made me sound like a professional.

'Rear entrance,' the maid replied in a weary voice, totally deflating my confidence as she shut the door in my face.

Fighting my way through the overgrown laurels to the back of the house I knocked on what I took to be the kitchen door and was eventually shown in by the same tired maid, who explained my duties to me.

'There's white wine and champagne in the fridge,' she said, pointing to what looked like a set of steel double doors, 'with plenty of red over there on the work surface. Should any of the officers require spirits you'll find them in the pantry.'

'Is it a military do then?' I asked, trying to make small talk as she busied herself adding the finishing touches to a tray of food on the kitchen table.

'Not really,' she said. 'More of a small reunion for some of my husband's oldest friends.'

Husband? This scruffy skivvy was the lady of the house? Jesus, my ma was right when she said real toffs didn't waste money on clothes. We continued in silence and I was grateful when the front door bell rang. Mrs Adelman scuttled upstairs to answer it, flinging her cardigan off as she went and shouting for me to 'bring some drinks up' after her. I poured out a selection of drinks, helping myself to a hefty glug of champagne before placing the glasses on a tray and taking them upstairs. It was a gloomy house and I wove through the rabbit warren of oak panelling following the sound of voices which eventually led to the dining room. At first glance I thought that this must be a bizarre fancy dress party. A couple of women wearing the same striped outfit as Mrs Adelman were watching delightedly as an elderly man in a jacket and trousers made from identical fabric to the women's licked the black leather jackboots of an equally decrepit SS officer. I hadn't noticed the yellow star on Mrs Adelman's dress before as her cardigan had hidden it from view, but seeing it now made me suddenly realize that the sinister theme of this little soirée was Nazis and Concentration Camp Victims. I stopped dead in my tracks, unsure of what to do or how to behave in such unsettling circumstances.

'Would anybody like a drink?' I heard my own voice saying as I shakily proffered my tray in the general direction of the group.

'Ah, good evening, Paul,' the man on the floor said, temporarily taking the heel of Himmler's boot out of his mouth to smile up at me. 'I'm Mr Adelman. Glad to see that you made it.'

'Would you like a drink, Mr Adelman?' My voice was beginning to make Minnie Mouse sound like a baritone.

'Not until he's finished polishing my boots,' Himmler roared, adding something in German which made them all laugh. I mumbled something about getting more drinks and fled to the kitchen to have a drink and a fag while I assessed the situation. The money was good and I was only required to stay for two hours – obviously things spiced up as the evening progressed and they didn't want me around to witness them, which suited me just fine. I could only guess at the history that spawned this peculiar reunion and the motives behind it, and the sight of two pensioners, one dressed in the uniform of the concentration camp and the other in full Gestapo drag, indulging in an act of sado-masochism on the dining room floor made me feel more than a little uneasy. However, it had taken two buses to get here and I was buggered if I was leaving without my money.

Judging by the number of times the front door bell had rung the party must be hotting up, and fortified by a couple of glasses of champagne I made my way back upstairs with a tray laden with drinks. If you ignored the fact that a lot of the male guests were dressed like extras from the History Channel's *Hitler in Colour* and that a woman was bent across the knee of an SS officer having her bare buttocks repeatedly whacked with a riding crop to a chorus of cheers from enthusiastic onlookers, I could've been passing the drinks around at any other gathering in a wealthy north London house amongst a group of elderly guests enjoying an aperitif before dinner and bridge.

As I washed glasses in the kitchen I mulled over the antics above. If the Adelmans were Jewish, and I knew they were by the presence of a mezuzah on the front door frame, and assuming there was a possibility they might at some time have been prisoners in a concentration camp, why would they want to revisit the horrors of the past? If they had experienced the nightmare of Belsen or Dachau, how could they now be making polite small talk in their dining room with a group of people who quite possibly might have been their captors? The notion was disturbing to say the least and not something I wished to dwell on. 'What they want to get up to is their own business,' I told myself, knocking back another glass of champagne quickly as Mr Adelman came down the stairs with my wages. 'Off you go now,' he said, pushing fifty quid and a bottle of wine into my hand. 'You've been marvellous.' Fifty quid for two hours' work! Jesus, at these prices I didn't care if they started experimenting on each other on the dining room table. Letting myself out, I staggered down the drive, slightly squiffy, in search of a cab.

Mr Adelman rang the agency the next day and sang my praises, prompting Pat to send me on more catering jobs. Mrs So-and-So of Chelsea Park Gardens would recommend me to her friend in Overton Square who would then enthuse over the telephone to her friend in Eaton Place and pretty soon I'd built up a list of regular clients. I'd even cook if required, thanks to a former client in Holland Park who taught me how to prepare and serve a three-course meal. She was a smart American who quickly realized just how inept I was around a kitchen and dining room, and instead of getting rid of me took me in hand, teaching me how to wait at table and how to rustle up with comparative ease a succulent roast leg of lamb, a simple New York cheesecake and, as a starter, smoked haddock and spinach soufflé, meticulously timing the cooking of this unpredictable dish with the seating of the dinner guests to ensure that it would arrive at the table in all its inflated glory and not in a state of wizened collapse. Thanks to word of mouth again I was kept pretty busy in the neighbourhoods of Knightsbridge and Chelsea, serving up the same menu of soufflé, lamb and cheesecake to each respective client and their guests. Gene Wilder was at one dinner party. He was an affable fellah who didn't seem to mind in the least when my slightly runny cheesecake slid off the serving spoon and, missing his plate, bounced off the table and on to his lap. 'Jeez, Paul, and here's me thinking you were a class act,' was his only comment.

I was enjoying myself cooking and catering, growing more proficient with each job. Mary Holland, the original Oxo Katie, showed me that a little Bacardi whipped in with double cream could transform a trifle and that it was a lot easier if you chopped herbs by putting them in a mug and attacking them with a pair of scissors. Even so, I secretly wanted the security of a regular job – one with holiday pay and sick leave entitlement and tea breaks and dinner hours and, dare I admit it, some semblance of a routine. I'd written after all sorts of jobs, including one as a trolley-dolly for British Airways. At my first interview, held at Heathrow Airport (there were three to get through in all), I was weighed and told that my weight had to be in accordance with my height and that as I was underweight I had to gain at least eight pounds before my second interview in six weeks' time. Each morning I religiously drank a pint of a hideous emulsion that professed to put meat on the bones of a cadaver, and every week I religiously weighed myself in the chemist's on The Broadway and was pig sick when I discovered at the end of six weeks that instead of gaining weight I'd actually lost two pounds. I went into a deep sulk, muttering to myself as I made my way home about all those wasted mornings retching over the kitchen sink as I forced that foul concoction down my throat. Who wanted to be an air steward in a smart uniform flying all over the world to exotic locations anyway? The only bloody difference between serving drinks to the passengers of British Airways and handing out aperitifs in Mrs Leighton Hunt's Mayfair drawing room was 35,000 feet.

It was at a small cocktail party in St John's Wood that I met Amy, a strikingly beautiful young woman who told me that she worked as an escort for an exclusive agency off Park

Lane, as indeed did all the other female guests at the party. I'd sort of guessed that they were on the bash, sensing that the incentive driving these beauties to act as if their corpulent Saudi Arabian companions were the most fascinating men on earth could only have been monetary.

'Do you have a fairly decent suit?' Amy asked me in the kitchen as I dragged more bottles of champagne out of the fridge to satisfy a never-ending thirst for booze brought on by the absence of the prohibitive laws of the gentlemen's own country. 'You see, sometimes we get a lot of hassle from doormen and security in certain hotels,' she said, lighting an ultra-slim cigarette. 'They are under the misapprehension that just because we are unaccompanied we must obviously be prostitutes.' She smiled slyly and winked, responding to my quizzical look by adding, 'I'm not a prostitute, I'm an escort. Prostitutes come down from the north on cheap day returns and give five-pound blow jobs behind King's Cross Station. I escort wealthy and powerful men to fabulous restaurants and night clubs and if they choose to repay my attentiveness with a gift of money or a nice piece of jewellery, well, it would be bad manners to refuse.'

'Yeah, but you're still flogging the same thing when all's said and done.'

'Different shop front, darling, and a more select clientele. Do I get the impression that you disapprove?'

A line of a song sprang to mind – 'Is it wrong if a girl takes pay for something she would do anyway?' – and I sang it to her to show I was far from disapproving.

'Look, love,' she laughed, sitting on the edge of the table, making herself comfy with a drink and her fag. 'This time last year I was living – no, barely existing – in a flat in Camberwell that the council were threatening to evict me from because I couldn't afford to pay the rent. My pig of a husband had walked out on me leaving me on the kitchen floor in a pool of blood and up to my ears in debt with two little boys to support.' Swigging her champagne back defiantly she slammed her glass down on the table and shuddered violently for a moment, whether from the shock of slugging back the champagne so speedily or from the memory of life back in Camberwell I could only guess.

'Look at me now,' she said, waving her empty glass at me for a top-up. 'Mine isn't a sad story. I live in a beautiful little house in Barnes, my two boys are being educated at one of the best schools in the country and I have a wardrobe of designer clothes – a mink coat for Christ's sake! – and, for the first time in my life, money in the bank, and lots of it. Let my detractors look down on me and call me a common prostitute. I prefer to see myself as a self-employed, highly successful businesswoman.'

She raised her glass, saluting the air before draining it in one, only this time without the shudder. So it must have been the Camberwell memory then that had caused it, I thought as I tried to visualize this sophisticated beauty standing in a mean little kitchen spreading the last thin scrape from a tub of margarine on to a slice of cheap white bread, failing to hold back tears of frustration at finding herself in hopeless circumstances that rendered her unable to provide a decent meal for her kids. I admired her refusal to accept her lot. Instead of spending her days in a Valium-induced stupor watching daytime telly and getting plastered on supermarket lager she'd chosen instead an enterprise that had turned out to be not only highly profitable but one that obviously suited her.

'What is marriage for some women anyway?' she asked defensively. 'Nothing more than a way of being kept in return for services of a sexual and domestic nature. Not for me, darling, not any more.'

I had to disagree with her on this, recalling my own parents' long and happy marriage.

'Then your parents were very lucky,' she sighed. 'Unfortunately for me I married a wife-beating drunk. Now let's get back to business. It's easier for a working girl to get into a hotel if she has a male companion with her, so how do fancy making yourself available to walk a few girls in? You'll make lots of money.'

'Wouldn't that make me a pimp?' I asked her in all honesty.

She laughed so hard she spilled her drink. 'Heavens no. Pimps are the scum of the earth. They're violent parasites who force their women on to the streets to work and then take all their earnings off them, frequently beating them up if they fail to bring home the bacon. No, you'll be a walker, an escort's escort if you like. Beats washing glasses and serving drinks. It's only a suggestion, but do think about it.'

I didn't need to think about it and wrote down my phone number for her. Wait till I get home and tell Vera about this.

CHAPTER 11

On the Bash

ON DAYS WHEN NEITHER OF US HAD ANYTHING TO DO AND not much money to do it with Vera and I would play games to amuse ourselves. Sometimes we'd be the women who help out at funerals, neighbours usually, the type who volunteer to make the tea and sandwiches for the recently bereaved on their return from burying their loved one, a pair of busybodies relishing their roles as indispensable citizens, waiting anxiously behind the net curtains for the funeral cars to return, the first glimpse of a chrome headlamp sending them hurtling into the kitchen to 'get that kettle on' or rushing to 'take those damp tea towels off the sarnies' in the parlour.

Vera and I would act out extremely lengthy and complicated scenes with the intensity and concentration of children at play, pottering anxiously about preparing for our pretend party of funeral-goers to return, re-enacting the rituals we'd witnessed when we were growing up that went on between 'the ladies who made the tea'. We'd peer out of the window waiting for the imaginary mourners to pull up in imaginary Co-op funeral cars, rushing to put the kettle on and standing in wait at the open door to offer a solicitous arm for the grieving widow to lean on, greeting her with a sympathetic 'Are you all right, girl? Get yourself sat down and I'll bring you a nice cup of tea and a little drop of whisky', enquiring further of the poor woman if she thought she would be able to 'get a little boiled ham sarnie down her'? It was all very funny and extremely well observed. Mike Leigh would've loved us, and no doubt if such behaviour were carried out in a theatre workshop or comedy club it might be considered 'improv'. We simply thought of it as 'playing', two daft young queens indulging themselves with a camp couple of hours' worth of re-enacting a Liverpool working-class funeral seen through the eyes of two old women.

Another game we enjoyed was factories. Based on Vera's extensive knowledge of factory life gleaned from his time employed as a machinist making pillow cases we'd rearrange the front room, putting two tables and chairs one in front of the other with Alma and Anne's sewing machines on them. Winding some of Angela's scarves round our heads we became factory girls, competing with the noise of the sewing machines and a transistor radio, blaring away on top of the sideboard as a touch of authenticity, to have a conversation. Vera once worked for a firm but fair supervisor called Joyce Forshaw, whom we resurrected to keep us in check. The imaginary Joyce would examine our work and tell us when to go for our break, which we'd spend in the kitchen, putting the factory to rights over a sausage roll and a mug of tea, discussing nonsense such as the finer details of Vera's daughter's forthcoming nuptials and whom we considered the prime suspect in the theft of the Christmas Club money.

When we weren't shouting out of the window for

imaginary kids to 'go to the shop for a few messages for us' we could be found leaping out of it playing *The Avengers*. I leaped with such gusto that I badly twisted my ankle, resulting in a trip to the Royal Northern Hospital and a week spent unable to put any weight on my foot. It never happened to Tara King.

We even had an imaginary friend, Kitty, a highly inquisitive old lady, the type they call in Liverpool an 'owld arse', who trailed round behind us, dropping in for a visit at the most inconvenient of moments. It got to the stage where Vera was paying for Kitty's fare on the bus and buying her drinks in pubs. When Vera got a tax rebate we made our way up the Seven Sisters Road stopping in every pub on the way for a large whisky for me, a ditto of vodka for Vera and as always a little something to keep Kitty lubricated. By the time we got to Finsbury Park we could barely stand, but as there was a fair on it seemed a shame not to go on any of the rides and we elected to throw ourselves with gay abandon on the mercy of the Rotor, a ride you very rarely see any more. It was basically a human spin dryer, a drum that revolved at great speed, sticking you to the wall with centrifugal force whilst the floor retracted from under you. Vera's shopping was scattered to the four winds together with his specs as we spun round and round screaming our heads off, much to the amusement of those looking down on us, Kitty no doubt amongst them, from the observation gallery above.

Kitty's still around today, still refusing to wear her false teeth and not as active as she once was, but then she's getting on now, two hip replacements and a little problem with her bladder, but she still manages to drop in now and then for old times' sake . . .

*

Amy rang me a week later. 'Get your Sunday best on, the boss wants to meet you,' she said, giving me the address of the agency off Park Lane.

I jumped into a tepid bath while Vera pressed the cream suit using a crusty tea towel that had been on active service for over a month, infusing my suit with a faint whiff of scorched bacon. There certainly appeared nothing sleazy or tacky about the escort agency selling its wares from a suite of rooms on the top floor of a smart mansion block. I pushed the buzzer marked 'Rowena Switzer' and was told to 'come up' by a friendly voice. I half hoped that it would be an emporium lit by beaded Tiffany lamps, with a pianist in a tux bashing out 'Hard Hearted Hannah' on a honky-tonk piano in the corner, the elegant madam leaning against it fanning herself languidly with a pearl-handled ostrich-feather fan while her girls, in a state of semi-undress, posed provocatively on shawl-draped chaises longues placed casually around the room. Getting out of the lift I could see that regrettably the agency's decor owed more to a provincial branch of a building society than to my vision of a New Orleans cathouse. Amy was there to meet me, looking every inch the society hostess in a black crêpe evening dress and diamonds.

'I've got a booking,' she said, giving me a kiss, 'so I must dash, but I'll introduce you to Rowena first.'

Rowena turned out to be as unremarkable as her premises, failing to live up to my idea of a brothel madam, and memorable only for an eccentric hairpiece, five shades of red lighter than her own, hanging perilously from the back of her head. She gave me the once-over and in the full glare of the extremely bright lighting of her office I became painfully aware that the cream suit possibly could've done with a bit of intensive care in the dry cleaner's before I came out in it.

Feeling provincial and awkward, I tried to position myself so she couldn't see the large stain I'd just noticed on my sleeve as I politely listened to her telling me that since I came highly recommended by Amy, whom she considered to be one of her best girls and trusted with her life, she was prepared to offer me the job of escorting her girls into difficult hotels.

'All my girls are high class,' she said, raising her eyebrows and putting me in mind of Mrs Dickie for a moment, 'and I expect them to be treated as such.'

And that was it. Another addition to my ever-expanding CV – I was a prostitutes' walker. Hang on a minute, what had Rowena said? Sorry, I was no common or garden walker, I was a *high-class walker* for *high-class prostitutes*, thank you very much.

I started work almost immediately. My first assignment was to get Shirley, a plump little peroxide blonde from Birmingham who made me question Rowena's definition of the term 'high class', into the Hilton Hotel for an assignation with a very important client.

''Ang on, will ya?' she shouted, teetering behind me as we made our way slowly down Park Lane. 'Slow down, you're like a fookin' whippet.'

Shirley had forced her fat little trotters into a pair of cripplingly high stilettos which had reduced her mobility to nothing more than a painful shuffle. We stopped just round the corner from the hotel so she could have a fag and force a finger down the side of her shoe in an attempt to take the pressure off her swollen insteps, which were rising rapidly like a pair of Yorkshire puddings.

'Ooh, these fookin' shoes,' she moaned, slowly lifting her

foot off the pavement in the hope of providing temporary respite from the pain.

'Why don't you take them off for a moment then?' I asked her, more for something to say than out of concern.

'Why? Because I'd never get the boogers back on again, that's why,' she replied, taking one long last drag of her ciggy before flicking it into the street. 'Just be glad you don't have to wear high heels for a living, duck. Now c'mon, let's get a move on. This won't get the baby fed.'

I managed to manoeuvre Miss Saltley Gas Works 1962 past the doorman without any bother, as fortunately he was pre-occupied getting some guests and their luggage out of a taxi. I marched briskly ahead with Shirley shuffling behind me as awkward as a cow on ice, her full-length leather coat trimmed in a fur of dubious origin flapping behind her. She would've been more at home with a Cherry B and cider on a hen night in a Blackpool Wetherspoons than with champagne in a Park Lane hotel.

We made it safely past the reception and slipped in behind a small group of elderly Americans waiting for the lift.

'He's a prince, this one, y'know,' Shirley confided in a voice that could've been heard across Hyde Park. 'Not that it's a big deal, of course – they're two a penny over there. There's a prince on every street corner.' The Americans pretended not to hear as Shirley explained her version of the House of Saud to me.

'They believe in big families, see, hundreds of wives with hundreds of kids. Must be a bloody nightmare at Christmas, not that I think they go in for it.'

Thankfully the lift arrived and we all piled in. As we ascended Shirley leaned towards me. 'D'ya know what the nice thing about Arab clients is?' she bellowed, breaking the silence.

'They're very handsome?' I offered, fully aware that the Americans were all ears.

'No,' she answered, matter of factly. 'They come quickly.'

Someone coughed and one of the American women hastily asked her group if anyone knew what time they were meeting in the lobby in the morning. Shirley yawned, unaware or perhaps just not caring that she'd caused a minor sensation amongst our companions. I stuck my hand in my trouser pocket and self-mutilated my leg, willing the lift to hurry up.

The corridor that led to the prince's suite seemed never-ending. Shirley's incessant chatter and her indiscretion in the lift had started to get on my nerves. I'm just going to dump her at the door and get the hell out of here, I told myself as I waited for her to catch up. The realization of just how sordid the situation actually was crept over me as I watched her waddling down the hall in her stupid shoes, a piece of mutton on its way to the slaughter, and my annoyance turned to pity and concern.

Before knocking on the door Shirley took a little mirror from her handbag and picked at her hair. 'Well, it'll have to do,' she said eventually, putting the mirror back up and tapping on the door.

'You look lovely,' I lied. 'Good luck.'

She squeezed my arm in response but as I tried to leave she pulled me back, muttering, 'Don't go. Not yet.'

We were ushered in by two armed bodyguards, gorillas in suits, who led us into the bedroom, where a large, swarthy man wearing a dressing gown over a white djellaba lay watching TV on a bed the size of a badminton court.

'Prince Abdul,' Shirley shrieked, showing a vast expanse of

thigh as she leaped on the bed and showered him with kisses. 'How I've missed you.'

Prince Abdul seemed equally pleased to see Shirley, grinning like the Cheshire cat over her shoulder at me as he patted her ample backside affectionately.

'This is Paul,' she said, getting off the bed and smoothing down her dress, the Brummie accent, previously as thick as a pan of chip shop mushy peas, replaced as if by magic by tones that sounded more Mayfair than Bullring. 'He very kindly escorted me here from the office,' she trilled, winking at me. 'Wasn't that kind of him?'

Her transformation from pint of northern mild to sparkling Park Lane cocktail was as instantaneous as it was startling. The metamorphosis from the whining lump of suet to the beautiful minx now curled up coquettishly in the armchair seductively toying with a bunch of grapes astonished me. This was no clumsy slapper, this was a seasoned pro, one who obviously reserved the act until she was on the main stage.

The prince slowly and with great dignity slid off the bed, fastening his dressing gown and holding his hand out to thank me. I wondered if Prince Philip would've been quite so charming if a complete stranger had marched into his bedroom and caught him in his nightie, but this prince didn't seem bothered in the least. Quite the opposite, in fact. Gesturing towards a table laden with food he encouraged me to eat something with cries of 'Please, please'. I quite fancied a butty but Shirley, throwing me a look from the chair that even I could recognize as a signal that translated as 'Get lost, I'm keen to get down to business', piped up and told the prince that I'd better not as I had to get back to the office.

The prince thanked me again and then said something in Arabic to one of the bodyguards, who showed me out, putting ten crisp twenty-pound notes in my hand as a thank you as I left. Good old Shirley. That's why she wanted me to hang around and made such a fuss of me. She wanted to make sure I got a hefty tip. My mother had been wrong all along. The wages of sin weren't death, after all. Sin was extremely well paid.

Rowena's clients were mainly wealthy Arabs, playboys who dumped their wives, kids and retinues of servants into rented Kensington mansions and went off and had fun partying non-stop in hotel suites with working girls. Rowena liked her Arab punters. Money seemed to be no object and many of the girls had earned a fortune out of them. Rowena was extremely fussy. Answering the phone one busy night she was asked by a prospective client how to get to the agency by tube. Before putting the phone down she replied curtly that she only supplied to the carriage trade and not, regrettably, to men who travelled on public transport.

There wasn't as much work as I'd been led to believe, but I'd hang round the office just in case, passing the time chatting to the girls and the two receptionists who more or less ran the place. The receptionists were strictly look but don't touch, and although they flirted outrageously with the clients, charming the pants off them and accepting presents with cries of 'Oh, Omar, a Cartier watch! You really shouldn't have', they were not for sale at any price. Despite this or maybe because of it they were in great demand and invited out to clubs and private parties in hotel suites after work nearly every night. I'd sometimes tag along, even though the likes of Tramp and the Saddle Room really weren't my scene, because it was interesting seeing how the supposed 'beautiful people' lived. I preferred the parties, for not only did I get to see inside some of London's grandest hotels but I knew that when the time came to leave it was a guaranteed dead cert that the host would shove a wad of notes in our hands for a taxi.

Vera was no longer pulling pints in the Sportsman. He too was now on the books of London Domestics and quids in thanks to a nice little earner cleaning for the wives of some of Rowena's best customers, temporarily domiciled out of the way in Kensington mansions that only the Saudis could afford to rent. Although these beautiful houses had endless bedrooms, magnificent kitchens and an assortment of elegant drawing rooms and morning rooms, the women chose to live and sleep together with all the children in one big room, forsaking the comfortable sleeping arrangements upstairs for makeshift camp beds. The kitchens remained untouched as meals were sent in from local restaurants.

The women spent the best part of the day shopping in Harrods. They seemed to spend for spending's sake, the proof of their many purchases piled high and mostly forgotten in the bedrooms: bedding, children's clothes, shoes, handbags and, in one room, over two hundred duvets. The majority of this booty was still there after the women had packed up and gone home and as Vera and I had never had the pleasure of sleeping under a duvet we helped ourselves to a couple, absolving our crime by telling each other that someone else would only take them if we didn't and that person more than likely didn't have to sleep under blankets so old they'd aged into something resembling mummified felt. I considered my duvet compensation for the many times I'd had to clean up mounds of human excrement from the sweeping marble staircase. Vera guarded his harem with the zeal of a possessive eunuch. He didn't want any strangers from the agency jumping on his gravy train and if extra help was required he roped either me or Angela in to help him. For something so simple as opening the front door to these women and then carrying their mountain of shopping in from the limo he was given a five hundred quid tip, so it was no wonder he was keen to keep this run of good luck to himself. Vera was the only cleaner in London I'd ever heard of who travelled to and from work by taxi and shopped in Harrods Food Hall for something for his tea.

It was an unsettling existence, washing dishes in the nursing home one day and sitting in the sun on the terrace of the Hôtel Negresco in Nice with a few of Rowena's girls as the guest of a French Canadian diplomat the next.

Since I fancy myself as a bit of a free spirit it really galls me to admit that I actually need a routine in my life. I do now and I did then and the day to day 'I don't know what I'm doing or where my next penny is coming from' lifestyle I'd been leading was getting me down. My self-esteem, to quote my aunty Chris, was lower than a worm's tit. Salvation came in the guise of Camden Social Services who, instead of kicking the front door in and sectioning me as they probably should have, rang up one morning and offered me a job.

Six weeks earlier I'd been for an interview for a job as a peripatetic care officer. This was a service, way ahead of its time, that had originally been set up by a remarkable Irishwoman named Maura Shanahan. Usually if a parent went into hospital leaving the children without a responsible adult to look after them, there was no alternative but to admit them into care. To prevent children from having to face the trauma of a children's home and possible separation from their siblings a peripatetic would move into the family home and care for them full time, allowing them to stay there and providing them with some normality in the face of an abnormal situation. 'Perries' also provided respite care, allowing an exhausted spouse or parent a much-needed break from caring for a loved one twenty-four hours a day, seven days a week.

I'd given up hope on the job as I hadn't heard anything from Maura since my interview and now here she was welcoming me into the fold and asking me if it would be possible to drop everything and come down to the office as they had a major crisis on their hands, one that required someone with my expertise and experience with children to handle it. Flannel and flattery, I fall for it every time, and with Maura ladling it on with a trowel I'd have agreed to look after Wednesday and Pugsley Addams. However, the Addams kids would've been a pushover compared to the family of Robinsons that I found in my charge. All five of them lived in a sparsely furnished basement flat in Kentish Town that the children had reduced to a semi-derelict shell of its former self.

Their mother Nora, a violent alcoholic, had recently died of a heart attack leaving her dysfunctional brood in the care of Camden council. Maura's policy of keeping families together was probably not the best idea for this lot. They hated each other. Margaret at fifteen was the eldest and her mother's daughter, spiteful, manipulative and an inveterate liar. She was forever escaping out of her bedroom window and going missing. Her brother Billy, a year younger, was a moody, deeply disturbed boy, prone to attacking his siblings at the slightest provocation with the nearest sharp implement to hand. The twins, Bernadette and Clare, a duo straight out of the *Village of the Damned* with their pale hair and blood-less complexions, hissed and spat at each other like a pair of baby adders. Clare was a religious fanatic who stole prayer books and holy pictures from the local churches and liked to parade up and down the darkened hall in the middle of the night wearing her communion dress, muttering prayers under her breath that sounded more like incantations and dark curses, while her sister Bernadette looked silently on from the top of the stairs. It was quite a shock to unexpectedly encounter her gliding down the hall at two in the morning, the light from the stolen church candle she was carrying casting strange shadows across her pale little face, already partially obscured behind a veil she'd made from all that was left of a pair of net curtains that had once hung in the kitchen but had been torn down in yet another argument. For me the youngest child Eddie was the most difficult. His cute good looks and diminutive size made him appear a lot younger than his years and it was hard to believe until you saw him in full flow that the dimples and curls hid a hyper-violent temper and a repertoire of swear words that would shock Barnacle Bill's parrot into silence.

Thank God for Barbara, whom I was to work alongside. She was an experienced perry, practical and patient, whom I found very easy to get on with, which was just as well considering we had to share a bedroom. Each day was like sitting on a time bomb. You never knew when the explosion would go off, and when it inevitably did all hell broke loose. I've seen Billy pick the television up and throw it through the window after an argument with Eddie, who wanted to watch a different channel. We went through tellies like toilet paper until eventually the office stopped giving us any more, making our evenings trying to amuse the little terrors doubly hard. One afternoon I foolishly took them to see *Snow White and the Seven Dwarfs* at the cinema in Camden Parkway. At the point in the film when the dwarfs make their journey home singing 'Heigh ho, heigh ho' Eddie came swaggering

across the stage, his minuscule frame casting a huge shadow
across the screen as he imitated the dwarfs behind him. His
response to the protests of the audience was a masturbatory
gesture. Needless to say we were thrown out, the manager
telling me never to darken his cinema's doorstep with my
brood again. Once outside the kids seized their chance and
ran off in all directions, leaving me roaring with rage and
frustration in the middle of Parkway.

As Camden didn't pay overtime we were given time off in
lieu which meant Barbara and I worked every other week, an
arrangement that suited us both as you needed a week off to
recover after spending 24/7 with the Robinson kids. We
rarely got a night of undisturbed sleep as there was usually a
drama to contend with, for as well as Clare's nocturnal
pilgrimages up and down the hall and Eddie's hyperactivity,
which allowed him to exist on half an hour's sleep a night,
there were the children's errant fathers to deal with. Each
child, apart from the twins, had a different dad who would
occasionally see fit to turn up in the early hours of the morning blind drunk and feeling extremely hard done by,
demanding to see their respective offspring.

There was no reasoning with these maudlin, self-righteous
drunks and they invariably turned violent when refused
access to the kids, who by this time were up and awake and
causing merry hell. We'd ring the police, but after a while,
annoyed at being called out to what they considered to be a
long-running domestic dispute, they stopped coming, leaving
the job of dealing with these nocturnal visits down to me.

Now, even if physically assaulted and regardless of the
circumstances, Camden Social Services' employees were not
allowed to retaliate or even defend themselves, in case the
assailant got hurt and consequently sued. Instead we were

expected to show our identification cards and explain in a loud but reasonable voice, 'I am a peripatetic care officer in the employ of Camden council. Please take that broken bottle you are waving out of my face and leave this instant.'

I tried the official approach once and once only, and received a slap in the mouth for my trouble. After that any drunken fathers were removed from the step by means of a smart tap over the head with a metal bin lid and a good shove from a hefty yard brush.

After three months working with the Robinsons I was beginning to feel that I was married to a woman named Barbara and together we were raising our five highly dysfunctional kids in Kentish Town squalor. Divine retribution, perhaps. But despite the Robinsons' many shortcomings, we found ourselves really caring for those kids, although we were desperate to find them suitable foster parents so we could get the hell out of there and back to our own lives.

Each night when the kids had finally settled down we'd sit over a pot of tea or, if the day had been particularly stressful, a bottle of wine, chain smoking and planning what we would do with ourselves when we finally got our very own 'relief of Mafeking'. Barbara's friend Beryl, an irascible little social worker with a dry wit who believed very much in telling it like it is, would join us in these 'at home with the Robinsons' sessions, offering practical advice and support when our nerve endings became so frazzled that they hurt. Barbara was planning to take a trip to north-west Poland by car to deliver much-needed medication, unavailable in Communist Poland, to her sick aunt who lived in a little town called Kamién Pomorski. Beryl and I agreed to go with her, God knows why. A fortnight in Playa del Ingles lying on the beach would've been a more suitable way to recuperate after four

215

months with the Robinsons than driving through Communist countries in November. However, the latter sounded more of an adventure and I duly applied for my visas and bought a Polish phrase book.

In the meantime we sat back rubbing arnica cream on our bruised shins and TCP on the teeth marks in our arms and watching, somewhat cynically by now, an endless stream of well-meaning but totally unsuitable prospective foster parents come and go. Just when we thought we'd finally got them off our hands Maura would ring to tell us that the placement had been unsuccessful as there had been some 'difficulties' – a euphemism for another nice home in ruins and Mr and Mrs Foster Parent on the verge of a nervous breakdown after just one night with the kids. Reluctantly, I'd pack my bag and set off for Chez Robinson, offering up a silent prayer on the bus to whichever deity would listen for some brave couple to please come along and rescue us.

Eventually, one did. Barbara and I weren't over-keen on them. They were like the Modern Parents from *Viz* magazine, having read all the books on modern parenting and attended all the courses and seminars. We felt that they put the children's disturbed behaviour down to our lack of skill. 'What they need is love, tolerance and a kind but firm hand to guide them,' Mr Modern Parent told me condescendingly as the kids piled into his beautiful car to be whisked off to Laura Ashley heaven in Richmond.

What they need is muzzling and a daily elephant tranquillizer, I thought privately, waving them off, hopeful that they had finally found a permanent home. No sooner was the car round the corner and out of our sight than I'm ashamed to say I turned into a lunatic, dancing and scream-ing exultantly like a prisoner who had just been liberated (which I had) and throwing what little was left of the crockery through what few windows remained intact. Unprofessional behaviour without doubt, but a bloody wonderful way to release four months of built-up tension.

Unfortunately the kids lasted no longer than a month in Richmond. They destroyed the house with its immaculate furnishings and were blamed for the eventual break-up of the Modern Parents' marriage, only this time there was no going back to Kentish Town. Instead, they were split up and placed in care homes. Not a successful result, then, despite the best intentions of everyone concerned. I hope that they had a happy ending.

CHAPTER 12

A Savage Debut

ON MY WEEKS OFF FROM THE ROBINSONS I SPENT MORE OR less every night in the Black Cap with Vera. We were mad for the drag acts. It was good to see the Harlequeens again, although they'd seriously upped their game since the last time I'd watched them. They were just as funny but their costumes were now magnificent confections of beads and feathers. Apart from the Harleys our favourite act was without doubt the Disappointer Sisters, a mime act made up of three queens called Reg, Roy and Graham – known respectively as Regina Fong, Rosie Lee and Gracie Grab-it-all – who, when not treading the boards of the tiny stage in the back bar, could be found blind drunk in the front bar screaming their heads off. This was no ordinary mime act. They were slick and inventive with wonderful costumes, elevating pub mime drag into previously unexplored territory. Reg's claim that it was always his intention to treat a pub audience as a theatre audience, crediting them with some intelligence, had certainly paid off.

He was a former dancer, a 'West End Wendy' who had appeared in the London production of *Fiddler on the Roof* and the films *The Slipper and the Rose* and *Oh! What A Lovely War*, as he never tired of reminding us. Reg was the brains behind the act, coming up with most of the ideas, choreographing the dance routines, designing the costumes and deciding who did what, making sure of course that he was always centre stage. He always wore a red wig and played the deadpan, hard-boiled member of the troupe. All in all it was a real eye-opener for me which went way beyond the clichéd image of the archetypal no-talent drag act mouthing along to 'Big Spender'.

Our favourite show was *Hollywood*, a twenty-minute spot that opened as a tribute to Busby Berkeley with the trio dressed as *Gold Diggers of 1933* chorines and went on to a series of impersonations of Hollywood stars before the climax of a full-blown Ziegfeld Follies type finale (on a budget of course) to the strains of 'Hooray for Hollywood'.

As well as the headlining act there were also a drummer and an organist who accompanied the live acts and a compère, a leggy young queen called Adrella, who sang, amongst other things, 'Three Little Fishes'.

Marc Fleming, or Aunty Flo as he was known to his regulars, was a very popular live act, a vicious-tongued old queen with a razor-sharp wit who berated the audience, in particular his band of loyal followers who gathered around the stage in an area known as the royal enclosure. It was a brave or, rather, very foolish person who dared to heckle the mighty Flo. Apart from being a brilliant stand-up there was no one to touch him when it came to the art of the put-down.

Coachloads of tourists would stop off briefly at the Cap for a quick drink and a gawp at the queers and drag queens. Aunty Flo would delight in abusing these hapless victims.

'Where are you from, darling?' he'd ask sweetly.

'Sweden.'
'Oh, Swedes . . . We feed them to cattle in this country.'

Rex Jameson's alter ego, the inimitable Mrs Shufflewick, was a drunken old slattern, the type you might have found propping up the bar of an East End pub in a battered hat and ratty old fox fur, knocking back the Guinness and regaling the customers with a salty tale of how she came to end up half naked at the back of a bus with a sailor and a fishcake for company. He'd created a three-dimensional character that was so credible I didn't realize at first that I was watching a man and not a little old woman. When 'Shuff' was on form he was sheer genius, but when he was paralytic, two sips away from being incapable, as he frequently was, I found the drunken ramblings of this tiny man dressed as a dirty old lady painful to watch, some of the audience delighting in laughing at him not with him.

I'd never heard of this Mrs Shufflewick until I saw him at the Black Cap. He'd been a big star in variety, radio and TV in the fifties and sixties, but times and tastes change and thanks to his drinking and growing unreliability managements were extremely reluctant to book him. So Shuff sought work in the only places left that would have him, the drag pubs, and some of his gags always made me laugh no matter how many times he told them. For instance:

'This sailor comes up to me and says, "You remind me of Elizabeth Taylor." I said, "Well, that's awfully kind of you. Is it my figure?" "Yes," he said, "it's gone for a Burton."'

'This sailor and me, we were standing outside the pub talking about this and that. I don't know what I said that upset him –

I know I'd mentioned the price of plums – but he suddenly went berserk and made a lunge at me. Well I shot down this side turning which I thought would be an escape route but turned out to be a cul-de-sac and I'm stood there with me back to the brick wall and me legs in two dustbins with a John West salmon tin where it mattered most, with the lid up. And there's him with his good conduct medals clanking away and his string vest at half mast, well, I thought, this is it tonight Gladys, death or dishonour. And then I thought to meself, well, I'm not bloody dying yet . . .'

Shuff collapsed one Sunday afternoon on his way to buy fags from his local shop off Camden High Street and died from a heart attack. I was shocked to hear that he was only fifty-eight. I'd thought that he was a lot older than that. At his funeral, they sang 'My old man said follow the van' as the coffin vanished behind the curtains and then retired to the Black Cap for a salmon barm cake and a glass of sherry.

To be honest, I'd never been interested in watching drag until I saw the acts at the Cap in action. It was very rare to see a drag act performing in any of the Liverpool gay clubs. The only one I can ever recall was a hairy-chested lorry driver from Manchester who appeared to think that a cheap black wig poking out from underneath a joke shop bowler hat and a tatty corset that looked as if it had probably once belonged to his grandmother instantly transformed him into the living image of Liza Minnelli. He was also under the misapprehension that to get big laughs all you had to do was shove a balloon up an ill-fitting crimplene dress and mime along (badly) to a recording of Dionne Warwick's 'Always Something There To Remind Me', preferably using a disc that had seen active service and was so heavily scratched it sounded as if Ms Warwick was frying chips when she recorded it.

The act was crude and offensive and I wasn't amused that I'd had to pay fifty pence to witness this freak show – fifty pence! A bloody fortune in the early seventies to have to cough up for the privilege of getting into Sadie's, and on a week night. What annoyed me most was that the audience seemed to be lapping it up. What was wrong with them? Couldn't they see how bad this crap was? I said as much to Billy the barman.

'That's because they're all pissed, love, so pissed they actually think that it is Liza up there. Just look at old Greta. She's ecstatic, God help her.' He indicated towards one of the more senior members of Sadie's clientele, a tiny wizened old queen, blissfully drunk, who was slumped against the wall by the dance floor, blowing gummy kisses and clapping along as Judy Garland's twenty-stone daughter tried to balance her massive girth on a bar stool while miming to 'Mein Herr' from *Cabaret*.

'Good on her at her age I say, getting out and about and enjoying herself instead of sitting in the bloody house on her own. Cider?' He took a drag of his fag and gently rested it on the edge of the bar while he dipped down daintily to take a bottle of cider from the shelf behind him. 'Mind you, she's always been lively,' he went on. 'She was a right one in the war, you know, not that I was around to see it, of course, way before my time. Glass?'

I shook my head.

'Yes, man mad, anything in a uniform, even the bus conductors weren't safe, on her back twenty-four hours a day. Broken 'earted she was on VE Day, poor cow.'

He seemed oblivious of the fact that he hadn't given me my

cider and there were a couple of people waiting to be served, carrying on with his potted history of the life and times of Greta regardless. 'They should have given her a medal for services rendered,' he said, giving Greta a little wave. 'Well let's face it, love, she entertained more soldiers, sailors, airmen and marines than Vera Lynn and Gracie fucking Fields put together.'

'Was she on the game then?' I asked, moving my empty glass across the bar towards him by way of a hint.

'Was she buggery. She was only too happy to give it away. Now as for *her*,' he said, ignoring my hint and the two restless punters still waiting to be served, who were now vainly waving fivers and their empty glasses at him, and turning his attention instead to the act, throwing it a look that Medusa would've given her snakes for, 'I say if you're going to indulge in this kind of tat trannyism then at least have the decency to keep it within the confines of your own home and not feel obliged to inflict it on a paying public.' He shook his head in disgust as he deftly opened the bottle of cider, plonking it down on the bar before me. 'It wouldn't have hurt her to have had a shave, would it? You'd think the least she could have done was shave her dirty great back before she flung a frock on.' He took my money and slithered towards the till, never once taking his eyes off the activity on the dance floor.

'Jesus tonight, poncing about in an 'alf-mast nightie with a chemo wig slapped on yer 'ead isn't drag, love,' he said, slithering back and giving me my change. 'I've seen the best and I know what I'm talking about. You can't put the likes of that dog in the same category as Ricki Renee, Laurie Lee and Danny, can you? Drag's an art and there's nothing worse than bad drag. It's an insult to both men and women and makes me want to grab a rope, organize a lynch mob and hang that out of the front window as a warning. Now who's waiting to be served?'

On the whole the majority of the acts who appeared at the Cap were polished professionals, although it has to be said that there were more than one or two who were complete and utter pony and trap. Some of them were so bad they deserved ten out of ten for cheek, for having the bare-faced effrontery to get up there in the first place, blatantly stealing other, more successful acts' routines and mannerisms and working cheap, undercutting the others. Watching these dogs prance about the stage I'd always remark that I could do better than that, anybody could.

The Disappointer Sisters were a big influence. If 'cool' had been in use back then we'd have described them as such. They seemed so 'today', unlike the old timers from another era who stood there and sang ballads in nice frocks leaving me stone cold. I couldn't see the point. There was no reason for them to be in a frock if all they were going to do was sing. They might just as well have worn a suit. Looking like a woman simply wasn't enough any more, it was what you did with it that made it interesting.

I wanted to get up there but be larger than life, a creature that was more cartoon than human. I wasn't sure yet. I wanted to get up on that stage and join in the mayhem at the circus that was part Weimar Berlin cabaret, part vaudeville and burlesque and yet quintessentially British, its roots steeped firmly in the traditions of music hall.

I certainly didn't want to pass as a woman and be able to walk down a street in full drag undetected – that was transvestism. Nor were my desires in any way sexual. There was no urge to don lacy apparel and sheer stockings and come over all girly – quite the opposite, in fact. Watching the acts at the Cap night after night I finally realized that what I'd wanted to do all along was perform, not as an actor but as a bump and grind, loud and lairy drag queen. Exactly how you went about joining the ranks of this sisterhood was quite another matter.

My next assignment as a peripapetic was looking after a girl and her three brothers while their mother went into hospital for a hysterectomy and their father into prison for alleged IRA activities. It was in another run-down flat, this time near King's Cross, that I found myself playing Mary Poppins for six solid weeks.

Luckily they were smashing kids, their ages ranging from four to ten, who were hardly any trouble at all to look after and seemed to live only for food and football, the girl included. I took them to see Arsenal play, only the second time I'd ever been to a professional match. My induction into professional football had taken place years earlier when Frank, our next-door neighbour, had taken me to see Tranmere Rovers play and the man standing behind me had done a beery wee down the back of my duffel coat through a rolled-up copy of the *Liverpool Echo*.

Apart from being woken each morning at the crack of dawn by Irish rebel songs played at full belt on the record player by Liam, the youngest boy, who liked to rouse the neighbourhood each daybreak with a selection from his father's record collection, life at King's Cross was fairly uneventful until the arrival of the children's aunty Rita, recently released from a spell in the nick and hot to trot. She was big and blowsy, Mae West with a touch of Blanche DuBois. Except this version had a thick Dublin accent. She was married and lived with her husband in Kilburn, not that she paid him much attention, but she'd taken to spending most of her time with us in King's Cross, more for its close proximity to her favourite boozer than out of any concern for the kids' welfare. Rita was a perennial good time girl and had got it into her head that in her sister's absence she'd be able to use the flat as a place to entertain her gentlemen callers.

One afternoon, returning to the flat unexpectedly, I was treated to the sight of Rita lying naked on the sofa with her flabby white legs wrapped round a big black arse that seemed to be pounding her into next week.

'He's a friend,' she grunted by way of explanation, waving at me over his shoulder. The 'friend', startled by the arrival of a third party, leaped off her as if she were an electric fence and hurriedly attempted to get dressed, shouting 'Sorry, sorry' as he hopped about the room pulling his trousers up.

I was extremely grateful that he'd reacted this way, as I didn't relish trying to throw him out. He was built like the proverbial brick latrine and a blow across the head from the penis that he was having trouble zipping his fly over would've been enough to stun me for a week, never mind a smack in the mouth from one of his massive fists. He was extremely apologetic, though, and I almost felt bad about walking in on him.

'Your mother's a nice lady,' he said, offering his hand for me to shake which I declined as I could see where it had been.

'She's not my mother,' I spluttered, looking down at Rita scratching her tatty head and yawning. Her lipstick was smeared up one side of her face and strands of her yellow hair were stuck to her forehead with sweat. I could see now that she wasn't naked but was wearing a flimsy bra that had started out in life as flesh-coloured but was now grey with age, one strap attached to a fraying cup by means of a safety pin having no doubt snapped from the stress of attempting to support the weight of her sagging breasts.

'Ah, don't go, Ernest,' she pleaded drunkenly, rooting around on the floor for her fags and matches. 'This is only Paul, he won't mind at all.'

But Paul did mind, and while Ernest beat a hasty retreat out of the front door I read the old slut the Riot Act. She seemed unfazed by my rant as if she'd heard it all before and just sat there yawning, scratching her crotch. I could see that she wasn't a natural blonde.

'Ah c'mon, give us a break will ya. The kids are all at school, no one was harmed,' she said eventually. 'I'm fresh out of the nick and gagging fer it. I get nuttin' of that owld eejit at home so you wouldn't blame me if I met a nice fellah in a pub and let me feelins get in the way of me common sense? I'm an owl fool, that's what I am. An owl fool.'

'You're an owl who-er,' I thought, leaving her to get dressed but deciding nevertheless to give her one last chance.

For a while she was the model of decorum, visiting every day bringing bags of sweets for the kids, a packet of fags for me and half a bottle of Bacardi for herself which she drank from a stainless steel goblet as she mooched about the kitchen, occasionally giving the table a cursory wipe with a dishcloth to show that she was 'helping'. She'd led me to believe that her husband was a monster, a red-haired giant of a man with a ferocious temper who when drunk, which by all accounts was twenty-four hours a day, was not beyond slapping his wife about.

'I should've left the owl divel years ago,' she'd sigh. 'The hidin's I've had off him.'

'Then why didn't you?'

'Because I love him, that's why,' she'd answer, adopting a

wistful expression and looking into the middle distance with big bloodshot eyes. 'As God is my witness I worship the very ground that man walks on.'

'But you live in terror of him,' I'd protest. 'He's a violent bully who batters you up.'

'And if he ever turns up here looking for me then for Jaysus' sake don't open the door, he'll kill the pair of us.'

Oh, great, just what I need, a drunken Finn McCool on the rampage.

He must have shrunk in the wash because when he eventually did turn up he turned out to be five foot nothing, with a cast in his eye and a stammer, his shiny, ill-fitting suit hanging off his puny frame, making him look like the stooge from a Benny Hill sketch.

One morning Liam, the youngest boy, wearing only a dirty vest, seized the opportunity of an open front door to escape. When I eventually realized that he was missing I took off looking for him in my bare feet, frantic that he'd wandered on to the busy road. Finally discovering him outside the station, barefaced and bare-arsed, I suffered the humiliation of seeing commuters on their way to catch their trains either averting their eyes completely or viewing the pair of us with a mixture of disgust and pity. A woman on her way out of W. H. Smith said that I wanted reporting to the social services for allowing a child to run around like that. Catching my reflection in the window, unshaven and unkempt, clutching a none too clean half-naked child, I could see why.

Getting back to the flat I found one of the neighbours from our house in Crouch End waiting for me. He explained that he'd answered the communal phone to a frantic Vera, who had been arrested coming out of the dole office and was being held at Hornsey Police Station. I was to go home to the flat and find the number of a pub in Liverpool called the Fountains and get a message to his dad that he'd been arrested for a series of burglaries he hadn't commited in Liverpool.

Vera hadn't been up to Liverpool for ages, not since his mother had died, so he couldn't possibly have gone on a crime spree breaking into the homes of wealthy Liverpool residents even if he'd wanted to. I could no more imagine Vera scaling a drainpipe with a stocking over his head and jemmying a bathroom window open in the dead of night than I could him coming home sober. It was a ridiculous notion. Besides, he had an alibi – me. I set off to Hornsey Police Station, Liam in tow, to prove Vera's innocence.

I went to the flat first to get the number of the Fountains from Vera's address book and rang them up. Pop, as Vera's dad was known, wasn't in the pub but the woman who answered told me that she'd send a message to him immediately to ring me urgently.

I peeled some spuds while I waited for Pop to ring back, genuinely concerned at the thought of Vera banged up in a cell just round the corner and thinking that it might be a good idea if I made him a bit of dinner and took it round to him at the station. The phone in the hall rang. It was Pop.

'All right, lad,' he growled. 'What's the score then?'

I explained what had happened and waited for Pop's reply.

'OK then,' he said after a momentary pause, sounding like a cop in an American police drama, 'I'll get things moving at this end. You sit tight, I'll keep you posted.'

Feeling a little reassured by Pop's grasp of the situation I sat Liam down and we had something to eat. I'd set some aside for Vera, a plate of corned beef, mashed spuds and peas sitting on top of a pan of simmering water to keep it warm. Covering it with another plate and wrapping it in a tea towel I took it down to the police station, hoping that if they searched it they wouldn't discover the note hidden inside the mashed spuds that read, *Don't worry, Vera, we'll get you out*.

The desk sergeant refused to give me any information apart from the fact that they were indeed holding Vera, and my protestations of Vera's innocence fell on deaf ears. Even though he promised to pass on the magazines, fags and corned beef dinner Vera never got them, nor did I get my plates and tea towel back. Thieving bastards.

When I explained to Rita what had happened to Vera she insisted on going up to the police station herself. Having met Vera a few times and liked him, she was determined to get him out. As she was a little drunk I couldn't risk letting her go on her own. With Rita as her counsel Vera would probably end up getting transportation, so I piled the kids on the back of the bus and we all made our way to Crouch End.

Rita had to pop into a pub first 'to calm her nerves' – this coming from a woman who didn't have a nerve in her body – while I waited outside with the kids. She wasn't in there long but when she came out she smelled strongly of whisky.

'Don't normally drink the stuff,' she explained as we trailed round to the police station. 'It has a tendency to make me violent.'

Consequently I was a little apprehensive as she approached the desk sergeant, one hand on her big fleshy hip which she rolled as she walked. 'This is Mr O'Grady,' she said grandly, pointing towards me. 'He is a social worker with the council and we would like to know why you are keeping his friend.'

'And who may you be, madam?' the sergeant asked, looking us up and down as if he'd just been invaded by gypsies.

He wasn't the one who'd been on duty earlier and didn't seem the type to suffer fools.

'Olivia Shelbourne,' Rita replied without missing a beat, 'Miss Olivia Shelbourne.'

I could feel my face burning as I clumsily explained the situation, but I could tell he wasn't listening to me. He was more concerned about a poster for death watch beetle that Liam had ripped off the wall and was waving about.

'Look,' he said to his siblings, 'there's one of them things we had in the bathroom.'

'What's your friend's name, sir?' the sergeant sighed wearily, watching me try and fail to get four highly excitable kids to sit down and keep quiet.

'Vera,' Rita piped, throwing the sergeant a sly smile. 'Vera. I'm afraid I don't know his surname, officer.'

'Vera? *His* surname?'

I gave the sergeant Vera's real name, squirming under his scrutiny as I tried once again to explain. 'Vera's a nickname,' I offered lamely, listening to my voice trail off as he shook his head in disbelief.

'He's being held until the arresting officers arrive from Liverpool tomorrow to take him back to be charged,' he said after making a phone call. 'That's all I can tell you for now. Thank you.'

'Why did you call yourself Olivia Shelbourne?' I asked Rita on the bus home.

'Well, you don't want to be giving the coppers your real name, particularly if you have a bit of form like me, it's common sense.' She settled down in her seat and started to lard some lipstick on.

'But why Olivia Shelbourne?'

'Well, Olivia, after Olivia de Havilland, y'know, the filum star, seeing as how when I was younger me da said I had a look of her,' she said, smacking her lips at her reflection in the window. 'And Shelbourne after the beautiful hotel in Dublin.' Comparing this peroxide bruiser attending to her maquillage on the back of a 41 bus to the ethereal beauty who played Maid Marian to Errol Flynn's Robin Hood I could only come to the conclusion that the drink must be extraordinarily strong in Dublin.

Vera was released the following evening, for as soon as the arresting officers turned up they realized that Vera was not the same person they'd nicked in Liverpool. Whoever they'd arrested was obviously someone close to Vera as he knew all his details, passing himself off as him.

'Look at me,' he said, safely back at home. His hand was shaking so violently it sent waves of tea crashing over the side of the mug he was attempting to pick up to wash a Valium down. 'Just look at the state of me poor nerves.' Another one with nerves of steel.

One of the other peripatetics had offered to mind the kids for me so I could go back to the flat for a couple of hours to see him. I wanted all the details. 'What was it like in there?' I asked. 'Being locked up?' I still couldn't believe that you could be locked up for two days for a crime that you couldn't possibly have committed.

'Terrible, Lily, terrible. I nearly went mad banged up all that time.' He spoke as if he'd just been released from the horrors of a long spell in solitary on Alcatraz. 'They took me glasses off me,' he screamed, outraged. 'In case I committed suicide with them, how stupid is that?'

Vera's eyesight is on a par with Helen Keller's and to take his glasses away was uncalled for. I ruminated on just how you'd go about killing yourself with a pair of specs while Vera had another go at drinking his tea. He found that rather than raising the mug to his lips the operation was more successful if he left it on the table, leaned forward, clamped his gob round the rim and sucked hard.

'I suppose you could break them and then cut your wrists.'

'What are you talking about?' Vera spluttered, a trickle of tea running down his chin.

'Killing yourself with a pair of glasses.'

'How the hell do I know?' he said, taking his off and wiping them shakily on his T-shirt. Had the Lovell Telescope at Jodrell Bank broken down then Vera's lenses would've made a more than adequate substitute. In fact he could've held them up to the sunlight, that's if his cell had such a luxury as a window, and burned the lock off the door.

'Come on,' he said, 'pop in the Cap with me for a drink on your way back to work. I certainly need one.'

Later on, as we stood drinking our lagers in the Cap, I noticed some leaflets advertising something called 'Regina Fong's Saturday Morning Madhouse'. What interested me was the bit at the bottom proclaiming that everyone was welcome to come along and do a number. It was all the encouragement I needed, desperate as I was to tread the boards of the Cap's tiny stage, and I made my mind up there and then that come hell or high water I was indeed going to get up and 'do a number'.

I'd taken the children to see their mother in hospital. She was a nice woman, a loving mother trying to raise her kids on what she received from the government and nothing at all like her errant sister.

When we got back to the flat I found I had unexpected

visitors, two men, one of whom was in the cupboard under the stairs. They turned out to be the children's uncle and his friend. The uncle emerged from the cupboard explaining that he was looking for a sports bag but as it wasn't there it didn't matter. They were affable enough as we stood around talking and drinking tea but I couldn't help sensing their unease. What was in that cupboard? I'd have a look later after they'd gone and the kids were asleep in bed.

Tucked away at the back of the electricity meter, wrapped in a carrier bag, I found my answer. A gun. I unwrapped the bag and stared at it, wondering what I should do now. I couldn't have four lively kids running around a flat with a gun waiting to be discovered by inquisitive fingers, nor was I prepared to put them and myself at risk by living in a possible secret armoury for the IRA. The uncle had either been looking for the gun when I disturbed him, which meant he'd probably be back, or been hiding it. Either way I didn't feel particularly safe that night and slept with one eye open.

In the morning, as I was about to ring Maura for her advice, the children's mum turned up. Having made up her mind that she was well enough to go home she'd discharged herself. I didn't want to worry her but felt I had to tell her about the gun.

'If you'd lifted them floorboards up you'd have found a few other bits and pieces,' she said resignedly. 'That bloody Gerry, I've warned him about using my house to hide his arms. Don't worry, I'll see that it's out of here by tonight and that will be the last of it. Forget you ever saw anything, d'ye hear?' I wasn't sure if I was to take her last remark as a piece of sound advice or as a threat and kept my mouth shut, telling no one apart from Maura, who replied somewhat darkly that she would 'deal with it'.

Since Mum was home and claiming that she could manage with a home help my services were surplus to requirements and I was free to go. Rita cried a little when I left. 'Keep in touch,' she shouted after me. 'And if you ever need a bed for the night you know where we are.' I hoped that I would never have to take her up on her offer.

It was basic to say the least, but as pub dressing rooms go, as I was soon to find out, far superior to the majority of rat-holes that the acts were expected to get ready and changed in. The bright fluorescent lighting picked out the glitter impacted on the bare concrete floor, the residue left behind by a lifetime of drag queens, making it sparkle in places, reminiscent of the rocks on Aladdin's Cave in Blackler's Christmas Grotto. A dress rail, hanging with a colourful assortment of the Sisters' costumes that I was slightly disillusioned to see didn't look quite so spectacular at close range as they did under the lights of the Black Cap's stage, ran alongside one wall. A long mirror hung on the other wall, the makeup shelf underneath pockmarked with cigarette burns and splattered with tiny yellowing pools of hardened spirit gum.

In the corner was the unheard of luxury of a sink, used by the acts not only to wash and shave in but also as a convenient lav. To reach the stage from this dressing room, you had to go down a couple of steps and past the gents' toilet. If it was a busy night it meant wading through the overspill of pee and if it was raining you got soaked as there was no overhead cover in the alley, so either way you got wet. Nevertheless, it was the tingeltangel, the gutter glamour, that I craved with an intoxicating eau de parfum all of its own. A combination of stale booze and fags, hairspray and sweat.

Reginald Sutherland Bundy aka Regina Fong was standing

in the door of the dressing room at the top of the steps haranguing the DJ.

'Oh, reeeally, de-ah,' he said, speaking in an exaggerated theatrical drawl, stretching the syllables out like strands of melted cheese, 'I don't need this hassle. The reason there are so many tapes, darling, is because there are quite a few of us all doing individual numbers. Now stop being so awkward and get back to your hutch. We're supposed to go up at one and I haven't even unpacked the slap yet.'

The DJ shrugged his shoulders and staggered back to his console at the back of the stage balancing an armful of cassette tapes.

'First no dresser and now the DJ giving me grief over the tapes. I don't know why I bother,' he said, peering down at me imperiously through hooded eyes. 'And what can I do for you, young woman?'

I found him quite intimidating in the flesh. He was tall, with a dancer's build and posture, and walked in that flat-footed way with his feet splayed out that ballet dancers tend to have.

'I'm doing a number,' I replied, suddenly overcome with shyness.

'Oh, are you now?' he said in an uninterested voice, flaring his nostrils and running his tongue over his sizeable front teeth. 'Then you'd better get ready, hadn't you, instead of standing out here gossiping.'

He stood by, letting me get past into the dressing room. Inside the other two members of the Disappointer Sisters were getting ready. Rosie Lee, perched on a stool in the corner languidly painting on a pair of eyebrows as thin as butterfly antennae, acknowledged me with a slight incline of the head. Gracie, over by the sink, was having a shave, talking non-stop as he hacked away at his face, stopping momentarily to stare at me blankly before carrying on where he'd left off. I felt awkward and very much out of place standing in the middle of the room unsure of what to do next.

'You can get ready over there, dear,' Rosie Lee said, solving my dilemma for me, pointing to a space at the opposite end of the make-up shelf. I could see him out of the corner of my eye watching me with some amusement as I self-consciously unpacked my few bits of make-up from a Batman pencil case.

'Is that the foundation you use?' he frowned, pointing to the tube of Max Factor liquid foundation, the sort that my aunty Chrissie used. 'You'll need a much heavier foundation than that for the stage, dear. The lights bleach you out and it would never cover.'

'Oh, shut up, Rosie,' Regina shouted over his shoulder, busy sharpening an eyebrow pencil he'd rooted out of an enormous fishing tackle box that he used to store his vast quantity of make-up in. 'Just because you've got skin like leather and need four coats of Dulux to cover it doesn't mean she has too. She's young, de-ah, remember it, youth? She's got young skin.'

Rosie Lee drew in his breath sharply. 'I'll have you know I have the skin of an eighteen-year-old.'

'An eighteen-year-old what, de-ah? Rice pudding?'

'As long as I never look as old as you, darling, I've no need to worry,' Rosie Lee said in honeyed tones laced with acid. 'Just take a good look at that face. Why, my dear, you've managed to break more veins than a vampire at an orgy.'

'Oh, shut up, Miss Lee, you're getting on my nerves.'

I watched them closely as they bickered and bitched and larded on the make-up. They used a stick of what looked like pink wax to flatten down their eyebrows and then covered them with a coating of glitter. Lips were painted a bright carmine red, and false eyelashes the size of a crow's wing defied gravity as they hung from the edges of turquoise eyelids. Three pairs of tights covered hairy legs. Chest and armpit hair, Reg insisted, must be Immacked regularly. He hated underarm hair, thought it an abomination on both woman and drag queens, regularly declaring to the others, 'I hope you've done the pits, de-ah, we don't want to see the Hanging Gardens of Babylon, do we?'

They didn't bother feminizing their skinny frames with padding or false boobs. Reg found them offensive. 'I'm not wearing a pair of humongous fake tits, de-ah. We're androgynous. You look at us and see a beautiful woman's face on the body of a boy.' I was to remind him of this statement some years later as he tried to force his ever-expanding girth into a Marks & Spencer girdle that was quite simply not up to the job.

For my debut at the Black Cap that Saturday afternoon, 7 October 1978, I thought it best if I went for the low comedy look rather than attempt high glamour as I had neither the resources nor the finances for sequins and feathers. From God knows where I'd unearthed a nineteen fifties black and white checked jacket that was too short in the arms and a matching pencil skirt so tight I could barely walk – add to this a pair of Lozzy's old high heels that added six inches to my height and a top-heavy picture hat decorated with a bunch of wax grapes I'd nicked from the fruit bowl on the table of the pugs' parlour of the nursing home in Regent's Park, and you had an accident waiting to happen.

'Divine hat,' Regina said, looking up at me. 'You're very tall, de-ah, what the fuck have you got on? Stilts? Never mind. Have you got your tape? I'll give it to the DJ.' Next to

Regina, resplendent in a black satin ball gown and an elaborately dressed hard wig, the kind you see on mannequins in shop windows, I felt, for want of a better word, a complete and utter twat, like some sad old tranny who'd dared to venture out into the world for the first time.

Rosie Lee, magnificent in platinum blonde wig and silver lamé dress, asked, 'Have you got a name, dear?'

'Yes, good point, Miss Lee. What's your name, dahling?' Reg said, wiping lipstick off his teeth.

'Lily Savage,' I mumbled.

'Larry Sausage?'

'No, Lily Savage.' I wanted the ground to swallow me up.

'Speak clearly, will you? I can't understand a word of that Liverpoolian accent. What number are you doing?'

'I'm doing "Nobody Makes a Pass at Me".'

'Is it autobiographical?'

'No, it's from a show called *Pins and Needles*. It's Barbra Strei—'

'I know where it's from, de-ah, thank you very much. Now move yourself, you're on next.'

I could barely breathe for fright as I stood outside the door to the stage waiting to hear the DJ announce me. What the bloody hell was I doing? Was it too late to leg it down the alley and vanish down Camden High Street? Maybe I should faint.

I could hear the DJ over the microphone trying to inject some enthusiam into his voice. 'OK, a first for you here at the Cap this afternoon, all the way from Liverpool, will you please welcome Lizzy Salvage!' Someone opened the door and pushed me out on to the stage. There was a smattering of applause and a few wolf whistles and I could feel my legs shaking violently underneath me, partly from fear and partly from the endless stream of large whiskies that Vera had ferried into the dressing room, with the added challenge of trying to keep my balance in Lozzy's killer heels.

As my eyes slowly became accustomed to the lights I caught sight of Vera's anxious face in the crowd. He was chewing his fingers down to the knuckle. I looked away, and tottered around the stage for something to do while I waited for the interminable intro to end and the song to begin. My mouth began moving automatically to Barbra Streisand's disembodied voice blaring out from somewhere behind me and slowly I began to loosen up and 'give it some welly'. Just as I'd started to enjoy myself it was suddenly all over and I was gratified to hear a decent smattering of applause following me as I made my way back to the dressing room.

'Well done, dahling,' Regina drawled, stepping out of his ball gown and into a pair of red satin trousers. 'You weren't bad, no, not bad at all. Help me with this zip, dahling. Our dresser has let us down – I don't suppose you'd fancy dressing us for the second spot? It's fairly uncomplicated, and we'll buy you a couple of bevvies . . .' He kept up the running commentary as he struggled to get into a sailor top.

'You've got something, you know, de-ah, raw of course but with a little polish . . . who knows? A word of advice though,' he went on, pinning a sailor's cap to his wig. 'If you're considering getting an act together I'd drop the name. Lily Savage is all right for a bit of camp but no one is going to take an act that sounds like an old scrubber seriously, dahling.'

CHAPTER 13

Invading Poland

TWO WEEKS AFTER MY DEBUT AT THE CAP, BARBARA, BERYL and I set off for Poland. Prior to leaving London I'd looked after a small boy while his mother had an abortion, and sat for three nights at the bedside of a sick old lady who had no one else to sit with her as she waited to die, and I was looking forward to getting away.

We'd chipped in and hired a beautiful bright red Ford Capri for our odyssey across Eastern Europe. Barbara was the designated driver since neither Beryl nor I could drive. I was also hopeless at map-reading. I can't even work out how to fold one back up, let alone read it. They baffled me then as they still do now, and the job of navigator was wisely entrusted to Beryl .

I sat in the back sleeping for most of the journey, waking up at intervals with the hump, moaning and whining, 'Are we there yet?' like a mardy kid you want to slap. Apart from the occasional toilet and coffee break Barbara drove the entire 577 miles to West Berlin without stopping, and seriously impressed by the woman's stamina I came to the conclusion that if she ever gave up working for social services she'd make a damn good long distance lorry driver.

It was dark by the time we arrived in West Berlin and had started to rain heavily, which did nothing to improve Barbara and Beryl's mood. By now they were near screaming point with exhaustion. After driving around for over an hour we eventually found our hotel, which turned out to be smart but disappointingly ordinary and nothing at all like Fräulein Schroeder's lodging house in Christopher Isherwood's book *Goodbye to Berlin*. I wanted to lie on a brass bed draped with shawls in a room illuminated by amber light, drinking schnapps and smoking a Café Crème cigar whilst listening to the distant sound of a gramophone playing hot jazz somewhere in the house.

Marching into the hotel we could have been mistaken for the zombies from *Thriller*. After fourteen hours in a Ford Capri, all Beryl and Barbara wanted was a meal, a hot bath and a good night's sleep. I had other plans. There was a city with a reputation for being shockingly sinful out there that I badly wanted to explore. Shaving, showering and changing into T-shirt, jeans and bomber jacket I quickly shovelled a plate of Kassler mit Sauerkraut down me in the hotel restaurant and hit the streets in search of the infamous cabaret bars of Weimar Berlin. My preconceived notions of Berlin night life, inspired by films and books, were forty-odd years out of date. The smoky waterfront bar with a vamp in a top hat sitting cross-legged on a barrel crooning bittersweet songs of the streets to a clientele of toffs, pimps, whores, sailors and queers now only existed on celluloid and in the end, to get out of the now driving rain, I ducked into a bar that was all but empty apart from a sad couple hunched morosely over their lager, numbed into a stupefied silence no doubt by the racket coming from a juke box in the corner belting out what sounded like the screams of the damned but turned out to be a genre of music known as 'German Rock'.

So much for Sinful Berlin. Having failed to find anything remotely decadent I returned to the hotel looking like the proverbial drowned rat to find myself unable to negotiate the electronic glass doors. In the end I resorted to hammering on the window, hoping to gain the attention of one of the piss-elegant crowd gathered in the lobby busy pointedly ignoring the tramp banging on the door. Eventually a member of staff let me in and muttering curses under my breath I made my way up to the room we were all sharing to save money, and was in bed and asleep by ten.

As we were driving down the Unter den Linden the next morning the indicators on the car ceased to work, resulting in a search for a garage with the necessary parts. Barbara drove to a police station and managed to convey what the trouble was by chanting 'Das indikator is kaput' and pointing towards the car. Eventually a copper who spoke some English sent us off to one of the few garages that were open on a Saturday and after a lot of fuss and fraying of nerves we eventually got the bloody thing fixed. At Checkpoint Charlie we nearly caused an international incident by attempting to cross over to the East with the wrong papers and after more fuss, bureaucracy and lengthy explanations we were redirected to a different route.

A sense of foreboding descended on the three of us as we drove into East Germany. On a grey autumn afternoon with the pale winter sun slowly setting on the depressing landscape it seemed the perfect setting for the grimmest of children's fairy tales. When we stopped at the edge of a small village for Barbara to have a look at the map I took the opportunity to get out and stretch my legs and have a fag, wandering down into the village to see if there was such a thing as a shop. It was only a small village, nestled at the base of a vast pine forest, a collection of ramshackle wooden houses lining a street that was no more than a dirt track. The place was deserted. Smoke curling out of the chimneys and the odd chink of light escaping from the gap between hastily drawn curtains were the only indications that this strangely disturbing little hamlet was inhabited. Jesus, it gave me the creeps. I wondered if these people stayed indoors after sunset for a reason. Vampires? Werewolves? Those woods looked like the ideal habitat for a lycanthrope, and I bet that somewhere in the middle of it lay the ruins of a castle in which a vampire was already up and cleaning his teeth preparing for a bite to eat.

I became aware that a woman was staring down at me from an upstairs window. She looked the type who was more than capable of abandoning stepchildren in dense woods, just as the man who appeared at the front door to see what this stranger in town was up to was every inch the sinister woodsman, no doubt experienced at hacking up grandmothers with the axe I could see propped up against the woodpile. Giving the couple a vague wave and a nod to show I was friendly and not intent on robbing their homes or biting their necks, I headed quickly back to the safety of the car.

We got lost. Again. Somehow we'd managed to come off the official transit route and were now driving around the back of beyond risking arrest at any minute. Barbara stopped the car and I got out to have a look at a road sign we'd just passed. It was pitch black and I couldn't make head or tail of what the sign was trying to convey. However, since I was out and about I headed towards a clump of trees for a much-needed pee. I didn't see the ditch hidden in the dark. One minute I was on terra firma, the next I was up to my waist in shit. I gave out a long loud howl of misery that no doubt had the locals reaching for the silver bullets in the belief that the werewolf was at large.

'Shut up and get in the car,' the two witches were shouting amidst screams of laughter. 'We're going to be banged up by the bloody Stasi any second.'

After a heritage tour of East Germany with all the windows of the car wide open to allow the overpowering stench of liquid manure to escape, we eventually found our way back on to the transit route that led to the Polish border. It was real Cold War stuff – searchlights, watch towers and armed guards with dogs who couldn't have been more surprised at the sight of our bright red Ford Capri if we'd pulled up in the Batmobile. The border guards instructed us to get out of the car and showed us the way to a small hut that looked surprisingly primitive in comparison to the rest of the set-up. In here we presented our passports and visas and, as it was compulsory, changed our sterling into zloty. The official exchange rate was appalling so we held most of our cash back, exchanging it later on the black market for a much better deal.

My first impression of Poland was that the entire country was lit by a forty-watt bulb. It seemed that the sun rose very briefly before buggering off quickly back to bed. In Warsaw Beryl and I had to share a sofa bed in the living room, an experience that she didn't want to repeat, claiming that she was astounded by the nasal dexterity of anyone who managed as I did to switch the light on with my nose every time I turned over. The Poles were a hospitable lot who insisted on getting out the brandy bottle the moment you set foot in their house. Polish brandy is lethal – ultra-strong rocket fuel that had me out of my mind after the third glass and consequently clambering over Beryl in the middle of the night, throwing up over both the arm of her pyjama jacket and the living room carpet before staggering to the bathroom and collapsing under the bath. It's to Beryl's everlasting regret that she failed to capture the image for posterity as I lay unconscious on the cold bathroom floor wearing only my Y-fronts.

The next day, when we gathered with the family around the table in the living room for lunch, the periodic waft of residual vomit reduced the pair of us to gibbering wrecks, unable to control the bouts of hysterical laughter that took hold of us at the most inappropriate moments during the conversation, much to Barbara's mounting fury and to bemused stares from the family. As Beryl remarked later, we did nothing for Anglo-Polish relations that afternoon.

Walking around Warsaw we felt as though the war was still on. Long lines of people, mostly women, queued patiently outside food shops, arms folded, chatting, accepting this way of life. A solitary department store stood depressingly empty, its windows bare except for a line of bottles containing a lavender-coloured liquid which I was later told was a cleaning fluid that was also popular as a cocktail with some of the locals.

Driving around we passed row after row of grey concrete buildings, depressingly neglected, and the monolithic Palace of Culture rising in the centre, built by Stalin and a constant reminder of Soviet domination. Among the beautiful older parts of the city I found the images that I'd sought in West Berlin: a ride around the dimly lit cobbled streets in a horse-drawn carriage, reminiscent of a scene from *Nosferatu*, a winding alleyway, the uneven walls of the ancient houses that stood on either side leaning dangerously inward with age, leading to an overgrown medieval courtyard with a rickety wooden staircase leaning drunkenly against the wall of a building as it rose up into the shadows. I could see in my mind's eye just how atmospheric Josef von Sternberg's lighting would've made this place – Dietrich dressed in mac and beret, fag hanging out of the corner of her gob as per usual, leaning languidly against the wall in the shadows on the stairs, her upraised face illuminated by individual shafts of moonlight heavy with cigarette smoke, pouring down on her from above. Oh, yes, I could see it all.

We visited the Wieliczka Salt Mine, the only visitors that day, but the guide opened up nevertheless and took us round the mine, treating us to a personal guided tour, leaving us alone to sit back and enjoy the solitude of the spectacle that is the underground cathedral, complete with crystal chandeliers carved from various shades of rock salt by the miners. Curiously, when we emerged from the mine we found that we were ravenous and even after wolfing down a substantial meal of meat and two veg in the only restaurant in town we still craved more and so ordered, and ate, the same meal over again.

Desperate for a night out I dragged Barbara and Beryl to the only bar in Kamień Pomorski, a watering hole, judging by the depressing decor, that had employed the interior designer responsible for provincial waiting rooms on northern railway stations during the Great Depression. We sat at the only available table, which just happened to be in the middle of the room, and drank our vodka, painfully aware that every hostile eye in the silent room was on us. The men all sported a mullet, obviously high fashion in these parts, as was yellow peroxide hair with a visible root growth of at least an inch and a healthy daub of startling blue eye-shadow for the women.

It is impossible to comprehend the horrors that took place in Auschwitz concentration camp as you stroll around on a warm autumn morning, impossible to come to terms with the knowledge that the initially innocuous-looking shower room you're standing in once echoed with the dying screams of millions of innocent men, women and children as they choked on the deadly fumes from the Zyklon B gas pellets. I'm not going to dwell on my visit to the former Nazi extermination camp. If you want to know more about it then I suggest you watch the History Channel or go on line and look it up. But I will admit that I was stunned by the sheer size of the place and that for a long time after I couldn't eat meat. The images I'd seen of life, or rather the destruction of it, imprinted themselves on my memory, surfacing to haunt me as I lay in bed late at night trying to work out just how and why the world went insane.

In Krakow my wish to lodge in a Fräulein Schroederesque lodging house came true. We stayed in an elderly lady's best front parlour, one of four rooms she occupied at the top of a crumbling mansion. The migraine-inducing wallpaper was adorned with holy pictures and religious icons pertaining to every saint in the Bible. Our beds, with their horsehair mattresses, were surprisingly comfortable. Barbara's lay underneath an enormous framed print of St Joseph, Beryl had the Virgin Mary, while I lay safe in the knowledge that Mary Magdalene was watching over me, which Beryl found rather apt. The next evening, after a delicious dinner of fish and potatoes in a dill sauce served with a side dish of my favourite delicacy, homemade pickled mushrooms, Fräulein Schroeder asked whether we would mind if she invited her friend over to meet us. Her friend turned out to be a tiny old lady in her eighties, a former Polish princess and death camp survivor who had watched as first the Nazis looted her family's treasures and priceless artworks and then the Communists relieved them of their land, home and titles. She was angry but philosophical, ruefully accepting her lot as she recalled grander times when the *szlachta* (the aristocracy) had strolled along elegant tree-lined avenues that bore the family name. Busts commemorating prominent and respected members of the clan had once adorned public parks and gardens. 'All gone, all gone now,' she said, drumming the table with gnarled fingers and staring into space, lost for a moment as she recalled a past life.

Fräulein Schroeder got out the ubiquitous bottle of brandy and I modelled a leopardskin stretch nylon polo neck I'd seen in a back street shop and couldn't bear to leave, having an inkling that it would come in very handy in the future, to approving nods of the head from our landlady and the princess.

The princess was a devout Catholic so I thought she might like a photo of Pope John Paul the Second, waving to the adoring masses from his balcony, one of a selection that Barbara's aunt had given me for my mother. I laid them out on the table for her so she could choose one. Her beady little eyes darted eagerly across the images of her hero and before I could draw breath she'd swept the lot from the table into the depths of her handbag. Oh well, I thought. Given the circumstances, I was sure my ma would eventually come to terms with the knowledge that she'd missed out on the chance to pass around amongst the members of a stunned Union of Catholic Mothers an actual, genuine photograph of His

Holiness himself. To compensate, I took back a souvenir plate bearing his image for her to hang on the living room wall, although secretly I thought it looked more like Hughie Green than Il Papa.

On the way home, after a long and boring drive along lonely roads, we turned a bend and were suddenly confronted by a scene straight out of *Close Encounters of the Third Kind* that turned out to be the East German border. We were hauled out of the car by border guards, and then they stripped the car of everything that was in it. Cases were taken down from the roof rack and ransacked, and a large mirror attached to a trolley was run under the car to make sure no one was escaping to the West by clinging on to the exhaust. One of the guards, a bullet-headed thug straight out of Union Jack Jackson in *Warlord*, pushed me into the back of the car indicating that I should remove the seat by screaming something unintelligible and waving a screwdriver in my face. At the best of times I wouldn't have had the slightest idea how you went about removing car seats, let alone semi-conscious at three in the morning with a gun-toting Neanderthal breathing down my neck.

'Schnell! Schnell!' he roared as I jabbed hopelessly at the upholstery with the screwdriver, hoping to find somewhere to put it. Screwdrivers are evil devices best left in the hands of dads and competent workmen and not entrusted to ham-fisted amateurs like me. He might as well have given me a divining rod for all I knew of what to do with it.

'Oh, for Christ's sake get out of the bloody way and give it here.' Barbara's mounting fury erupted. Pushing the guard out of the way and pulling me from the back she removed the seat herself, cursing at the top of her lungs and comparing the guard to a rather uneducated porcine species.

I looked at Beryl and mouthed the words 'labour camp'.

On the last leg of our journey on the ferry we stood on deck watching the approaching white cliffs of Dover wondering why the lyricist of the song had chosen a bluebird, a species uncommon to our native shores, and not the more home-grown seagull to fly over the fabled cliffs, coming to the conclusion that it was probably something to do with the fact that a bluebird made a far more acceptable symbol of hope than our native screaming, swooping shite-hawk.

'Are you glad to be home?' I asked Beryl.

'What do you bloody think?' Her squawk rivalled the gulls circling overhead. 'After that ordeal?' Pulling her scarf closer to face into the wind she slowly started sniggering. 'Having said that, it was bloody funny though. What did you think?'

My recollections seemed to have been shot in mono-chrome, hard to distinguish from images imprinted on my memory from the early *Frankenstein* and *Nosferatu* films. A trip back in time to a land of perpetual darkness, a place seemingly shunned by sunlight, with brandy and doughnuts for breakfast and pickled mushrooms and fresh dill for tea. A complex land of primeval forests, graveyards illuminated by candlelight on All Souls night, oppression and ugliness, humour and beauty.

'Well . . .' I tried to find words suitable to define our experience.

'Exactly,' Beryl said, reading my mind. 'Through the looking glass and back again, matey. Through the bloody looking glass.'

CHAPTER 14

Manila

BACK AT WORK, I FOUND MYSELF CARING FOR THREE SISTERS recently abandoned by their mother in a Swiss Cottage slum of unimaginable squalor. I arrived to find Maura opening every window in the flat in a vain attempt to get rid of the overwhelming stench of poverty and neglect. Our kitchen in Crouch End could get in a state, with the sink frequently piled high with abandoned dirty dishes and the odd dried-out tea bag hanging from the leaning tower of crockery by way of ornamentation, but I'd never seen anything in my life like the kitchen I was standing in. You couldn't even see the sink for the mountain of plates and rotten debris that covered it, pouring over the side and on to the floor. What little food there was in the broken old fridge was moving, having decomposed months ago, the packet of cheap supermarket mince now a breeding ground for a teeming mass of maggots. The smell took your breath away and I rushed back outside to throw up, Maura close behind me.

'We're getting the Blitz Squad in to clean it up,' she said. 'It'll be a different place in a couple of days once it's been cleared out and fumigated and with some new furniture. Those little girls have been sleeping together on a piss-wringing mattress on the floor with no bedding, just a couple of coats over them.' A classic case of a family who'd slipped through the net. Social services hadn't been aware of this lot until the neighbour rang them up, worried about the kids. Of course, first sighting of the health visitor and the mother did a runner.

The three little girls had obviously been pitifully neglected and, in addition to the many bruises and welts on their emaciated frames, they were crawling with nits and scabies, which they promptly passed on to me.

As promised, the Blitz Squad lived up to their name and I moved in with the girls. Understandably, after a lifetime of abuse and finally finding themselves free from the tyranny of their mother, they transformed from timid little mice into spitting, hissing, hair-pulling hell-cats. Finding foster parents for this tribe wasn't going to be easy and my heart sank at the realization that my stay in Swiss Cottage might not be a short one.

Since the girls had never been to the theatre I thought it might be nice to take them to see *Annie* at the Victoria Palace. Maybe they'd relate to the story of the plucky orphan girl who overcame adversity to find happiness with a new father? After the debacle with the Robinsons at *Snow White and the Seven Dwarfs* I made sure that I sat behind the girls so I could keep an eye on their every move, just in case they fancied getting up on stage and joining in 'It's The Hard-Knock Life'. Miss Hannigan, the irascible drunk who ran the orphanage, played to perfection by Sheila Hancock, struck a chord with me when she vented her frustration in the song 'Little Girls'. I could empathize with this poor woman, driven to the end of her rope by the monsters in her charge, and offered up a silent prayer that the same fate wouldn't befall me.

On the bus home the girls were rapturous, jabbering like excited monkeys as they discussed the show among themselves. 'Well, we're not going anywhere,' I heard the eldest say, 'until a billionaire offers to foster us, right?'

Their social worker was going to love me.

'Who are you staring at?' I asked, aware that Amy, the youngest girl, had been studying me intently for the last five minutes, a habit in children that gives me the creeps. It's like they know something you don't.

'You should be Miss Hannigan,' the Midwich Cuckoo came out of her trance to observe.

Charming. So this was how the child saw me: an old piss-pot with an evil temper, and female to boot.

'No you should, you'd be good.'

Was my slip showing or something?

I remembered this conversation on the bus twenty years later, in my dressing room at the Victoria Palace, larding on the slap to play Miss Hannigan in the 1998 revival of *Annie*. The child was a prophetess.

I'd worked so many hours since becoming a peripatetic that I wasn't surprised to find out I was owed over four months' time off in lieu. It's all very well having lots of time off if you've plenty of money but as usual I was skint, so I got the Access card out of hiding to buy presents and together with Vera returned home for an extended Christmas break. The weather was foul, I was housebound thanks to a heavy fall of snow and trapped with my ma for a memorable couple of days with no electricity and water cascading through the bedroom ceilings from the pipes in the loft which had burst, as they always did whenever the temperature dropped. My cup runneth over.

I was actually contemplating not going back to work. The money was lousy, I'd been repeatedly attacked, caught nits and scabies and seen enough human degradation to last me a lifetime, added to which a tooth infection that had made my face swell up like Jabba the Hutt wasn't helping my bleak mood. Soon I was writing my resignation to Maura. Unemployed again, but this time of my own volition

Towards the middle of January, Maura rang to ask if I'd consider coming back to work early as a job had come up she really needed me for. It was the usual story: mother in hospital leaving a two-year-old and an eighteen-month-old baby, lovely little kiddies, at risk . . . It would be better if a man went in as there was a history of violence with the father.

'Didn't you get my letter of resignation?' I asked her.

'Of course I did, but I took no notice and put it in the bin. It's the weather getting you down, that's all,' she replied, adding hopefully, 'So we'll see you on Monday then?'

And so I went back, and moved into a furnished rat-hole in Camden Town to look after the two 'lovely little kiddies'. Two nights later the father, on the run from the police, turned up drunk and, mistaking me for his girlfriend's latest squeeze, tried to kill me. I locked myself in the bathroom with the two kids, who by now were extremely distressed, and prayed the door would hold, leaning heavily against it as he tried to kick it down. Thankfully he gave up after a while, transferring his attentions to the room next door.

'I'm going to burn the fucking place down,' I could hear him ranting as he smashed up the furniture. 'D'you hear me? Burn it down to the ground.'

It was now or never. I had to make a run for it. The kids were in their pyjamas so I wrapped them in towels, picked them up, took a deep breath and opened the door. If Dame Kelly Holmes had seen me running she'd have given up there and then. I was nothing more than a blur as I legged it down the hall, out of the door and down the stairs and didn't stop running till I reached the High Street. I'm amazed that I didn't slip on the snow and ice and can only assume that I was moving so fast my feet weren't actually touching the ground, à la Billy Whizz.

So here I was, trudging along Camden High Street in heavy snow at ten o'clock on a Sunday evening, carrying two frightened kids wrapped in towels and searching for a phone box that hadn't been vandalized. The Pearl White of the Peripatetics. All I needed was an ice floe to cling to with a couple of wolves howling in the distance. Whoever said that the streets of London were paved with gold obviously hadn't visited Camden Town. The streets were paved with dog shit and drunks, plastic bin bags filled with festering rubbish piled high on the pavement spilling over into the road. The bin men, or refuse collectors if you like, along with just about everybody else were on strike.

'First you can't get your hands on a bloody loaf,' my mother had said on the phone, 'now you can't even bury your dead. Bloody gravediggers going on strike, there's coffins piled high up in Landican Cemetery and you can't get a space in the mortuaries and funeral parlours for love nor money. I hope I don't drop dead in the next couple of weeks, that's all I can say. We'll be overrun with rats next and what's that Callaghan doing about it? Sweet bugger all, that's what.'

Typically, all the phones in the tube station were broken, the ticket booth was closed and there wasn't even a guard about. In desperation I fought my way through a crowd of punks gathered outside the Electric Ballroom to ask a bouncer if there was such a rarity as a phone I could use. The Lurkers and Adam and the Ants were playing and it was bedlam but the bouncer was a gent and after a brief explanation he escorted me and the kids downstairs to the office. Bemused punks glared at me as I pushed past with the kids, a couple of them aggressively asking what I thought I was doing bringing kids into a club.

'Earning a living,' I shouted back. They must've thought I was a courier for a baby farmer. While I waited for the police the manager got me a drink and an orange juice for the two-year-old, who was bawling his head off. The baby, on the other hand, seemed oblivious to the noise and commotion coming from the club and slept contentedly in my arms, Adam and the Ants seemingly having a soporific effect on him.

The police came and took us off to a children's home in Hampstead. As I had left my coat behind in my haste to get away from the kids' father I had no money and no means of getting home to Crouch End, but the police were un-sympathetic. 'Sorry,' one of them said as they were leaving, 'but we're not a taxi service.' The woman who ran the home rang for a cab and lent me a fiver. Why did Maura have to go and ignore my resignation?

I hammered on the flat door for ages until eventually Rip Van Vera was roused from his slumber. I could hear him squawk-ing, 'Hang on, hang on, will ya,' as he made his way to the door. He had on a knee-length baggy T-shirt with 'Oh Bondage, up yours!' written on the front and a pair of flip-flops. He looked like Gandhi at a Sex Pistols concert.

'What's happened?' he quacked, firing a barrage of questions at me. 'I thought you were at work? Where's your keys? And your coat? What's gone off?'

Huddled over the feeble gas fire in the bedroom, sucking on a cig for warmth, I briefly explained.

'Oh,' he said. Unimpressed, he took off his glasses and got

back into bed, mumbling as an afterthought before slipping back into the arms of Prince Valium, 'Guess who was in the Cap tonight?'

'Who?'

'Ryan. He wants you to ring him, I've got his number for you.'

Ryan, as you may recall, was my old squeeze from Liverpool. He was in London for a few days and we arranged to meet for a drink. I hadn't seen him since his last visit to London when I'd rudely given him the cold shoulder and I wondered how our relationship stood.

Would we pick up where we left off in Liverpool in spite of my treatment of him or were we now 'just good friends'? He seemed more than happy to see me but I got the impression the Love Boat had capsized and we were sailing into different waters on the good ship Platonic. As the night drew on I began to regret letting this one slip through my fingers and wondered if it wasn't too late to patch things up.

Ryan was going back to the Far East to work for an oil company in Manila and he was insistent that I should join him in the summer. Was this the offer of a reconciliation? I couldn't tell, he was so hard to read. Anyway, whatever the outcome, a chance to visit a place as exotic as the Philippines was hard to turn down and the more I thought about it the more determined I was to get there.

Since he wasn't offering any help towards the fare, I wondered where in hell I was going to find the price of an air ticket. The answer came courtesy of my fairy godmother, the good old Inland Revenue again (that's the last time you'll ever hear me describe them so favourably, I promise), in the form of a sizeable tax rebate, out of which I bought an open return.

I flew the 6,679 miles via Amsterdam, Rome, Karachi and Bangkok, sending postcards to my mum and Vera at each stop-off. This was an epic adventure for me and I was as excited as a pig in a ditch full of truffles for the entire journey, taking everything from the menus to the sick bag home with me as a souvenir.

After spending twenty-four hours cocooned on a plane the riot that was Manila airport came as a complete culture shock. It was overwhelming. The first thing to hit me was the heat, followed by the sheer volume of noise from the traffic and the mass of people gathered outside the airport. Ryan came to meet me. He was living in a small apartment in a hotel in the Malate district, an area with a distinctly Bohemian atmosphere. Artists, writers and those in the entertainment industry tended to gravitate towards Malate and despite the Marcoses' dictatorship an interesting and varied nightlife was beginning to flourish. The apartment turned out to be small and basic, shower and toilet with one double bedroom separated from the kitchen/living area by a set of sliding doors. There was also a small balcony overlooking some shanty houses and a dilapidated water tower, and for those who fancied sunbathing or a swim there was a small pool and a roof area with views across the city towards the harbour.

I liked the Tropicano Apartments on sight. The decor was very '60s Americana, the type of place where you'd expect to find McGill from *Man in a Suitcase* in reception. The staff were incredibly friendly, as were the majority of fellow guests; the only drawback was the wildlife. Walt Disney cockroaches, an unwelcome and unavoidable presence in all buildings in the city, had the tendency to scuttle up the wall or across the floor when you least expected it, their crazy antennae waving like the arms of a wailing widow in full flight. The tiny green lizards that darted across the bedroom ceiling worried me the most. I lived in constant fear that one would lose its grip and fall into my open mouth as I lay sleeping below and so, as a precautionary measure, I slept with my head under the pillow.

Walking around the streets of Manila was like stepping into a musical. Everybody sang. All you had to do was turn the radio on and if a popular song was playing then the whole bloody street would join in. It got on my nerves at first, as did the constant smiling. Having lived in London for a while I was unused to passers-by greeting me with a cheery 'hi', for if anyone behaved like that on the streets of Camden Town they were invariably drunks or nutters or both and were not, under any circumstances, to be encouraged. My first impression of Manila wasn't good, in fact the place horrified me. It was all so different and after a couple of days I'd had enough and wanted to go home, just as my mother had when as a young wife and mother she'd first visited my father's family on the farm in Ireland. Well, they do say what's in the bitch comes out in the pup . . .

Back in Liverpool, Ryan and I had had what Mills and Boon would have described as 'a fleeting but highly intense affair' which naturally had cooled since my move to London, particularly on my side. Previously we'd never spent more than a couple of days at a time together and now here we were, living in a small apartment and attempting unsuccess-fully to recreate a relationship we'd once shared in what seemed like another lifetime. We were no longer the same people. We'd changed – not radically but enough to make a big difference – and at times the air was as heavy with tension as it was with the sour smell of citronella mosquito repellant. Light the blue touch paper and stand well back.

*

My introduction to what the city had to offer in the way of cuisine and nightlife got off to a bad start. Walking around the unfamiliar streets, I was introduced to the horror that is *balut*. Seeing I was curious as to what a young boy carrying a large wicker basket and calling out '*BALUT!*' at the top of his lungs was selling, Ryan called him over. Underneath a grubby piece of flannel was a basketful of eggs.

'Here, try one,' Ryan said, buying an egg off the boy. 'They're nice.'

I don't like eggs. If I'm in the mood I can just about manage a small plateful of them scrambled on toast, but a hard-boiled egg? Not for all the tea in China.

'This is different, not like your average egg,' he persisted. 'Crack it open and have a look.'

I held the warm egg wrapped in a piece of newspaper tentatively in the palm of my hand while the boy deftly peeled the shell back with a small knife. To my horror, what lay inside was a creature straight out of *Alien* – the nearly fully formed embryo of a boiled chick wallowing in a glutinous grey liquid.

'Suck, suck,' the street vendor instructed, urging me to hold the egg up to my mouth and draw the monster out.

'It's a delicacy,' Ryan remarked casually. 'Get it down you, it's supposed to be an aphrodisiac.'

I tossed the egg into the street and threw up. The kid laughed like a drain, clapping his hands as I ranted on about dirty filthy bastards mid-retch.

'Go on, bugger off,' Ryan laughed, dropping a couple of dollars into the boy's basket, 'and see if you can find anyone selling corned beef hash and chips.'

As always I wanted to go clubbing, and Ryan said he knew of a place across town called the Oddball which made Sadie's back home in Liverpool seem like the grand salon of the palace of Versailles.

'They have shows on in here,' Ryan said, paying the entrance fee to the reptilian lad on the door, who despite his youthful appearance bore all the hallmarks of a canny pro. The club was stifling hot, nothing more than a claustrophobic sweat box devoid of any form of air conditioning, the fetid air thick with cigar smoke and the smell of clammy bodies. The motley clientele was made up of grubby teenage boys and seedy middle-aged men. Seated at the table next to ours, a corpulent Australian, his shirt soaked through with sweat, was slyly fondling a semi-naked boy, who was curled up on his lap giggling like a geisha.

A spotlight hanging dangerously from the ceiling pointed towards the tiny stage and unexpectedly flooded the gloom with light, reflecting off the mirrored wall behind and temporarily blinding everyone. No fancy lighting in this establishment then to herald the arrival of cabaret time, no compère to warm the punters up before bringing you on stage with an encouraging 'Let's have a big hand for a fabulous act.' At the Oddball it seemed to be a case of get your bony arse out on that stage, do your stuff and then get off. The Disappointer Sisters wouldn't have approved, that's for sure, and I wondered how the local drag fared.

The first act on the bill was a scrawny lad who unceremoniously trotted out and impaled himself on a litre bottle of Coca-Cola. My jaw hit the floor. The fat Aussie next to me starting cheering and bellowing for more. More? What in God's name did he do for an encore? Make a crateful vanish? To quote Frankie Howerd, my flabber had never been so gasted.

The next act on the bill was a young man who bent over, spread his cheeks apart and systematically opened and closed his anus like a sea anemone, enough of an act to stir the sweaty old men who leaned forward eagerly in their seats for a closer look. I'd had enough. Winking sphincters was not exactly what I was expecting when Ryan mentioned there was cabaret, so picking my jaw up off the floor I got out of there smartly, Ryan following close behind.

'What kind of a place was that?' I ranted at Ryan in the street, genuinely appalled by what I'd just seen. 'What are you doing bringing me to a club full of dirty, sweaty old bastards salivating at the sight of a couple of manky little scrubbers shoving half the bar up their arse? It's disgusting!'

'Climb down off your high horse, will ya, this isn't Birkenhead, it's the Philippines – a third world country with a maniac in charge busy running it into the ground. Those "manky little scrubbers" as you call them are probably kids from the country who've arrived in this shitty city to find the only work they can get is sitting on bottles in a sex show.'

I got the feeling my outburst had rattled him.

'There's no job centres here, you know, no social security. Nothing. They do what they have to do or starve, so don't be so bloody snotty. Good God, do you realize that in some parts parents are selling their kids for sex for the price of a few days' food?'

No, I didn't know. I'd assumed that the lads on the Oddball were in that line of work because they were born hustlers and chose to be. Manila wasn't quite shaping up to my expectations. There was no evidence of banyan trees and coral sands and Nellie Forbush and the whole kit and caboodle that *South Pacific* on the telly of a Sunday afternoon had promised, just a dirty, sprawling, poverty-stricken metropolis.

'I'm 'omesick.' It came out before I could stop myself.

'Oh, for God's sake, don't be soft, you daft get.' Ryan put

his arm around me, laughing. 'Stop acting like a prissy old schoolmarm. Manila's a great place, you've just got to go with the flow. Why are you so uptight? Loosen up. C'mon, we'll go to a bar you just might like.'

Famous last words, as my mother would've said.

Gussie's bar was nothing spectacular but it had bucketloads of atmosphere. A dimly lit smoke-filled room, intimate you might say to be kind, with a smattering of punters, two of whom I was cheered to see were American sailors, not the best-looking boys in the fleet but sexy nevertheless in their naval whites – sitting around a dance floor that was no bigger than your average coffee table. I was also happy to see that the entertainment didn't include anything untoward involving Coke bottles, just three lads with a drumkit, piano and guitar attempting to make music.

'It's quiet tonight, you should come later in the week. The band is much better at the weekend, very good,' Gussie the owner said, wincing slightly at the sound of the trio massacring 'Blueberry Hill'. 'Now, you want something nice to drink?'

You couldn't help but like Gussie, a friendly middle-aged Filipino who rarely moved from his perch on a barstool next to the till. There he sat night after night like a wise little Buddha, surrounded by postcards, paper currency from all over the globe and yellowing photographs of customers past and present tacked to the walls, constantly chivvying the sad young Filipina who helped him behind the bar.

'I know she only works at two speeds, slow and stop,' Gussie confided when the girl had vanished out of earshot through the beaded curtain that led to the kitchen, 'but she's my sister's girl and needs the money, so I'm training her to tend bar.' Gussie employed a lot of family members. The boy on the drums was a relation, which explained a lot, as was the young waiter.

'They're all students, studying hard. I do what I can to help.' Gussie sighed, shaking his head as he watched his niece wander aimlessly around the club in search of the customer who had ordered the plate of beef tapa she was carrying.

'Over in the corner, the gentleman in the corner, you silly girl,' he shouted, trying to be heard above the racket the band were making. The nephew on the drums also sang and was now busy mangling the lyrics to 'Moon River' while bravely trying to keep up with the rest of the trio who were playing something that sounded more like the theme from *Goldfinger*.

'Would you like a little snack?' Gussie asked, all smiles, offering me a menu.

Through what was left of the threadbare bead curtain I'd been able to take a good look at the tiny galley kitchen beyond and watched, appalled, as a family of mice scuttled back and forth along the water pipes underneath the sink.

'No thanks, I've eaten, honestly I'm not hungry, thanks all the same.'

Nothing, not even extreme starvation (which I'd be nearing if I didn't eat something soon) would induce me to sample the cuisine from Gussie's kitchen. Since I'd been in Manila I'd reverted to the fussy eating habits of my childhood, and if I was dubious about the origins of the meat in my burger in the restaurant of a relatively good hotel then a snack served with a side order of mouse droppings on toast from Gussie's kitchen was most definitely out of the question.

The toilets were a huge no-no as well. Just a hole in the floor from which emanated the heart-stopping stench from years of warm effluent. My mother, who could've written *The Michelin Guide to Good Public Conveniences*, would've dropped dead at the sight of this unsavoury latrine, I thought, breathing through my nose, desperately trying to resist the urge to retch as I willed what seemed to be the longest pee in history to hurry up and end so I could get the hell out of there and back to the bar.

Despite these minor setbacks I grew to love Gussie's and became quite the regular.

In a place called Pagsanjan Falls, where the only way to get to the famous falls is by shooting the rapids along the Bumbungan River in a traditional Filipino *banca*, the oleaginous manager of the dilapidated chalet complex we had the misfortune to spend the night in proudly showed us around our 'suite'.

'This is the best room in Pagsanjan,' he gushed, 'the Royal Suite.'

'Oh yeah? Who was the last member of the royal family to kip here then? King Kong?' I said snidely, looking around at the dubious bedding, the fag burns in the nicotine-stained mosquito net and the tatty sixties rattan dressing table minus one of its drawers. Royal Suite indeed.

'Would you and your friend like anything for later?' he leered.

'Like what?' I got the general idea that he wasn't talking about Ovaltine here.

'A couple of boys? Nice boys, very young.'

'No thanks, we're fine, we don't want any boys.' Ryan moved quickly, steering him towards the door, sensing that I was about to go off like a rocket.

'A nice young girl then?'

He just wouldn't give up.

'Listen, you dirty old bastard.' I moved towards him and started to push him firmly out of the door. 'I don't want either a boy or a girl. Do you understand?'

'Ah! Yes, I understand, you want a man!' he leered, rubbing his crotch suggestively and sucking the air through his teeth, forgetting that he was meant to be leaving and trying to make his way back into the room. 'You want me to come back? I'm a big man, very big.'

My flesh didn't exactly crawl, it slithered and I could feel every hair on my body twitching like the whiskers of a nervous rat.

'OUT!'

Children appeared to be dispensable here, nothing but chattels to be exploited and casually sold off for a few bucks. It was very depressing and made worse by the realization that there was absolutely nothing I could do to prevent it. In places like Pagsanjan paedophilia was endemic.

The room was unbearably hot. Unable to sleep, I lay on the bed next to a snoring Ryan and watched the ceiling fan slowly rotating above me, a hopelessly inadequate antiquity that squeaked with every turn, useless at providing respite from the stifling heat but unbeatable as a jolly carousel ride for every flying insect within a twenty-mile radius that appeared to have congregated in our Royal Suite. They'd obviously heard on the mozzie grapevine that there were two tasty slabs of burned English flesh on the menu.

I was eaten alive. Mozzies were dancing the Rose Adagio on my flesh, zipping in and out of one of the many convenient holes in the net like dive bombers for a quick Bloody Mary, forcing me in the end to get up and douse myself in another gallon of the noxious but ineffectual mozzie repellant. I went outside to escape from the choking fumes of the spray. It was cooler out here with a hint of a breeze, the air alive with the noise of a million chirping crickets. Sitting down on the step to enjoy a fag and admire the myriad stars in the night sky, I heard footsteps approaching along the boardwalk. I turned to look. The manager was slobbing along with a couple of pubescent boys in tow. He knocked quietly on the door of a room a few doors down and after brief negotiations delivered the boys to the unseen occupant as if they were nothing more than a room service snack.

I went back to bed before the grease-ball noticed me and felt obliged to offer his wares again. I seriously wanted to kill him. Just as well we were leaving for Manila in the morning.

It was hotter than mooching through hell in a pair of gasoline drawers and I'd been walking along Roxas Boulevard for what seemed like hours until eventually I came across a sign-post pointing me in the direction of the recently opened Metropolitan Museum of Art, an oasis in the desert. I quickly headed for it, more with the intention of escaping from the heat and availing myself of the café, if there was such a thing, than to gaze upon the artworks.

For the last couple of hundred yards I'd been aware that a boy on a bike was trailing me.

'Hi,' he shouted after me, 'hi, are you Australian?'

I quickened my pace, refusing to be hustled or to engage in any sort of conversation whatsoever, but I'd underestimated this one's persistence. Ignoring my cold shoulder, he dismounted and chattered away incessantly as he walked his bike alongside me. He was small and wiry and couldn't have been any older than sixteen. His coal-black hair, shining in the sunlight like an oil slick, looked as if he'd used gloss paint to comb it back with and his top lip bore the scar from a harelip, which far from marring his good looks seemed to enhance them.

'You mind if we talk?' he chirped. 'My name's Joselito, pleased to meet you. What's your name, buddy?'

271

'Look, I'm not interested,' I snapped, hoping he'd go away.

'OK, OK, I only wanna talk. Say, are you Australian then?'

'No I'm not, I'm English.'

'Ho! I have a cousin who lives in Bir-ming-ham, maybe you know her?'

'I shouldn't think so.'

'In a town called King's Heath, you ever been?'

Jesus, would he ever take the hint and bugger off?

'Look, I'm going in here now,' I said, stopping outside the museum. 'Nice to meet you but I have to go now.'

'You want me to come with you? I can show you where the Picasso is.'

'No, I'm all right, thank you.' I sniffed, aware that I was beginning to sound worryingly like my mother.

'Hey, I don't want sex with you, oh, no-noo sir.'

'Good, I'm glad to hear it because I don't want sex with you either.' Cheeky little sod. What did he mean by that? What's wrong with me then?

'So, buddy, you want me to come with you?'

'All right,' I said, worn down by his doggedness, and instantly regretted my rash decision.

'I'll put my bike away,' he shouted, running towards the car park. 'Wait for me. Hey, what's your name?'

'Paul,' I called after him, causing him to stop and turn round and shoot me a quizzical look.

'Pearl?'

'No, Paul, it's my accent, I'm from Liverpool.'

'Wow!' He suddenly became very excited. 'Liverpool! The best football team in the world!'

You could write what I know about the beautiful game on the nipple of an amoeba and I seriously hoped that he didn't want to strike up an in-depth discussion about football as I wouldn't be able to participate. I needn't have worried; I wouldn't have been able to get a word in, Joselito did all the talking. Sat in the café drinking his Coke that I'd had to force him into accepting, he told me that Kenny Dalglish and Jimmy Case were gods and his greatest wish was to see Liverpool play at Anfield one day. He looked at me as if I'd slapped his face when I let slip that although I'd only lived a train and a bus ride away I'd never been there.

It turned out Joselito was twenty-two and not sixteen as I'd previously thought. He lived with his mother and numerous siblings in one of Manila's many shanty towns and to help support his family he drove a Trike, a taxi motorbike with a covered sidecar familiar on the streets of the capital. He and his brother rented it, sharing the workload. He'd been on his way to visit an uncle recovering from an illness when he'd spotted me and was now asking if I'd like to go with him.

'I'll take you on my bike.'

'Oh, I don't think so.'

'Yes you will, c'mon, c'mon.'

Ten minutes later I was sat on the back of a bike that was two spokes away from being classified as a deathtrap, weaving in and out of the heavy traffic with Joselito pedalling hell for leather as if we were taking part in the Tour de France.

'You OK, buddy?' he shouted over his shoulder, turning to look at me.

'I'm fine, just keep your bloody eyes on the road, will ya.'

Please God, let me survive this bike ride and I'll never be bad again . . .

Joselito's uncle lived in a shanty town that ran either side of the railway tracks. There seemed to be as many mangy dogs about as there were people and the children, oblivious to the dangers of oncoming trains, played happily among the railway sleepers. The squalor that I frequently found myself in with some of my Camden clients bore no comparison to the shack where Joselito's uncle lived, no bigger than your average garden shed and constructed entirely out of debris – corrugated iron, bits of wood, roofing felt, lino, cardboard, anything considered suitable for housing material that had been scavenged off the rubbish tips.

His uncle slept in a makeshift bed behind a shower curtain that divided the solitary room. I thought he was in his sixties at least and was shocked when Joselito told me that he was only thirty, prematurely aged by the ravages of cancer. It was all very depressing and I found it hard to comprehend that people were forced to live like this. Despite his obvious pain, Joselito's uncle greeted me warmly, reacting with the same delight that Joselito had shown when I told him I was from Liverpool. 'Ah, Liverpool,' he exclaimed, 'Kenny Dalglish!'

I was glad to get out of the fetid air of the little room and into the open again. A crowd had gathered outside, curious to see who the foreign visitor was. A young girl, another of Joselito's relatives, held out a baby for me to see. She was beautiful, no more than a few days old and wrapped in a snowy-white shawl, shining like a pearl in the midst of such squalor. What chance did she stand? I wondered, growing up in the face of such adversity.

'I'd better go home now,' I said to Joselito, anxious to get away from this place. He instantly offered me a lift on his bike. Despite my protestations there was no turning this persistent kid down and reluctantly I got on the back again.

'You seen the sunset over the bay yet?' he asked. 'It's very beautiful. I'll take you, yes?'

He was right, the sunset was beautiful. We sat drinking cans of Sprite and watching it slowly set blood-red in the sky, the experience only slightly marred by the stench coming from the harbour.

'When Madame Marcos had a party on her yacht in the bay, she floated barrels alongside filled with Chanel No. 5 so the air would smell nice for the guests,' Joselito told me proudly, throwing his empty can of Sprite in among a mound of rotten flotsam and jetsam gathered on the shoreline. 'Isn't that clever?'

No, I didn't think it was clever at all. How could he speak with such pride and affection of a woman who showed so little regard for her people, floating barrels of expensive perfume in the harbour when the citizens of Manila existed in abject poverty all around her?

'She loves the people,' he said simply, 'and they love her.'

It seemed pointless to argue so I said no more on the subject. I'd already got into trouble in a shop for making remarks about the Marcoses and I didn't want a repeat performance. I'd laughed at a highly romanticized portrait of the lady, which looked like a crude attempt at emulating a Pierre et Gilles photograph. There were pictures of the Marcoses, Imelda in particular, all over Manila but this one took the biscuit. Here she was, depicted as a latter-day Madonna – by that I don't mean she was bumping and grinding in a conical bra, no, I'm talking about the Virgin Mary, who, to the best of my knowledge, didn't go in for such a carry-on, that being more in Salome's line of work. Anyway, here's Imelda complete with halo sitting on a gold throne gazing adoringly towards the heavens and cradling a sleeping child in her arms. That was comical enough but what really set me off were her eyes. They were crossed, giving her a pained expression as if she were sat on an elaborate lav, badly in need of a heavy-duty laxative.

'This has got to be a send-up, surely?' I said to Ryan.

'Leave it, will you. Stop taking the piss.'

'But look at her, she's got a gozzie eye.'

'Will you shut it.'

'She wants shootin'.'

Ryan could see that the two men behind the counter were becoming increasingly agitated at my reaction to what was obviously a prized possession and, hastily paying for his ciggies, he dragged me out of the shop.

'You can't say things like that about her within earshot,' Ryan admonished me. 'She's a saint here. The Filipinos won't hear a bad word about Imelda or her old man, so keep your bloody gob shut in future or we'll be the ones getting shot.'

'But they're a pair of gangsters,' I protested.

'Even so, that kind of talk will get you arrested. This country will eventually come to its senses, but until then do us a favour and keep your bloody big trap shut, eh?'

By the time we got back to the hotel I was in agony. Every part of my body ached from the journey home on the back of Joselito's bike, the saddle of which had been whittled away with age to the width of a pencil. It was akin to sitting on a blunt axe. Outside the hotel a young Australian walked by. You could tell he was Australian, blond, tanned and healthy, sunshine in a pair of shorts.

'Phew,' Joselito whistled, 'there's a hot-looking guy. Oh man, look at those legs.' He was salivating, licking his lips appreciatively as Bondi Beach Boy swaggered past. 'Oh, I love Western boys,' he drooled, 'Australians, Americans, English, Dutch, you name it.'

Vanity mixed with an element of hurt pride caused me to ask him why, if he had such a passion for Westerners, he didn't fancy me.

'Oh no,' he said, horrified, 'you're too old.'

Over the hill at twenty-three! Oh well, I did ask. With that we parted, him to his job driving his Trike and me to consider plastic surgery, pulling the skin of my face back in the bathroom mirror to assess if a facelift was in order.

Tension was mounting between Ryan and myself and we argued at every opportunity. I wanted our relationship to revert to the way it had been in the early days, just me and him. Unfortunately a lot of water had passed under the bridge since then and Ryan had moved on, taking the cold shoulder that I'd given him back in London as a sign that the feeling was mutual. I accused him of having it away with everyone from the room service boys to the doormen, until inevitably our verbal spats led to a full-blown fight, wrecking half of the kitchenette in the process.

Having had enough, Ryan vanished for three days on a trip with some friends to one of the islands. I headed for Gussie's and got drunk.

I poured my heart out over the bar to Gussie. 'Why does he make me so angry?' I moaned. 'Why do we always end up hating each other?'

'The answer is simple, you love him,' said Gussie, topping my glass up. 'Perhaps you should tell him.'

Oh Christ.

I got so drunk that night that I got up and 'sang'. The only number in the band's extremely limited repertoire that we both knew was 'Summertime' and telling the bemused drummer to 'give it plenty of welly' I took off around the dance floor, murdering that lovely song in a voice that my ma always compared to the sound of a lump of coal caught underneath a cellar door, slowly stripping off down to my underpants as I went. I'm cringing with shame as I recall it. However, at the time the fact that I was standing on the dance floor of a busy club wearing nothing but my underpants didn't faze me in the least. Oh, the curse of the demon drink!

On the plus side, the crowd (it would've had to be packed that night) went wild. Westerners didn't normally throw caution to the wind and behave in such a manner, especially in a place like Gussie's, and as my new-found confidence grew, fed by the applause and cries for more, I gave them a bit of patter which, in my drunken haze, appeared to go down very well. Wisecracking with the crowd, I even managed a comeback to an American who asked me why I wasn't taking the underpants off.

'Because I'll catch cold,' I replied coyly, a feeble retort and one nicked from Gypsy Rose Lee, I know, but very effective nevertheless at the time. Asking my audience if they would be so kind as to return the clothing that I'd tossed among them with such gay abandon, I left the dance floor to a tumultuous roar of appreciation. Flushed with the sweet smell of success, I drank every drink that was bought for me and had to be poured into the sidecar of Joselito's Trike when Gussie eventually managed to persuade me to go home.

The following afternoon I awoke fully clothed. It seemed ironic that I had been happy to take them off in a club but apparently hesitant to do the same when it came to bedtime. It was a hot afternoon and I was as dehydrated as Tutankhamun's mummified corpse but after a couple of gallons of bottled water and a cool shower I felt as good as new, which, unfortunately, isn't the case these days. Now I've supposedly grown up, a hangover nearly kills me. I just can't do it any more and, sadly, nor do I want to. After a heavy night on the lash I found that I was having to lie down in a darkened room for at least forty-eight hours with a sign saying 'Do not resuscitate' hanging at the bottom of the bed. Hangovers are self-inflicted and a waste of time, so I don't bother and on the rare occasion I do, boy, do I regret it the next day.

But back in my early twenties a hangover was easily shaken off and I tottered out into the sultry afternoon sun in search of breakfast. Outside the Holiday Inn, Joselito pulled up alongside me on his Trike.

'You OK?' he asked. 'Phew, you had plenty to drink.'

'I don't care, I enjoyed myself.'

'Hey, you never told me you were in showbiz.'

'I'm not.'

'Well, you should be, you're very funny.'

'Nah, I wasn't. I was drunk, I made a bloody fool of myself.'

'No, you were good.'

This was music to my ears.

'Well, the singing maybe not so hot . . .'

OK, no need to nit-pick.

'But you're a funny man, you made everyone laugh.'

Right, that was it, as soon as I got back to London I was going to get an act together. I was bursting to get on a stage and show off and didn't care in what capacity as long as somehow I got to scratch this persistent theatrical itch and achieve my ambition.

'You like to watch the striptease?' Joselito asked.

'No I don't, thanks,' I said, recalling the cabaret at the Oddball club, 'I don't want to watch some lad sitting on a coke bottle.'

'No, this is ladies.'

'I don't want to watch ladies sitting on a Coke bottle either.'

'No, this is the striptease.' He mimed taking off an imaginary glove. 'Very classy club. I'll take you tonight, yes?'

I was aware of a street of clubs that was popular with men looking for a 'girly show'. And so that night I found myself in a seedy little club, transfixed by the unimaginable sight of a young woman smoking a cigarette, and not with her mouth. Ryan had told me that what few sex shows there were in Manila were tame in comparison with the Patpong dives in Bangkok. Even so . . .

'Let's go,' I said to Joselito. 'I don't want to watch this kind of thing.'

'No, wait,' he said, pulling me back down into my seat. 'Wait till you see the big lady, she's very good.'

The big lady turned out to be a portly redhead of indeterminate years, who one moment could've passed for twenty-five until suddenly, before our very eyes, she'd trans-formed, as if we were catching a glimpse of her through the mirror of Dorian Gray, into a haggard old lady who really shouldn't be taking her clothes off in public. Judging by the size of her heavily lacquered bouffant hairdo that refused to move an inch as she swayed across the stage in time to the three-piece band's version of 'Rock Around The Clock', throwing her head back defiantly every now and then, she must've shared the same hairdresser as Imelda. Clinging to the side of it like a dead bird caught in a hedge was one of those strange confections of feathers and net that women wear at weddings and are called fascinators.

Her heavily made-up face was swollen and strangely out of shape. I realize now that this was due to the work of an inept plastic surgeon but then I thought she'd been fighting. She certainly looked like she'd gone a couple of rounds with

David Haye, especially around her puffy eyes. Parading about the stage, waving the side of her green sequin dress back and forth suggestively, she fixed us all with an unnatural smile that instead of having the desired effect of being seductive came across as slightly unnerving.

I wondered if she'd had one too many as she seemed a little unsteady on her feet. She clumsily unzipped the dress and struggled out of it, revealing a pair of sagging buttocks and wobbly thighs pitted with cellulite and threaded with varicose veins. Turning to face the audience she proceeded to gyrate and violently bump her hips, thrusting them towards us, making little snake-like movements with her tongue, darting it swiftly in and out in what she must have mistakenly believed to be a provocative manner. Unhooking her bra to reveal a pair of rock-solid breasts that might have been augmented with two substantial grapefruit, she slowly got down on the floor, naked now apart from a tiny G-string, arching her back to reveal a bird's-eye view of her crotch which she proceeded to slowly stroke.

Here it comes, I thought, expecting the inevitable array of merchandise worthy of the conveyor belt on *The Generation Game* to come streaming out of her. Thankfully she suddenly changed position, leaning towards us on all fours and unsuccessfully attempting to jiggle her rock-hard breasts by a series of violent shudders and shakes of her shoulders which gave the impression that she was in the middle of a violent fever. Nothing short of an earthquake could get those cement-packed puppies to move, nevertheless – to give credit where it was due – she certainly persevered. She was still giving it lots of tongue action, thrusting it furiously in and out, perhaps a little over-enthusiastically for her own good as in her pre-orgasmic state she managed to dislodge her top set of false teeth. Momentarily she lost her composure as she hastily shoved them back in her mouth before they fell out completely. She concluded the act by whipping the G-string off, giving us a quick flash and then daintily skipping off the stage to muted applause. I whistled approval for this brave old girl with the ferocity of a steam train because thanks to my cousin Marjie, who taught me how to whistle with two fingers in my mouth, I can shatter glass and I am deeply indebted to her for this much-envied skill.

'She's very old,' Joselito told me as the brave lady left the stage, waving. 'It's said she danced for General MacArthur in 1946 when Manila gained her independence.'

I had no reason to disbelieve him. We went on to Gussie's for a drink afterwards. I was a little apprehensive at first about showing my face in there again after my impromptu strip, concerned that I might have gone too far and committed the cardinal sin of 'making a show of meself', but I had no reason to worry as I was given a hero's welcome. It was a Saturday night and the joint was jumping. Gussie seemed very flustered as one of his waiters hadn't turned up and he was running around behind the tiny bar like a headless chicken, trying to keep up with the demand for drinks.

'I'll help you,' I offered. 'Pass me a tray and a notepad and pen and I'll take some orders for you.'

Without hesitating he handed them over and I set to work. Soon I had a tray piled high with drinks and was hopping from table to table serving customers as if I'd been working there all my life.

I'd noticed two women who always sat at a table by the door, two unremarkable middle-aged ladies dressed in short-sleeved cotton blouses and black slacks, their hair pulled neatly back from faces devoid of any make-up. Above the club there was a hotel of some sort. Certainly there were rooms for rent as these two ladies seemed to be doing a roaring business taking gentlemen upstairs for a quick 'massage'. I soon learned to point in their direction any customer who asked me if I knew of any action going, wink-wink. Here I was, working in a whorehouse again, albeit temporarily, but long enough to put me ma in hospital if she ever found out. Personally I relished the notion that I was peddling drinks in a salacious bar and only wished the job was permanent. It certainly beat the Showplace or the RAFA club back in Birkenhead and it was infinitely preferable to wiping arses for Camden Council.

I helped Gussie out over the next couple of nights, earning a considerable amount in tips. Having a Westerner wait on tables, especially a gobby one, was virtually unheard of, so the customers tipped the novelty act heavily. I even plucked up the courage to say a few words and introduce the band. Oh, I was loving this job but unfortunately all good things must end, as they did when the usual waiter came back. He happened to be Gussie's nephew and because blood is thicker than water I regretfully handed my tray over and went back to civvy street.

When Ryan returned from his trip I was secretly gratified to see that he was the colour of an overboiled beetroot. 'Had a nice time?' I asked, slapping him hard on the back and making him leap into the air with pain like a Loony Tunes cartoon character.

'Listen, let's call a truce and start again,' he said. 'Why don't we go somewhere together, just you and me, see if we can't work things out, eh?'

And so for my birthday Ryan very generously took me to Hong Kong. I'd heard so much about this place from my seafaring uncle Hal and cousins John and Mickey who made regular trips there that I felt instantly at home. Mickey had been engaged to a Chinese girl he'd met there and they were about to be married but at the final hurdle she jilted him by letter, breaking his heart in the process. He was killed in a car accident not long afterwards. The girl was from an extremely wealthy family who lived on the Peak, Hong Kong's most exclusive residential area, and I can just imagine their reaction when she told them she wanted to marry a merchant sailor from Birkenhead. It was doomed from the start. Poor Mickey.

In the only gay club in town, a place called Dateline, Ryan was surrounded by a bevy of oriental youths who clung on to him like a litter of Siamese cats from the moment he set foot in the door. They left me well alone, probably sensing my hostility towards them, and instead I sat on my bar stool enveloped in an emerald green haze, jealously watching Ryan lapping up all the attention.

'Excuse me.' I turned to find a young Malaysian at my side. 'My friend likes you and would very much like to say hello to you.'

I knocked back what was left of my hideously expensive whisky and Coke and slid off my stool, shooting Ryan a look that said, 'Curl up and die, shithead,' as I mooched off to meet the friend. He was sitting at the back of the club in a dimly lit booth. The Malaysian go-between introduced us and I held out my hand to shake his but he ignored the gesture.

'Oh, by the way, he's blind,' the Malaysian said, motioning me to sit down.

I didn't want to ask the obvious, like if he was blind then how did he know that he fancied someone at the other end of the club, so I shut up and sat down, grinning uncomfortably. Ryan was going to love this, the only offer I get all evening is from a blind man and an elderly one at that with a face that could stop a clock.

'Hello,' I said in a voice that reeked of forced joviality. 'My name's Paul, pleased to meet you.'

'He doesn't speak any English, Pearl.'

'No, it's Paul.'

'Yes, that's what I said, Pearl.'

'No, it's PAUL, P-A-U . . . Oh, sod it, what's the point?'

We sat in silence. Eventually the Malaysian leaned across the table and asked me if I'd like to come home with them.

'What for?'

'For sex, of course.'

'What, with him?'

'No, with me. He likes to watch.'

'How can he watch when he's blind?'

'He uses his fingers to see.'

'No thank you, I'm with my boyfriend and I'd better get back.'

'Bring him as well,' he shouted after me as I returned to the bar.

Ryan was on his own, his harem had vanished elsewhere, and so we sat down and got very drunk. When I told him about my encounter with the Malaysian and his blind sugar-daddy he predictably roared with laughter. He was still laughing when we got back to the hotel, telling me that I should have gone back with them as the blind old man might have mistaken my myriad mozzie bites for Braille and he was curious to know what they might spell out.

'Probably "For Sale",' he laughed as I jumped on his back and dragged him to the floor. We rolled around the hotel corridor play-fighting until eventually we lay in a heap, too drunk and exhausted by our exertions to move.

I could hear Gussie's voice in my ear: 'Tell him, tell him how you feel.'

And so I did.

He lay there in silence for a moment and then suddenly got up, brushing himself down before offering me his hand and helping me to my feet.

'I used to love you,' he said quietly, 'once upon a time back in Liverpool, but that was a long time ago. I was in bits when you left to live in London and even more so after I came down to see you and you didn't want anything to do with me. Well, it's too late to go back now, things can never be the same. You do realize that, don't you?'

I nodded.

'Now get to bed and I'll see you in the morning,' and planting a chaste kiss on my cheek he went off to his room, leaving me alone in the corridor. It seemed our Mickey wasn't the only one to have his heart broken in Hong Kong. Must be a family tradition, I reflected, making my way to my own bed.

On my return to Manila there was a letter from my mother. I wrote lots of letters back then, phone calls were expensive and so I was busy writing to almost everyone I knew on a daily basis. She'd sent me a clipping from the *Liverpool Echo*. Aunty Anne had entered a competition to write a poem about Liverpool and had won. There was a photograph of her, smiling proudly at the camera on the Prince's Landing Stage in her best coat. Her poem had been printed in quite a large column alongside her picture:

> Oh dying Port of Liverpool,
> No more your liners sail,

> The Prince's Stage deserted now
> Could tell us many a tale
> Of rich and poor and emigrants
> Who sailed with hopes so high
> Of a brave new land in another land
> But leaving with a sigh
> As they gazed their last at the Liver Birds,
> Soaring to the sky,
> And the homeward-bounders' hearts that thumped
> As the stage hove into view
> Oh Liverpool, my Liverpool
> What have they done to you.

Hopelessly sentimental, but enough to reduce me to tears of homesickness. Maybe it was time to go home? Ryan was moving on to a new job in Jakarta anyway so I had no choice. In the short time that I'd been in Manila I'd gone from loathing the place to falling in love with it. I'd even managed to get over my revulsion towards the food, happily wiring in to *lumpiang bahay*, a sort of Filipino egg roll, and a bowl of *pancit molo*, a dish similar to won ton soup, although I still fled in horror at the sight of the dreaded *balut*.

I learned that the people were very special indeed, hard-working and resourceful, enduring life's many hardships with a smile and a song – a cliché with a Disney twist, I realize, but true nonetheless, and the more I got to know these people as individuals the more I admired and respected them. I was really going to miss all the folk I'd made friends with – Gussie and his customers, the manager of our hotel and his heavily pregnant wife, an elderly expat who lived in the apartment below us and occasionally invited me in for tea, the kids in the street who greeted me every day, but most of all I was going to miss Joselito with his enduringly optimistic outlook on life and sunny good nature.

As fate would have it, the day I was due to fly home all DC-10 aircraft had been grounded following a major accident in Chicago and the airways were in chaos. Manila airport was heaving with people trying to get home as I joined one of the seemingly never-ending queues to check in. Ryan slipped a twenty-dollar bill inside my passport, hoping that a little bribe might just guarantee me a seat. It didn't. The Philippine Airlines steward behind the desk was above such blatant corruption and slid the bill across the desk with a sniffy but pointed 'I think you'll find you've left some money in your passport, sir.'

After a wait of over ten hours I was finally allocated a seat on a Pakistan Airlines flight to Bangkok. It was time to say goodbye to Ryan. He hugged me self-consciously.

'Try to keep out of any trouble, eh?' he said. 'I'll see you around.'

I grunted in reply as it was all that the lump in my throat would allow. I gave him one last wave as I entered the departure gate and then he was gone. As I've said frequently, I'm hopeless when it comes to saying goodbye.

No sooner had the flight taken off and we'd all settled down to read the in-flight magazine than I found myself in trouble. The plane had developed engine failure and was falling from the sky. The cabin shook violently, sending luggage in the overhead lockers flying into the aisles, all the oxygen masks popped out and from somewhere over the screams of panic a voice was telling us in broken English to adopt the brace position.

A group of Italian women in the row behind me cried out

like the Wailing Women, clutching their rosary beads and appealing hysterically for divine intervention. I was strangely calm; nothing to do with nerves of steel, I just firmly believed that I was invincible, confident that my time wasn't up yet and convinced that even if the plane were to crash then I would undoubtedly survive.

The plane didn't go down. Instead it turned back to Manila and all the passengers were put up in a nearby hotel for the night with the promise of a flight in the morning. After oversleeping and nearly missing the flight the next day thanks to a heavy night in the bar with a couple of Germans, I finally made it to Bangkok, although the airline had other plans for my luggage and sent it off to an unknown destination on a long holiday all of its own. At Bangkok airport I was told that there wasn't much chance of me going anywhere for the next couple of days as all flights were full.

Outside the airport I was mobbed by taxi touts. The most dogged of the lot won the day and I ended up agreeing to a guided tour of Bangkok for what I now realize was an extortionate price. At the temple of the Emerald Buddha I met a girl who looked like a forties film star, dressed in a crimson jumpsuit with a matching turban and spiky red heels.

'This place is Hustle City,' she drawled in a thick New York accent. 'Ya gotta watch 'em like a hawk or they'll fleece ya first chance they get.'

I thought her the ultimate in sophisticated glamour, the Lana Turner of the Temples, and it wasn't until she removed her enormous tortoiseshell sunglasses that I realized that underneath the slap she couldn't be much older than me.

'The name's Roxanne,' she said, 'Roxanne Casey from New York City, pleased to meet ya.'

She was in the same predicament as me, unable to get a

flight home and stranded in Bangkok where she'd spent the previous night sleeping on the floor at the airport. I asked her how she'd managed to look like she was about to step on to the red carpet at the Oscars, remarkable in the circumstances.

'The washroom, the goddamn public washroom.' She shrugged. 'What else is a girl to do? But I sure as hell don't fancy doing it for much longer. Y'wanna get outta this heat, go for a beer? See if we can't figure a way how to get the hell outta here?'

Roxanne was quite rightly suspicious of the taxi driver, wanting to know how much the 'son of a bitch' was charging me and haggling furiously with him before she agreed to let him take us any further.

'OK,' she said, once she'd managed to bring the price down to a sum she considered respectable, 'take us to the Oriental Hotel.'

She explained to me in the back of the cab that it was the best hotel in town and we stood a good chance of meeting a couple of guys there who might be able to 'help us out'. 'A couple of nice guys, businessmen looking for a little company,' she said, sitting back in her seat, 'who in return will put us up until we can get a flight.'

I seriously doubted Roxanne's hair-brained scheme to get us bedded down for the night but pretended to go along with it for something to do. I couldn't imagine anyone lusting after me, man, woman or beast, not unless they were into extremely rough trade as I was still wearing the same clothes that I'd left Manila in – jeans, T-shirt and flip-flops. I also hadn't shaved for a few days and my hair, which badly needed cutting, was as high as the proverbial Maori's hut. And it wasn't the only thing that was high. Having overslept and nearly missed my flight to Bangkok, I'd had no time to shower or even clean my teeth and I was conscious that I must be more than a little ripe.

Tagging along behind Roxanne, who sailed into the Oriental as if she owned the place, I grinned sheepishly at the doorman, surprised that he'd let me in, and followed Roxanne to some tables and chairs in the busy lobby.

'Holy Mary, Mother of God!' Roxanne exclaimed when she saw the prices on the drinks menu, ordering two beers never-theless. 'Now all we gotta do is sit tight and wait for a couple of big fish to swallow the bait.'

I was content just to sit in the cool of this beautiful lobby lis-tening to the piano and people-watching. Roxanne was certainly attracting lots of attention from both men and women – it would have been hard not to notice her in that jumpsuit and turban, she put the colourful flower display to shame – but to her growing chagrin no 'nice businessmen' approached us with the offer of bed and board until eventually, after what seemed like an hour, a man made his way over to us.

'Quick. Look interesting,' Roxanne hissed as he gave us the once-over before settling himself at a table next to ours and unfolding a newspaper.

Leaning across to him and waving a cigarette she asked coyly if he had a light. Lowering his paper, he gave her a look that managed to convey that he was used to being hustled by a more superior calibre of con woman in hotel lobbies and, indicating the lighter sat on our table, asked her why she didn't provide her own.

'It's broken,' she simpered sweetly.

'I don't smoke,' he replied curtly, getting up and moving to another table. 'But I'm sure one of the waiters will provide you with a book of matches if you ask.'

'What is it with these guys? They all celibate or something?' she protested, watching him go.

'C'mon, let's get out of here, we're wasting our time.' I was anxious to leave, worried that any minute now we would be thrown out.

'OK by me,' she said, gathering her few possessions and marching smartly across the lobby towards the exit. 'The place is a bore anyway.'

On the way back to the airport I asked the driver if he could recommend a shop that sold jewellery. My sister had a thing for what she called 'Siamese silver' and I wanted to see if I could find something to take home that was within my limited price range.

The driver took us to a shop. 'The best prices in Bangkok,' he said.

'He probably gets commission for every dumb mug he takes here,' Roxanne said, looking around her. 'Jeez, what a load of crap.'

She haggled like a trooper with the shop assistant over a bracelet of 'Siamese silver' that I wanted to buy.

'Silver my ass. Leave this thing on overnight and you'd wake up with verdigris poisoning. I'll give ya five bucks for it.'

My sister got her bracelet but we were not so lucky when it came to getting a flight out. At check-in we were told again that there were no seats available on any flights and that unfortunately for us we were at the bottom of a very long standby list.

Roxanne took herself off to the washroom to change for 'bed' and re-emerged a different woman, dressed in jeans and a T-shirt. With her face scrubbed clean of make-up and her squeaky-clean shoulder-length blonde hair freed from the confines of the turban, she looked like a little girl.

Trying to get to sleep in a small plastic chair is impossible, no matter how tired you are. In the end I joined Roxanne on the floor, where she at least had a jacket to cover her and a holdall for a pillow. We talked for hours until Roxanne finally fell asleep. I lay on the hard floor trying to get comfortable, wondering what the hell I was going to do. The little money I had left wouldn't last much longer and it looked like I was stuck here for days, maybe a week. I could just picture myself starving, my clothes in rags, harassing people on the streets of Bangkok for the price of a meal. No, I had to get out of here and as I lay on the floor a brilliant if devious scheme to get us home slowly unfurled in my mind. Roxanne's luggage had gone AWOL, as had mine, so what we'd do was this: we'd go to the offices of the airlines for which we were on the waiting list and tell them we were diabetic and that since our luggage containing the necessary supplies of insulin had gone missing we were now in danger of going hyperglycaemic as the little we had with us in our hand luggage was running out fast. Brilliant.

'Hypergly-what?' Roxanne asked the next morning as I explained the plan over breakfast in the airport café.

'Hyperglycaemic, it's what happens to a diabetic when they need insulin.'

'How do you know this shit?'

'I used to look after kids who had it, so I know all the facts. It's worth a try.'

'OK, I'm in.' She took a slug of coffee and peered at me over the tortoiseshell sunglasses. 'Now run all the details by me again.'

I managed to dissuade her from putting on the warpaint and the crimson jumpsuit, explaining that she looked more vulnerable au naturel.

'I'd rather die than be seen without lipstick,' she moaned. 'You're a goddamn sadist.'

In the office of KLM I gave a performance worthy of an Oscar, keeping my fingers firmly crossed as I relayed my sorry tale to the nice lady behind the desk, not wanting to tempt fate by telling such an outrageous lie. Eyes brimming with tears, I'd managed to convince myself that I was about to go into a coma at any minute by the time I'd finished. The nice lady was very concerned and after a few phone calls she managed to secure me a seat on a flight leaving for Rome that night. Making a mental note to God promising to make amends for telling such a whopper, I went in search of Roxanne. She was coming out of the offices of Pan Am with a huge smile on her face.

'Guess what? They're putting me on a flight to New York tonight,' she shouted excitedly, rushing towards me and giving me a kiss. 'They said I could use the first-class lounge while I waited, and I got you a pass as well. You're a genius!'

Roxanne went to town in the first-class lounge, availing herself fully of the facilities in the ladies' washroom to transform herself from all-American girl back into forties vamp. We exchanged addresses and made promises to keep in touch and then went our separate ways, never to see each other again. Once safely on the plane I was beside myself to find that I'd been allocated a seat in business class. After a lovely dinner I settled down in the luxury of my enormous seat and went to sleep. Heaven.

CHAPTER 15

The Glamazons

FIVE DAYS AFTER LEAVING THE TROPICANA APARTMENTS AND still wearing the same clothes, I'd finally made it home. It was Friday afternoon, Vera was out and there was someone sleeping in my bed.

A tousled mop of curls appeared from beneath the blankets. They belonged to Chrissie, a queen I'd seen around the clubs in Liverpool and wasn't very keen on. He was camper than a Dora Bryan film, mincing around Sadie's screaming like a one-man ghost train. Underneath the mane of corkscrew curls lurked a face that could have been very pretty if it wasn't set in a permanent scowl, and his mean little mouth framed by a pencil-thin moustache always puckered up as if he were sucking a mouthful of sherbet lemons. Appearances were deceptive, as despite his delicate looks he was as hard as nails and ferocious in a fight. I once saw him come to blows with the cloakroom attendant from the Bear's Paw over something as petty as a spilt drink. The attendant, himself a tough little queen, rose to the challenge when Chrissie 'offered her out' and they set about each other like a pair of psychopathic Shih Tzus fighting over a bone, until eventually Chrissie put an end to the matter by belting the poor queen over the head with a chair. I was wary of Chrissie; he was not one to cross.

'Hiya, queen,' he screeched as if we were long-lost friends. 'We didn't know when you were coming back. Vera's at work.'

'Vera? Work?'

'Yeah, she's working behind the bar of the Black Cat.'

'It's Cap.'

'Whatever, she's 'avin' a ball anyway, pissed every night. You haven't got a vogue going spare, have yer? I'm crawling up the wall here in desperation for a little whiff.'

I threw a packet of duty-free at him and asked if he'd like a cup of tea.

'Ooh, I'd love one – no milk please,' he said, slithering out of bed in his vest and underpants to get a light from the gas fire, 'an' I wouldn't mind a little bit of toast with that if you're making any, queen.' There was more than a hint of Uriah Heep about Chrissie when he was attempting to ingratiate himself.

'What are you doing here, Chrissie, if it's not a daft question?' I asked as I waited for the kettle to boil.

'Well, you see, Lil,' he said, taking a deep drag on his fag, pulling the strap of his vest over his bony shoulder as delicately as if it belonged to an elegant satin chemise, 'I had to get out of town. It was closing in on me, y'know? Well, I had the promise of a job down here so I rang Vera and asked if yous'd mind if I crashed here for a couple of days.' He took another pull on his fag, idly flicking the ash in the general direction of the fireplace and missing. 'You don't mind, do you, Lil? I've tidied up.'

That was an understatement. The place was transformed;

for the first time in months I could see the bedroom floor.

'I've done all the washin' and hung up every scrap of clothing. I've also scrubbed this dump from top to bottom. You two are a dirty pair of bastards, I thought you'd been broken into when I first got here, the state of the place.'

I left him to get dressed and made the tea, unable to believe that for once the kitchen sink was devoid of dirty dishes and our motley collection of mugs were now hanging from cup-hooks on the end of the shelf. Chrissie had been very busy in my absence: an army of spring-cleaning fairies couldn't have done a better job. I took a look in the front room and saw the turquoise lino shone like a lake and the net curtains that had previously been a smoky grey were now a gleaming white.

'How was the Far East then? You've got a smashing tan,' he shouted from the bedroom. 'Did you have a good time? We thought you were never coming back. Work's been on the phone looking for yer, you'd better give 'em a ring.'

'Thank God you're back,' Maura was saying on the other end of the phone. 'Now I realize you still have a month to go before you're due to come back but a job's come up that really only a man can do.'

This sounded ominous. It was obviously an unsafe house with a drunken father who'd kick the door down in the wee small hours, hell-bent on killing me. Why did I leave Manila? Why didn't that bastard Ryan say, 'Come with me to Jakarta'?

'He's an elderly gentleman suffering from dementia. His wife, who is also his full-time carer, badly needs a break so we're going to provide a bit of respite care while she goes off and has a holiday.'

'How long is the assignment?' I asked, crossing my fingers and hoping to God that it would be a short one.

'Three weeks.'

My heart sank. Three weeks looking after a demented old man 24/7. I'd go out of my mind along with him.

'Now he's a big fellah,' Maura went on. 'Very strong despite his age and prone to violent outbursts towards strangers, but apart from that he's a nice owld boy. His name is Mr Pantucci and he loves his classical music.'

Great, dodging blows to Mahler.

'When do you want me to start?'

'Monday morning. Now write the address down and I'll meet you there.'

I went off to get a pen.

'Everything all right, Lil?' Chrissie was munching on a piece of toast and smoking at the same time as I rooted around for a pen. It was always the same, you could never find one when you wanted one. I swear to God we had Borrowers living behind the wainscot who specialized in biros.

'If you wanna pen, they're all in the kitchen drawer. It'll probably take you a while to get used to a bit of order.' He yawned. 'Oh well, I better have a wash. I want to do a bit of shopping, I promised Vera I'd get something in for later. Watcha fancy?'

I took the address down off Maura and hung up the phone with a heavy heart. It was going to be hard to adjust after Manila. I felt displaced, unsettled and the prospect of three weeks' solitude with a crazy old man did nothing to cheer me up.

'Anyway, Lil, welcome home,' Chrissie shouted, heading for the bathroom. 'It's nice to have you back.'

Yeah, welcome home, Lil, wherever home was.

*

Vera and I were sat in the kitchen catching up over a pot of tea and twenty duty-frees when Chrissie arrived back from the shops, carrying a highly varied assortment of goodies. 'I've got bacon, bread, beans, sausage, a bottle of wine and a pork pie, oh and half a bottle of whisky for you, Lil, to welcome you home.'

Strangely none of this was carried back from the shops by the orthodox means of a carrier bag. Instead he produced this seemingly endless stream of merchandise from deep inside the recesses of his overcoat, a garment that Fagin had obviously left him in his will. 'I've gorra bit of cheese somewhere,' he said, rooting around an inside pocket, 'and a couple of jars of sandwich spread as well.'

'I thought you had no money, Chrissie?' Vera asked, examining the bottle of wine.

'I haven't.'

'So where did this little lot come from then?'

'Where d'ya think, soft shite?'

Vera gasped. 'Are you mental? Shoplifting when you're on the run from the pol—' He tried to swallow his words as they came tumbling out but it was too late. The cat was out of the bag.

'Are you on the run from the police then?' I asked, trying my best to sound casual, as if I was used to harbouring queens on the run every day of the week. 'What did you do?'

'Nothin' much, just a bit of shoplifting.'

'And she's at it again now. You're gonna get your collar felt, Chrissie, if you don't watch out – and where did you nick this little lot from? I hope it wasn't out of Mrs Bhakta's.' Vera was referring to the lady who ran the corner shop, who we both loved because she allowed us to get things on tick.

'No, it wasn't Mrs Bhakta's, it was the Co-op if you must know.'

'That's all right then,' Vera said, changing his tune. 'In that case open that wine and I'll make a little sarnie.'

That evening we went to the Black Cap to witness Vera in action behind the bar. The feisty Irish landlady, Babs, had given him the moniker 'McGoo' after the short-sighted cartoon character. At closing time she would hammer a shillelagh forcefully on the wood panelling in the front bar in an attempt to coerce the stragglers to drink up and go home. 'McGoo! Are you pissed again?' she would cry as an inebriated Vera staggered ever so slightly while supposedly collecting glasses.

There was a group of queens from Leeds who lived in a big flat over a shop on the Holloway Road. They were notorious for throwing wild parties that invariably culminated in a mass orgy in the front bedroom and I recall one of them, Regina, drunkenly lurching around the landing, naked apart from a vest, screaming, 'Have any of you bar-stards seen my jeans and a leather thong?' I'd become friendly with Paul, known to the residents of the flat as 'Joyce', a nurse who worked in the special clinic at my old stomping ground, the Royal Northern Hospital. 'You wouldn't believe the amount of male genitalia that slips through my hands on a daily basis, luv,' he'd say. He was easy-going and a lot of fun and, like the rest of us, no slouch when it came to having a good time.

He was in the Cap that night and we stood together watching a particularly appalling mime act with a critical eye.

'I could do better than that any day,' I said for the umpteenth time as one of them launched into the ubiquitous knicker routine. Among other items, the artiste produced a dead plant from inside a pair of voluminous bloomers, to the strains of 'I Never Promised You A Rose Garden'.

'I know, luv,' Joyce agreed. 'A pile of crap and they're earning good money for that. Do you know, a double act can earn thirty quid – that's over a hundred quid each a week if you work every night.'

'Really?' The seed that had been planted long ago began to stir.

'We should get an act together, we'd be brilliant. I love nursing but I fancy a change – and you should see me in drag.'

I looked at Joyce doubtfully. He was broad-shouldered and what my ma would call big-boned and in no way feminine to look at. I tried to visualize him in drag.

'Here, I'll have you know that I look fabulous in a frock, luv. Better than half of this lot,' Joyce boasted, indicating towards the stage. 'I've always wanted to get an act together and go professional. So what d'ya reckon?'

The seed was germinating at an alarming rate and was about to burst into full bloom.

'Bugger it, why don't we then,' I said, suddenly getting very carried away with the idea. 'What's stopping us?'

'Well, first we'll have to find someone to make costumes.'

'And cheaply,' I butted in.

'Because there's no way I'm going on stage in public wearing charity-shop tat.'

'I can do that,' Chrissie piped up casually. 'I can make costumes.'

'You?' Joyce and I sang out in unison.

'For your information I served a five-year apprenticeship with a master tailor in Birkenhead,' he said, adding grandly, '*I* am a couturier. One of the finest.'

'What do you charge?' I asked, hoping it wasn't some astronomical figure that we couldn't afford.

'Well normally I'd be way out of your price range, but

seeing as how you're putting me up, I'll do it in lieu of rent. Now get us a drink before I change my mind.'

Chrissie was indeed a genius on a sewing machine. He was totally unique, a jack of all trades. Not only could he design, cut out and sew remarkable costumes, he was also a dab hand at covering a three-piece suite, painting and decorating, and could nick a packet of bacon from under the store detective's nose in the Co-op before she had time to blink. In addition, as I was to find out over the years ahead, he was a highly complex character, as unpredictable as the weather, with quicksilver mood swings and the possessor of a viperous tongue that could cut you to the quick. Life with Chrissie around was certainly never dull and I knew within the first few days of our meeting that we would end up friends for life. He was funny, daring, loyal and capable of extreme kindness and bore with enormous courage the stinking, rotten illness that eventually carried him off. Remembering him now, vigorously slapping Oil of Ulay on his face in the mirror over the mantelpiece while getting ready to hit the Vauxhall Tavern for the night out, I really wish he was still around.

'What are we going to call ourselves then?' an excited Joyce asked.

'How about "the Sisters" something?'

'How about the Sisters Shite? Is anyone going to the bar then?'

'How about the Glamazons?' I suggested, recalling the name of a troupe of extremely tall Ziegfeld Follies showgirls I'd seen in a book.

'The Glamazons?' I could see Joyce mulling the name over in his mind. 'The Glamazons? Ooh, I'm not sure, luv.'

'Well we're both tall, hence the Amazon bit.'

'Aye, but who's to say we'll be glamorous?'

'You will be once I've finished with you,' Chrissie said, finishing off what was left of his pint. 'That's if one of you tight bitches buys me a bleedin' drink.'

'All right then, Glamazons it is, luv. Now what we having?'

The next day was Lesbian and Gay Pride, or just plain Gay Pride as it was known back then, and Vera, Joyce and I were on the float that belonged to Zipper, the gay bookshop that Kate and I had wandered into many moons ago. It had rapidly expanded and metamorphosed into a successful enterprise.

Also on the Zipper float was Reg, who had broken his leg at the Alexandra Palace Drag Ball. Having had more than a few large brandies, he'd fallen off one of his stilettos as he was leaving and consequently was in a hip-to-ankle plaster cast. It was a bit of a performance getting him on the back of the lorry and even trickier getting him off it at the other end after he'd consumed the best part of a bottle of vodka en route.

In those days Gay Pride wasn't the big corporate affair that it is today. Even so, there was still a big turnout for the march through London to the rally in Hyde Park. There was a lot of abuse from Christian groups and gangs of yobs as we passed by. I remember a bus driver, his face contorted with hate-fuelled rage, shouting from his cabin, 'You all want gassing, you dirty bastards.'

'God bless the queens, darling,' Reg calmly replied, toasting him with a can of warm Budweiser. 'And fuck you!'

None of us was shy in telling our detractors just where to get off and we all gave as good as we got, and for every homophobic heckler it was heartwarming to see that there were just as many sympathetic supporters happy to cheer us on. It was exhilarating hanging on to the back of that lorry.

There was a real sense of freedom and, above all, defiance in the air as the various tribes of gay men and women from all over the country gathered together to let the world know that 'We're here. We're queer. And we're not going shopping!'. The loudspeaker on our float belted out 'Y.M.C.A.', a song that I loathed, but in this instance I happily gyrated along to it with the rest, not caring for once what anyone thought.

A rather worthy journalist ran up to our float with his tape recorder.

'I'm with BBC Radio Four,' he said, holding his mike up to Joyce. 'What do you think of Jeremy Thorpe?'

The former leader of the Liberal Party had recently been on trial at the Old Bailey, charged with the attempted murder of a former male lover. (The jury later acquitted him.) The press had had a field day and it was still a much-discussed topic.

'As a gay man,' the journalist panted as he ran alongside our float, 'how do you feel about Mr Thorpe?'

'She's all right, luv,' Joyce replied dead-pan, 'but I wouldn't turn me back on her.'

That night at the Cap, Joyce, who by now was also working part-time behind the bar, told Babs that we were getting an act together. Her immediate response was to offer us a booking, act unseen, on the forthcoming Bank Holiday Monday afternoon.

'Thirty quid,' she said. 'Two twenty-minute spots, that's if you can get it together in time.'

'Oh don't worry, we will, Babs, we will,' I promised, my mind going into overdrive. I was determined that come August the Glamazons would have some form of act, conveniently ignoring the fact that for the next three weeks I'd be out of action as I cared for Maura's 'nice owd fellah'. Never mind, I told myself, I'd use any spare time to plan and devise an innovative act, the like of which was going to slay the punters of the Black Cap.

Maura had lied when she described Mr Pantucci as 'big'. He was a Goliath and, despite a pronounced stoop, he towered over me.

'This is Paul. He's going to look after you for a little while,' his wife was telling him, rubbing his arm encouragingly and trying to sound enthusiastic. 'Say hello to him then, dear.'

Mr Pantucci, glowering angrily, lunged towards me and grabbed me by the throat, shaking me like a rag doll.

'No, dear.' His wife gently rebuked him as if talking to a small child, prising his fingers from around my neck. 'That's not how we behave towards guests, is it?'

Three weeks of this. Jesus, I'd be lucky to survive.

'He's really very gentle once he gets to know you,' Mrs Pantucci tried unconvincingly to reassure me. 'He's a big pussycat, honestly.'

Yeah, a sabre-toothed tiger.

'The district nurse comes every morning to help wash and dress him and then again in the evening to help you put him to bed. Oh, and speaking of bed, my husband is inclined to get up and wander during the night so I'm afraid you'll have to sleep in the same room as him. You'll find a cot bed next to his. You don't mind, do you?'

Maura suddenly became very preoccupied with a print of Mozart hanging on the wall. I did mind but given the circumstances I had no choice but to agree.

The wife's unwillingness to leave her husband in the hands of a stranger was touching, despite her obvious need for respite from caring for a man with advanced dementia twenty-four hours a day. She was tearful when we finally persuaded her to go, reluctantly getting in the taxi with a worried expression on her face.

'You will take good care of him, won't you?' she pleaded anxiously. 'He really is a dear, we've never been apart for this long since the day we got married and I'm loath to leave him. I wouldn't dream of it ordinarily, it's just that I'm a bit tired. You do understand, don't you?'

A bit tired? That was an understatement. She was exhausted and deserved a medal, let alone a temporary break. Her frail exterior belied the fact that underneath lay a woman of steel, determined to continue to provide the best care she could manage for her husband, despite herself being on the verge of collapse from nervous exhaustion. I tried to put her mind at ease by giving the impression that she was leaving her spouse in the hands of a seasoned professional, and with a sinking heart waved her off for a well-deserved rest at her sister's in Bournemouth.

'OK then, Mr Pantucci,' I said, returning to the front room and trying to sound cheery. 'What would you like for your lunch?'

'GET OUT!' he shouted, hurling a telephone directly at me but thankfully missing.

'Good luck,' Maura said, smartly stepping into the hall out of harm's way and making for the front door. 'If you need anything, just call the office.'

I wondered what were the chances of 'the office' supplying me with a straitjacket and some horse tranquillizer as I watched her close the door behind her, leaving me alone to face a furious Mr Pantucci.

'Would you like a nice cup of tea?' I announced in my phoney cheery voice.

'Bugger off!' he roared, scattering a pile of ancient *Radio*

Times magazines in my direction. 'And take that bloody dog with you.' Oh dear, as well as Mr Pantucci to deal with there was an imaginary dog to walk.

'OK,' I said, beating a hasty retreat to the kitchen. 'I'll just put him in the back yard.'

This was going to be fun.

The worst aspect of being a carer is the solitude. Apart from visits from the district nurses and the home help, who tidied up and did the shopping, I saw no one. For three weeks I never left the flat and at times the loneliness was crippling, particularly in the early hours of the morning when I sat listening to the shipping forecast on the radio after I'd finally managed to get Mr Pantucci off to sleep. There was a framed photograph on the mantelpiece of a handsome young army officer astride a horse, smiling proudly at the camera, and it was hard to connect this vital young man with the decaying old ruin fighting the demons that had invaded his mind alone in the dark next door. In those gloomy moments I wondered what would become of me, and the unstoppable tide of advancing years and the inevitable afflictions that came with it made me question my own mortality.

While I bent over to feed Mr Pantucci his dinner one evening he took me unawares, catching me in a powerful headlock, pulling me down and submerging my face in a bowl of tomato soup on the tray on his lap. I really thought my time was up and that I would drown or at the least end up with a broken nose. 'What an ignominious end to a life not yet fulfilled,' I could hear Maura telling the police as she identified my body the next day. 'Drowned in a bowl of soup.'

Thankfully his grip slackened after a while and I was able

to wriggle free but it was a long time before I was able to face tomato soup again.

The cot bed that I slept on was pushed close to Mr Pantucci's bed because of the limited space in the cramped little bedroom, and a good night's sleep became nothing but a distant memory. During the spasmodic moments when he actually slept he snored like a bear, breaking off to have a rant every now and then. Once I was woken by the sensation of warm water running across my face. Happily dreaming that I was having my hair washed, I was content to lie there until it suddenly dawned on me that my dream was in fact reality.

I opened my eyes and there in the half-light was Mr Pantucci standing over me, his striped pyjama bottoms around his ankles, his ageing testicles swinging like two golf balls in an old sock, peeing all over me.

Occasionally, as we sat listening to one of his favourite concertos on the coffin-sized radiogram in the living room, there would be moments of lucidity when he would regain control over his mind. 'Please forgive me,' he'd beg, appealing to me with sad eyes, 'I can't help myself.' It was heartbreaking.

Mrs Pantucci rang me nearly every night to see how we were getting on, concerned about the husband she obviously sorely missed. Desperate as I was to get home myself, I'd nevertheless convince her that everything was running smoothly and that she should stop worrying and enjoy her rest, otherwise what was the point of the exercise?

Glancing through a Sunday tabloid that the home help had left one morning, I was shocked to see a double-page exposé of Rowena Switzer's escort agency. A journalist, passing herself off as a potential escort, had infiltrated the agency, befriending the girls and even going out on a couple of dates. It was all there, a highly dramatized account of 'The Sordid

Prostitution Racket on Park Lane!' and because of this woman's handiwork Rowena and a lot of the girls, Amy included, had been arrested and the agency closed down. Reading the journalist's story, I came to the conclusion that the girls who worked for Rowena were infinitely more honourable and decent than the woman who worked for this Sunday paper.

When the three weeks were finally up and Mrs Pantucci came home, I ran down Abbey Road with the sheer exuberance of any creature that has been freed from captivity and released into the wild. But the experience of caring for Mr Pantucci left me with a profound respect for all full-time carers. All too frequently they are conveniently neglected by the system and left to 'get on with it', regardless of age or capability. I went straight from this job to a week in a caravan park in Great Yarmouth with a group of Peripatetics and an assortment of underprivileged kids. I had seven little Asian boys in my care and I recall that we all had a whale of a time. However, I was also starting to panic that our act would never be ready for Bank Holiday Monday.

'You can't beat a good shite first thing of a morning,' Chrissie declared, waltzing out of the bathroom and into the kitchen. 'I feel like I've shed ten pounds.'

Vera, who was in the process of taking a bite out of a slice of toast that he'd just dipped into the runny yolk of his fried egg, started to retch violently.

'I'd leave it for half an hour before you go in there,' Chrissie said wickedly as Vera ran past him and into the toilet to vomit. 'That kebab I had last night must've been off.'

Perversely, the sound of Vera vomiting has always made me laugh. Chrissie, knowing this, did his best to set Vera off every morning, even going so far on one occasion as to serve up a cat turd studded with bay leaves on a saucer for breakfast. It wasn't hard to make Vera sick, the sound of me gagging as I cleaned my teeth was enough to have him projectile vomiting.

'Oh well,' Chrissie said, helping himself to Vera's breakfast, 'I suppose I'd better get on that sewing machine and run up another incredible creation. You better get yourself into town. I need lining material, some more of that white fringing and fabric for those flapper outfits.'

'How many yards shall I get?' I asked.

'Depending on the width, I'd say you'll need about three,' Chrissie said, running an experienced eye over me.

'What about Joyce?'

'Oh, at least ten. She's bigger than you, particularly around the back.'

'Ten? She's not that big.'

'She's getting there though.' Chrissie loved to tease Joyce about his weight. 'No, get four yards for Joyce, that should do it. Oh and don't forget the zips. Metal ones only please, not those useless plastic things. My costumes are couture and when that Regina Fong gets a load of them she's going to have a thromby. Vera, get out of that lav, your cup of tea's getting cold.'

My first port of call was 58 Dean Street, W1, a record shop that specialized in the more obscure soundtracks to films and shows – at a price. It was managed by a wily old queen called Derek, who had the uncanny knack of parting you from substantial amounts of money by screaming, 'Have *I* got something for *you*?' and disappearing through the beaded curtain into the back of the shop, to emerge with an LP which he'd clutch to his chest as if it were a sacred relic.

'There is *the* most fabulous track on here that's very you, darling,' he'd say tantalizingly. 'No one will have heard it before, and certainly no other queen will be doing it. Shall I pop it on for you so you can have a listen?'

He played me a raucous bump-and-grind number sung by Dorothy Loudon called 'I've Got To Get Hot', the very funny lament of an aspiring opera singer forced to support her 'grey-haired mother' by stripping.

'How much?'

'Twenty-five quid.'

'Twenty-five quid!'

'Well, it's the only copy in London after all, and you have to admit that the number is guaranteed to bring the house down! So what do you think? Do we have a deal?'

Recklessly I'd hand over twenty-five pounds that I could ill afford, desperate to secure the number that was going to be the talk of the drag circuit at any price, unaware that Derek gave every drag-queen the same persuasive spiel.

'Oh, before you go I'd like you to hear something else that you may be interested in. A truly fabulous album by Sandra Church – she played Gypsy in the original Broadway production, but then you know that. There's some wonderful strip numbers on it, very you. Would you like to hear it?'

Fifty quid lighter but with the satisfaction of knowing that I was the proud possessor of some original numbers never before heard in the gay pubs of London (or so I thought), I made my way to a theatrical fabric shop to buy something knockout for the finale costumes. The solitary assistant who worked there was forever bunging me free feather boas, diamanté necklaces and yards of material. I don't know why, he didn't want anything in return – no quick fumble in the stock room, nothing – it was always a puzzle. I came to the conclusion that he either hated his employers or felt sorry for me, but whatever the reason I was only too happy to accept a bag of contraband in among my purchases. This time I'd bought some fabric that I'd seen in the window. It was a garish lime-green sateen and covered in a design of clefs and musical notes.

'What the hell is that?' Chrissie screamed when I got it home. 'Couldn't you find anything more hideous?'

I thought that it was interesting and unusual if nothing else.

'It's fluorescent,' I protested.

'Fluorescent! Jesus, like it needs any help to be seen.'

Within a month Chrissie had managed to turn out a set of beautifully made costumes on Anne's antique Singer sewing machine. We no longer had a spare set of bed sheets as Chrissie had used them to make patterns.

'Of course I'm used to using calico,' he said, pinning half a sheet to my chest, 'but I suppose this is what you get when you work with amateurs.'

'Will these sheets be OK though?' I asked him, ignoring the slight even though I knew he wasn't far from the truth.

I was driven, a drag-queen-in-the-making possessed, and if Chrissie needed calico then I'd throw myself on the mercy of the little man in the fabric shop until I got the length, if you'll pardon the expression, that Chrissie demanded. Being fitted for a costume by Chrissie was akin to torture. He'd stand you on a chair and insult you as he casually stuck pins in you as if you were a voodoo doll.

'You haven't got a curve on your body, you're just straight up and down and if you want my honest opinion then I think you'd be better off sticking a bulb in your gob and standing in the corner with a lampshade on your head than traipsing around the stage of the Black Cap with a shape like that. No

312

offence, Lil, but it breaks my heart to think that my beautiful couture gowns are going to be hanging off your skinny arse.

'However,' he went on smugly, 'with my beautiful figure I could carry off a sack. Lots of men have told me that.'

'I think you'll find what they actually said was you should be carried off in a sack – and dumped, preferably in the river.'

This kind of Ugly-Sisteresque banter was the stuff of life to Chrissie. He thrived on it and I was aware that we were sounding exactly like Alistair Harlequeen and Tony Page that afternoon in Formosa Street in what now seemed a lifetime away.

'Camp' he simpered with an evil smirk, sticking a pin in my arm.

'OW!'

'Oh sorry, Lil. Did I catch you? It's this sheeting, it's wafer-thin. Bit like yourself.'

Chrissie was also a wind-up merchant par excellence but it was better not to rise to the bait as the mood might turn ugly. Then Chrissie would go off into one of his sulks, rocking back and forth on the end of his bed lost in a world of his own, when what I really wanted was him chained to the sewing machine and running up another couture gown.

'Are you sure you don't want me to get you the proper stuff?' I asked again. 'I'm sick to death of hearing about bloody sheets.'

'You don't have to put yourself out, this'll do just fine thank you very much. Listen, when I was inside I used to use newspaper.'

He realized that he'd said too much and to cover his embarrassment started fussing unnecessarily over a dart in the sheeting.

'Have you been in prison then?' I asked cautiously, not

wanting him to clam up on me. Not that I need have worried.

'Has Rose Kennedy got a black frock? Course I have.'

'What were you in for?'

'Oh, nothing much.' He shrugged, feigning an air of non-chalance as he busied himself with his pins. 'I nicked the polio box off the counter of Burton's in Grange Road, got six months. I wouldn't have minded but there was fuck all in it anyway, the miserable gets.'

Once the cat was out of the bag, Chrissie's tales of prison life became legendary. Even if he was prone to gross exaggeration and you never really knew if he was spinning you a tale or even if he'd spent any time in nick whatsoever, he enjoyed playing the hardened con and he had a willing audience in me and Vera.

'You wouldn't believe what I've done for two Swan Vestas and a Park Drive,' he'd brag, helping himself to one of your fags.

I spent hours listening to my ever-growing collection of LPs for suitable numbers and became totally engrossed in the process of editing them down and cutting songs together, obsessing until the joins were undetectable. It was all done on a music centre that I'd got on the HP from the electricity board around the corner. When finally I'd got together what I considered to be two strong twenty-minute shows we set about clumsily rehearsing them in Joyce's flat.

Babs had let us use the Black Cap at first. We rehearsed in the afternoons when the bar was closed but I felt uncomfortable as the staff would watch us as they cleaned up and stocked the bar, offering suggestions and sniggering. Even Regina popped in one afternoon. 'You need to use the hands more, darling,' was his critical response to our lack of terpsichorean talent.

'The hands are very expressive. Movement should be fluid and elegant,' he drawled, rolling his flexible wrists and positioning his hand in the manner of a shop window mannequin to demonstrate. 'But carry on, I'm sure it will be all right on the night.'

I preferred to rehearse in private so it was off to Joyce's to annoy the neighbours below as we clumped around, devising some form of dance routine to 'Lullaby Of Broadway'. I'd become friendly with a lot of the acts by now, in particular a young Liza Minnelli-obsessed drag queen called David Dale, the possessor of an incredibly mobile face that he could contort into a million expressions and a pair of rubber lips he could do the most extraordinary things with. David, or Doris as he was known to his friends, was a seemingly inexhaustible whirling dervish on stage. He didn't just stand there moving his mouth like a goldfish gasping for air to whatever soundtrack was play-ing, he put his heart and soul into it. With Doris it really was a case of 'Every Little Movement Has A Meaning All Its Own' and, like me, he idolized Regina.

'I'm grooming Miss Dale to be my protégé,' Regina told me one evening in the Cap after I'd bought him a drink ('Large brandy, darling'). 'Rosie Lee is threatening to quit the act. Mrs Norris told her that it was undignified for a queen to be dragging up after she's hit thirty, silly cow, and as it's her thirtieth birthday soon I'll be looking for a replacement.'

He paused to take a hefty slug of his brandy, sucking it through his tombstone teeth and then exhaling loudly as if he'd just sipped petrol.

'Between you and me, dahling, I think Miss Dale would be divine in Rosie's part, don't you?'

I wanted to shout that I'd be great in Rosie's part but since I was commited to the Glamazons I silently knocked back my cider and kept my thoughts to myself, agreeing that David Dale would indeed be ideal for the job.

David was extremely inventive. He got a group of people together, including a young teenage girl, to perform a version of *The Wizard of Oz* and as well as playing the Cowardly Lion he choreographed, directed, got the tape together, designed and made most of the costumes and hats and was responsible for ringing round the pubs and clubs to get the bookings. He was also prone to throwing the odd hissy fit, as we all were, and there was many a drama and intrigue among the cast of *The Wizard of Oz*. I went up to Newcastle in the back of a white Ford Transit van with them to play a club called the Copacabana and ended up in bed with the Tin Man.

It was David who pointed me in the direction of Fox's, a shop in Covent Garden that specialized in theatrical make-up. It was run by the indomitable Fred, who knew everything there was to know about slap. He it was who taught me how to glue three pairs of eyelashes together until they were the required length and thickness of a Lido showgirl's. I practised getting the make-up right at home, caking it on until I was satisfied that I'd arrived at real drag queen slap, surprised and a little dismayed to find just how much it aged me.

I had no idea where to buy wigs until eventually I stumbled upon a small shop in King's Cross. The range of colours was limited, mostly black and brown and the closest that they had to a blond was a silver grey, but I bought a handful and took them home to Colin, a hairdresser friend from Liverpool who now conveniently lived locally. He transformed them with a flick of a tail comb and a couple of cans of lacquer into something slightly more flattering and less like a bag full of dead rats.

As the great day of the Glamazons' debut approached I could barely sleep or eat. We were having a full dress rehearsal in the front room of the flat a few days before when my interpretation of 'I'm Still Here' from *Follies* was annoyingly interrupted by a ring on the front-door bell. We instantly went into a blind panic as we always did when the doorbell rang. I peeped through the dirty net curtains to see a policeman on the steps.

'It's a copper,' I hissed, sending Chrissie bolting for the safety of the bathroom. 'It's no point pretending we're not in, he must've heard the music halfway up the street. Go and see what he wants, Vera.'

'Why do I have to go?' Vera quacked indignantly.

'Cos you're not in drag, that's why.'

The bell rang again, only more persistently this time. Vera and I hopped up and down as if we were on hot coals, flapping our hands about and silently panicking.

'Oh for fuck's sake, I'll go, luv,' Joyce announced, making for the front door.

The copper was a pro. He didn't miss a beat at the sight of Joyce in a Bri-Nylon leopardskin halter-neck dress and black beehive wig, nor was he looking for Chrissie. He merely wanted to know if we had any idea whose car it was parked outside on the pavement.

Bank Holiday Monday had finally arrived. I was up at the crack of dawn and banging on the door of the Black Cap way before opening time to make sure I was ready to go on at one o'clock. Chrissie declined to help in the dressing room, declaring, 'D'ya think Norman Hartnell hangs around to pull the Queen's zips up? I don't think so. Anyway, I want to watch from out front.'

Lozzy designated herself as dresser, wearing a white overall and a pincushion on her wrist as her badge of office. She was now living in a cosy little flat in Victoria Mansions on the South Lambeth Road. We'd tried out bits of the act at one of her regular parties before a conveniently inebriated and good-natured audience and Lozzy was eager to get involved. She loved showbiz, even if it was in a pub, and busied herself making lists and checking costumes. As I slowly unpacked my make-up, laying it all out in readiness on a hand towel the way I'd seen the pros do, I began to have serious self-doubt. What if we die on our arse? What if we are so abysmal the audience laugh us off the stage, or even worse hurl bottles and pint pots? I'd never show my face in public again. What the hell was I thinking of, arrogantly assuming that I was good enough to get up on the Black Cap stage, on a packed bank holiday no less, a premier date in any seasoned act's diary, and perform for a paying public?

'Would you like a drink? A whisky or a cider?' Lozzy asked, interrupting for a moment my train of negative thoughts.

'No thank you,' I replied primly. Real pros never drank before a performance and I intended to start as I meant to go on. Joyce, on the other hand, had no such qualms and was busy quaffing a bottle of Martini.

'For the nerves, luv,' he offered apologetically.

The opening number was a military big band song from a show starring the two surviving Andrews Sisters called *Over Here*. I'd gone to Laurence Corner, a shop off the Euston Road that sold army surplus, and purchased two olive-green ladies' jackets belonging to some branch of the American women's armed forces, a couple of khaki skirts with matching shirts and ties and some smart GI's hats to pin in the wigs. I was quite pleased with these purchases, having managed to clothe the opening number for next to nothing in what I considered to be two very smart and undoubtedly flattering outfits.

However, in the cold fluorescent light of the Black Cap's dressing room my heart sank as I stared at our reflections in the mirror. Even though Colin had worked miracles with what little hair there was on the King's Cross wigs, they still looked like a pair of National Health teasers, the kind that were given out to cancer patients who'd undergone chemo. We looked grotesque in them and while I would have won first prize in a 'Pat Coombs as a clippie in *On the Buses*' competition, Joyce, on the other hand, was a dead ringer for one of those stereotypical bull-dyke women's prison officers frequently seen terrorizing the vulnerable in black and white American movies set in a women's detention centre.

Apart from standing in the alley waiting to go on, rigid with fright as the we heard the DJ announce us, I have very little recollection of the performance. The pub was packed and the response was fairly respectable, nothing earth-shattering but at least they didn't boo us off. As soon as we got home I collapsed on the bed. Having had quite a few drinks after the show, I was a bit pissed and down in the dumps as it had all been such an anticlimax. I hadn't enjoyed it that much and felt in my heart of hearts that the act wasn't at all special and we still had a long way to go. What we needed was something different, preferably funny, if we wanted to be noticed. As I dozed off to sleep the phone in the hall rang.

'That was Babs,' Vera said, coming in from answering it. 'She said that the Dueragon Arms has been on the phone and they want to book you for tonight. Joyce is up for it if you are.'

Oh Christ. All I wanted to do was go to sleep.

'Go on, you might as well, think of the money.'

Vera was right, it was stupid to turn good money down and wearily I dragged myself into the bathroom for the second shave of the day. The skin on my face was going to resemble a quarter of corned beef at this rate.

The Dueragon Arms in Homerton was a famous East End pub that had once been run by Gay Travers, an East End legend in his own right.

'I do hope you're glamorous,' Mae, the current landlady, whined as we introduced ourselves. 'We had the Harlequeens on last night. Fan-tas-tic! Took the roof off. You should see their costumes, must've cost thousands, all those feathers and beads . . . Are yours anything like that? I mean after all with a name like the Glamazons you sort of expect something . . . well, glamorous, don't you?'

'We're a mixture of comedy and glamour, luv. We've got some beautiful finale costumes,' Joyce lied with authority. 'Wait till you see them.'

Mae didn't seem very impressed when eventually we trotted out in the fluorescent lime-green sateen fishtail dresses, in fact I think she visibly flinched from the glare.

'Well, thank you very much,' she said later, handing over the thirty-five quid fee in the dressing room. 'Don't be put off by the reaction, it's a very nice little act you've got, a bit gay but very nice. It's just that it's not the sort of thing that appeals to my punters.'

Really? And here's me thinking that we'd gone down all right.

'What my punters like is drag that's either funny or looks like real women. Now take Lorei Lee, they don't come any funnier and he looks fabulous, got a nice cleavage as well. And then there's Terry Durham. Well, he's got real breasts, a lovely pair they are, better than most women's. He strips right down to a tiny g-string and a pair of tassels and then plays the accordion. Wonderful act.'

'He wants to watch he doesn't get pleats in his tits,' I snapped, shoving costumes into my case. It was obvious from her tone that we wouldn't be invited back so I saw no reason to keep up an air of polite gentility. I was tired, hungry and growing more irritable by the second and this patronizing drivel was getting on my nerves. It seemed that if you wanted to please Mae you had to jiggle a pair of tits with a bunch of beads and feathers hanging out of your bum.

On the way home in the taxi after I'd dropped Joyce off I sat and thought about what Mae had said. She was right. She had only confirmed my own suspicions that the act was boring and if we were to carry on then it was time to up our game. Oh well, back to the drawing board.

The next morning I was up bright and early to look after a family of children who wanted to know why my face was covered in glitter, but seemed satisfied with my explanation that I'd been clearing out a cupboard and had an encounter with an extremely sparkly Christmas tree. Thankfully this job was more or less nine to five, leaving me available for all the work that would soon be pouring in for the Glamazons.

I was hopeless at ringing round the pubs for work. It felt like begging, particularly when it came to haggling over the fee with a landlord who had no idea who you were or what you were like, and if it had been left up to me the Glamazons would never have worked again. Eventually Joyce took charge and managed to fill a few dates in an otherwise empty diary.

At the Royal Vauxhall Tavern, in what felt like a rough part of sarf London, the acts who performed there worked on the bar. Some of them shot up and down it fearlessly on roller skates, whereas I was a little more cautious and tottered gingerly along in my saloon girl's outfit, miming to Madeline Kahn's 'I'm Tired' from *Blazing Saddles*. There was a bit of a Wild West saloon feel to the place anyway. The crowd were rough and ready and looked as if they were more than capable of eating their young alive. The dressing room was a rat-hole and if you didn't fancy strutting your stuff atop the bar then there was a swing for you to show off on. It was exhilarating swinging higher and higher over the heads of the crowd, and above the noise I could hear Joyce from behind the curtain muttering to our dresser, 'She's going to kill herself out there.'

I've read a few articles over the years about how the Royal Vauxhall Tavern was once a famous music hall where the likes of Marie Lloyd frequently performed, and even how Queen Victoria once paid a visit (hence the Royal) en route to the palace. Although it's built on the site of what was the Vauxhall Pleasure Gardens the tavern has no such romantic past, starting out as a humble lorry-drivers' pub until the sixties, when the landlady jumped on the drag boom band-wagon and started putting on acts to entertain the mainly heterosexual working-class audience. It hadn't changed much since then apart from the audience, who, while still being very working-class, were now mostly passengers on the lavender bus. Neither had the decor altered much over the years. I thought it was a dump. South London seemed like another country compared to Crouch End and I didn't particularly care if I never set foot in the Vauxhall again. Little did I know that it was to become my spiritual home for over ten years and that in time I would learn to love every brick in the place.

If I thought the Vauxhall Tavern was bad, then nothing could prepare me for the Elephant and Castle pub over the road. It's now one of those ubiquitous Starbucks coffee shops and I wonder if the clientele have any idea of the building's history as they sip their caffè lattes. The Elephant and Castle, or the Elephant's Arsehole as I came to call it, was without doubt one of the sleaziest pubs in London. The patrons of this watering hole were a ragbag assortment of drunks from the doss house next door and hard-bitten rent boys and their dubious punters. There were frequent fights and it was said that if you'd been barred from every other pub in London then the Elephant and Castle would be more than happy to accommodate you. Sat at the end of the bar, an incongruous figure among such lowlife, was a smartly dressed middle-aged lady in a neat little suit with pearls at her throat and a head of nicely waved hair, ever so 'refeened'. She acted if she were running an elegant hotel bar, apparently oblivious to the winos and down-and-outs staggering around her as she dispensed bonhomie with the charm of the chairperson of the Harrogate Rotary Club. There was no dressing room; in the Elly you got changed in the none too clean ladies' lav and the odd ladies (and I mean odd) who used it always, and quite rightly I realize now, berated us for being there.

'Take it up with the management,' Joyce would tell them, fighting me for space in the tiny mirror over the sink, 'and shut the door please if you're going to have a slash. We can see what you've had for your dinner.'

A further black spot on the Elly's copy book was the reduction in fee. 'We can't afford to pay as much as our competitors as we are a much smaller establishment, but we can guarantee you regular bookings,' the Annie Walker clone would say, smiling sweetly as she handed us our twenty-quid fee for the night.

I hated working at the Elly. It was the last chance saloon,

the end of a road that I hadn't even started on yet, and I felt that we were finished before we'd begun as we stood there bumping and grinding to a bunch of uninterested losers. And yet, years later, the Elly was to be the birthplace of Lily Savage. It was there that I first abandoned the tape and found the courage to pick up the microphone and talk.

It was in a record shop in King's Cross called Mole Jazz that I first heard Brenda Lee's unique recording of 'Saved' complete with the opening of 'Bringing In The Sheaves' – and had an epiphany. In a blaze of light I could see a vision in which both Joyce and I were dressed as Salvationists, me as the fallen woman newly reformed after a life of drink and debauchery and rejoicing that she'd been 'Saved' and Joyce bringing up the rear as the chorus, going hell for leather with a tambourine. I rushed home to make a tape.

I would come on in an old kimono and a wig full of rollers, clutching a gin bottle, to Phyllis Diller's version of 'One For My Baby And One More For The Road' and at the denouement, when I eventually collapsed from a combination of grief and drink, Joyce would appear dressed in the uniform of the Salvation Army, complete with bonnet, to Julie Andrews's rendition of the hoary old music-hall lament 'She's More To Be Pitied Than Censured'. Then I would join her in a uniform of my own for 'Saved'. Perfect except for one thing. Just where does one go to get a Salvation Army outfit?

Shamelessly I gathered up the kids I was looking after and took them with me on the bus to Denmark Hill and the William Booth Memorial Training College, the very heart of the Salvation Army. My plan was simple. I worked for social services, the kids would prove that, and one of the centres where I worked was putting on an amateur production of

Guys and Dolls and we needed to borrow a couple of uniforms for the larger lady. I didn't like lying to them at all – the Catholic guilt really kicked in and I was full of remorse – but I needed two Salvation Army outfits and I could hardly say I wanted them for a drag act, now could I?

I left the children waiting in the large, airy reception while a squeaky-clean young male officer escorted me to a room upstairs. I felt the kids gave me the air of a Maria von Trapp and I nearly burst into a chorus of 'I Have Confidence' as I skipped up the stairs after Officer Squeaky Clean. The officer who interviewed me was sweeter than Snow White and gave me a selection of ancient uniforms to look through. I chose two of the largest, hoping they would fit us, and a couple of bonnets and left a donation of fifty quid that I hoped would atone for my sins.

Returning to the reception area, I found the children drinking orange juice and eating biscuits supplied by the saintly Officer Squeaky Clean. 'You do a very good job,' he told me kindly, which made me instantly feel like the biggest piece of shit that ever slid across a pavement.

I really do have the greatest admiration for the Salvation Army. I've seen at first hand the remarkable work they do and since that autumn afternoon in 1979 I've always made the odd donation. Once a Catholic, eh?

Joyce howled with laughter when he saw the uniforms, which were falling to bits and stank of mould. Mine looked as if it had been around since the First World War but apart from being a little short in the arm they were a reasonable fit. Chrissie patched them up and made a few alterations and we launched the new act at a pub called the Nashville in Hammersmith that same night. It went down a storm and for the first time since we'd started out we left the stage to the satisfactory sound of deafening applause. As a finale Joyce stripped off his uniform and bonnet to reveal a minuscule gladiator's outfit underneath that Chrissie had thrown together out of half a yard of black leatherette, a tin of gold model paint and a few studs and chains, and swapping his tambourine for a bugle he launched into 'You Gotta Get A Gimmick' from the musical *Gypsy*.

After a quick change I joined him in another of Chrissie's five-minute creations: a set of pink chiffon moths' wings attached to a tiny sequined bra from which two strategically placed tassels hung limply. Covering my crotch and my modesty was an oversized sequin butterfly fashioned out of an old pair of tights and a wire hanger, again with a tassel that swung between my legs. It would take a general anaesthetic to get me to put on something like that 'costume' today in private, never mind in public, but I didn't give a damn then and even had the nerve to go out to a club in it afterwards.

John Gleason, the affable Irish landlord of the Nashville, liked to book two acts for his Wednesday night cabaret. It was a great pub to work in. The stage was huge and lit by a professional lighting rig and the dressing room, surprise, surprise, was a decent size and fit for human habitation. We shared the bill that night with a mime act called Stage Three: Jimmie, John and David, known in certain circles as Elsie, Connie and Miss Hush. Don't ask.

David, aka Miss Hush, was the brains behind the act. An inventive window-dresser by day, he designed and made all the costumes and elaborate feather headdresses, styled the wigs and not only painted his own face each night but did the other two as well. Hush's make-up was a work of art. He took his time applying slap as it was a ceremony he enjoyed. He would pause every five minutes for a fag and a hefty swig of 'the baby', half a litre of Coke mixed with half a bottle of vodka. Hush never went to a booking without stopping at an off-licence en route. 'Just pull over here a minute, will you, wench, while I pop in the offy for the baby.'

Hush's speciality was to strip to 'Put The Blame On Mame' dressed in a wig and costume identical to the iconic black satin one worn by Rita Hayworth in the film. He really was extraordinarily glamorous – he literally oozed glamour – and you'd never think that the big bloke in the checked shirt and jeans was the same person as the smouldering redhead slowly removing her shoulder-length glove on stage. Like Joyce, his bulk made him look curvy and voluptuous whereas I just looked like a long streak of piss.

Hush also spoke a different language. 'I'm just going to the bar to collect the handbag' translated as 'I'm off to collect the night's fee.' Wigs were shyckles and an offer of 'getting a nice bit of jarry down the screech at the latty' meant 'come to our house for your tea.' Elsie spoke the same lingo only more fluently. He was the oldest of the trio, bossy and opinionated with a pronounced lisp, and referred to himself in the third person as 'yer mother'.

'Yer mother don't tell no liesh, babesh, but I've seen better nets hanging in a window,' he once said to me, alluding to the net coat that the drag queen on stage was wearing as a tribute to Dorothy Squires. Elsie was very possessive of 'Dot' and whereas other acts who impersonated the fiery Welsh singer would send her up, invariably staggering on stage pretending to be drunk and waving a bottle of Gordon's gin, Elsie's Dot was delivered straight as a tribute to his idol. Since Hush's day job as a window-dresser meant he had access to all manner of goodies, feathers in particular, Elsie's Dot Squires gown was magnificently trimmed in yards and yards of luxurious white ostrich feathers tipped with turquoise, courtesy of a window display at Allders in Clapham. Elsie closed his eyes and literally shook with emotion as he mouthed the words to Dot's dramatic rendition of 'Till', every last one of those turquoise-tipped feathers quivered in unison, putting me in mind of a little plump quail going about the delicate process of laying an egg.

I liked Elsie, he was a real character and very funny, and it was he who encouraged Joyce and me to join him and the rest of the gang at the Escort Club in Pimlico. On admittance you were given a paper plate with a solitary lettuce leaf and a slice of luncheon meat to get round the licensing laws' requirement that the club serve each patron a meal.

It's commonplace now to see a troupe of drag queens parading through the streets but back in '79 it was quite brave to walk around brazenly in drag on a Wednesday night, particularly if you were dressed as a moth. We stopped the traffic as we sashayed across the road and into the club. I ended up getting hammered and falling off my bar stool, as you do when you've drunk your body weight in cider. I managed to kick Joyce in the back, sending him rolling down a couple of steps and sliding across the dance floor like a large sequined stone in a game of curling.

'I'm going to knack you,' he roared from his position on the floor, picking his wig up and slamming it hastily on his head back to front. 'And just look at me good purple, it's destroyed,' he bellowed with dismay on discovering the large tear in his brand new purple sequined frock.

I'd finally conceded that the lime-green fishtails with the music notes were hideous. Thanks to the nice little man in the West End, I came home with a bale of purple sequined fabric that Chrissie transformed into two evening gowns. Joyce's good purple had been his pride and joy and now it was ruined. I flapped me wings and got out of Joyce's way double smart and hid in the lavs until mercifully Hush stepped in, offering to repair the frock. And so, when the club closed, off we trooped to their house in Purley, a tiny whitewashed two-bedroom cottage on the main Purley Road that one day Vera, Joyce and I would move into. Six drag queens and Vera. Now there's a title for a sitcom . . .

The owner of the house we'd rented a flat in for nearly three years suddenly decided that his tenants were responsible for the rates – not just the current ones but also for the two years that he was in arrears. This left us with a rent that was unaffordable. We fought him with the help of the Citizens Advice Bureau but, as so frequently happens, the little guys lost and as we couldn't and wouldn't pay the astronomical rent increase our landlord served us with eviction papers. I'd hoped to get a few months' grace before he slung us out by the devious means of taking him to a gay club and getting him drunk. Then I'd chat him up and get him to change his mind. That was the plan. However, pissed as a fart and overcome with passion (and who would blame him?), he made a clumsy lunge at me, sticking his tongue in my ear in a gesture of wanton lust. When guilt overcame him and he thankfully retracted it, he would slump to his knees, dragging Vera and me with him for a bout of prayer and self-flagellation, right there in the middle of the Rainbow Rooms, Manor House.

Finding an affordable flat in an accessible location in London at short notice is asking the impossible. We'd scanned the

Evening Standard and *Time Out* to no avail, and with less than a week to go before the landlord sent in the bailiffs we still hadn't found anywhere to live.

Desperate times call for desperate measures and I went in search of a key I still had somewhere that belonged to the flat of an elderly client who had died over a year earlier. She was very old and sick and the hospital, realizing that they could do no more for her, sent her home to die in her own bed. As she had no living relatives and no one to care for her, the job of looking after her in those final days was left to me and a home help.

It was a small flat, just one room with a tiny kitchen and bathroom, and each time you turned the gas on for the oven or ran a bath the walls and windows ran with rivers of condensation.

Edna, the lady in question, had been an orphan. She went straight from the orphanage into domestic service as a nanny and a life sentence of caring for a succession of rich people's progeny. Dotted around on top of the mantelpiece in cheap gilt frames were old black and white photographs of these children to whom she'd given so much of herself, and yet here she was at the end of her long life, alone apart from a total stranger in a damp little bedsit in Camden, waiting to die. It was sobering stuff sitting with her in the wee small hours of the morning, listening to her shallow breathing growing weaker and the constant tick of her bedside clock counting down the hours.

Before she died, Edna told me that there was a little money wrapped in an old sheet in her wardrobe drawer that she'd like me to have. She explained that since she had nobody else to leave it to she'd like me and the home help to share it. I took no notice at the time as she was saying a lot of things that didn't make sense; only that morning she'd called me Maud and asked if I'd laid the nursery table for the children's breakfast.

Edna died peacefully at three in the morning. She'd woken up and asked me if I'd warm her some milk and when I returned from the kitchen she was dead.

There'd been a spate of deaths since the nights had drawn in. A few weeks prior to Edna's death, I'd let myself into the home of an elderly gent and found him lying dead on the hall floor, with his arm outstretched, grinning obscenely. But that was small fry compared to the morbidly fascinating tale of the old lady who was discovered burned alive in her kitchen in King's Cross. She had just lit the gas and was about to put the kettle on for a cup of tea when she'd had a stroke. That was bad enough, but unfortunately for this poor woman the plate rack over the stove combined with the recess wall had held her upright, positioning her over the stove in such a way that the flames from the gas ring slowly roasted her alive, burning through her chest. Rivers of fat had bubbled out of the charred hole in the back of her cardigan to cover the kitchen floor. The smell was disturbingly similar to that of frying bacon and for a very long time afterwards quite a number of Peripatetics couldn't even consider a bacon butty without retching.

Thankfully Edna's death was in nowhere near as traumatic. I understood what people meant when they said that loved ones had 'just slipped away', for that was what Edna had done, tranquil and untroubled. I covered her with the sheet and then went round to the phone box to ring the police and an ambulance, who, judging by the amount of time they took to turn up, put the collection of an old woman's corpse at the bottom of their list of priorities. Surprisingly, considering the *Exorcist* saga when I'd jumped into bed with my ma because I was scared to sleep in my own bed, I didn't mind being alone with Edna's body. She was a nice old girl and if I did feel the jitters creeping up on me I reassured myself that, as she wouldn't have harmed a fly in life, there was little chance of her suddenly rising from under the sheet reincarnated as a flesh-eating zombie hell-bent on ripping my throat out. Nevertheless I opened the front door to let some air in and watched her from the safety of the front step just in case she moved.

As I smoked my fag I noticed that the sheet over her was covered in stains. Resignedly I went in search of a clean sheet, not wanting the police and ambulance services to think she'd been neglected and allowed to lie in a dirty bed. As I was getting a clean sheet out of the wardrobe drawer I had a look to see if there really was any money hidden. I was sceptical but underneath the bedding I felt something very much like a wad of notes. Pulling the bundle out, wrapped in a towel just as Edna had said, I sat back on my heels with the blood pounding in my ears. How much was here? It could be thousands, millions even, although I doubted it as the wad really wasn't that big.

A thought suddenly occurred to me. What would it look like if the police turned up right this very moment and found me on my knees with a stash of greenbacks in my hand and an old lady dead in the bed behind me? They'd think I'd murdered her. Quickly I undid the elastic bands and unwrapped the tea towel with trembling hands. There was a wad of notes all right, a decent-sized one at that; it was just a shame that they happened to be pre-decimalization ten-shilling notes.

After the ambulance had taken Edna's body away, I left a

note of explanation for the home help, washed up the milk pan and mugs and let myself out into the cold of the early morning.

And now here I was, almost a year later to the day knocking on Edna's door to see if anyone had moved in. I had a story worked out in case someone answered the door – about how I was one of Edna's great-grandchildren – but there was no need for me to go into my patter as no one seemed to be home. I tried the key and, as I'd hoped it still worked. Quickly I let myself in before any of the neighbours saw me, and found the place exactly as I'd left it a year earlier. The note I'd written for the home help was still propped up against the ashtray with a crumpled packet of Winstons in it and the indentation of Edna's body still visible in the mattress.

Time had stood still for the last twelve months and it seemed that the council had completely forgotten about this place. Time to change lodgings!

Before we abandoned ship, Chrissie and I drew a series of obscene and highly graphic cartoons depicting Vera and the landlord in compromising sexual positions on the living-room wall. Vera wasn't amused in the least and went round the room closely examining them, sniffing with disgust while Chrissie and I rolled around on the floor, beside ourselves with laughter.

Late one Friday night we finally said goodbye to Crouch End. Rolling up a couple of mattresses and securing them with pairs of old fishnet tights, we left in style in a black cab. I was sad to leave the place that'd been my home for the past three years, as were Chrissie and Vera, and even though I hadn't liked it at first we'd had some good times there. Angela had long gone, working in theatre in Northumberland, and I told myself as the taxi drove off and I took one last look at the place that it was right to be leaving. Not that we had much choice in the matter: the bailiffs were arriving in the morning to evict us, led no doubt by the self-righteous landlord.

We'd made frequent trips to Edna's, washing down walls and floors and packing her personal items away in bin-liners, squashing them into the only storage cupboard in the hall. Vera didn't fancy sleeping in Edna's bed and nor did I but Chrissie had no such reservations.

'That's a good-quality horsehair mattress, that is,' he remarked, dismantling the iron bed frame to make more room. 'I don't care who died in it. You don't think you sleep on Crown bedding in the nick, do ya?'

The living conditions were cramped for one person, let alone three, added to which we had mountains of drag hanging from the picture rail and lining the walls and the enormous blond bouffant wig that Hush had created was perched on top of the telly. Things had changed since we'd met Miss Hush. He'd sold us old costumes that he no longer had any use for, including a pair of crinolines complete with hoops that were now wedged behind the bathroom door. Hush pointed me in the direction of Hairaisers, a wig shop on Lisson Grove that sold wigs in every colour and size including the white-blond that I'd searched in vain for. It was one of the major requirements for the look I had in mind, that of a big blonde hard-bitten slapper. He also made us new costumes quickly and cheaply, much to Chrissie's annoyance who had been made redundant since Anne had reclaimed her Singer sewing machine.

After a couple of months living together in what was beginning to feel like a theatrical hire shop we were really getting on each other's nerves. All those petty grievances that had been simmering away suddenly erupted, resulting in a punch-up between Chrissie and me. He'd been in one of his moods and we'd had a bit of a set-to in a West End club called Scandals, for which he'd been thrown out. When I got back to the flat he jumped on me with eyes like a bedlamite, hitting me over the head with a heavy glass vase and sending blood splattering up the walls. I in turn went for him with the bread knife, fully intending to kill him before he did me, while Vera, trapped on his mattress in the middle of the room, searched frantically for his glasses that had been kicked across the floor in the struggle. The police turned up. Chrissie made a swift exit, leaving it to me to explain. He vanished into the night and across the river to stay with Lozzy in Victoria Mansions and we didn't speak to each other for over a year.

I didn't go home for Christmas. We had a booking at the Black Cap on Christmas Eve and another in an East End pub on Boxing Day and, believing you should never turn work down, I spent a jolly Christmas Day with Joyce and his flatmate instead of my family.

I was growing increasingly unhappy living at Edna's. Not being one of nature's squatters, I was tired of lying to the persistently inquisitive neighbours and living in constant fear of a knock at the door. My new year resolution was to find a flat, but although bookings had increased we still weren't earning a lot of money from the act and I certainly couldn't afford to give up the day job yet. Still, there were some good offers of work for the coming year: a three-week tour of the north and a month in a club in Denmark plus the bookings we had in town. Maybe things were starting to look up after all.

On New Year's Eve I dropped in on a family I'd been working with for the last few months. After cajoling the father every day, I'd eventually worn him down. Tired of my lectures, he'd finally roused himself from his stupor on the sofa, had a shave and begun to care for his remarkable children for the first time in his life. He'd really smartened up his act and as a New Year's Eve treat, instead of spending it in the pub, he was taking his family for a pizza and then on to a firework display. The flat was tidy, the kids were happy and there was food in the fridge and I knew that I was no longer required.

This display of domestic harmony had an effect on me and I suddenly felt the urge to get in touch with my own parent. I rang her from a stuffy phone box stinking of tobacco and pee at the station before catching the tube up to Camden Town to see 1980 in at the Black Cap.

'What are you doing tonight?' I asked her.

'Oh, I'm just getting ready to go out. I'm going on a cruise on the *Royal Iris* up and down the Mersey with a fellah I met at mass,' she replied casually.

'Really?'

'Don't talk bloody soft, I'm just about to get into my nightie and watch *Murder on the Orient Express* on the telly. You know I can't bear New Year's Eve. I'll be glad when it's over.'

So would I. New Year's Eve made me fretful. Whatever I was doing, as I waited for the clock to chime midnight, I was always tense, and in the back of my mind there was a niggling suspicion that I wasn't having quite as good a time as I should be and that somewhere else a wild party was in full swing that I was missing out on. Tonight was a big one: the dawn of a new decade. I really felt that instead of standing pressed against a wall with half a pint of lukewarm cider in a Black Cap packed with people I hardly knew, I should be celebrating in the grand style, dancing on a table perhaps, drunk on champagne at somewhere like the Café de Paris, the air thick with balloons, streamers and champagne corks, with all my friends and family around me, dancing frantically to a big band.

'You shouldn't be staying in on your own tonight,' I said, suddenly saddened by the thought of her alone on New Year's Eve. 'Why don't you go up to Aunty Anne and Chrissie's or our Sheila's?'

'Oh, I can't be bothered,' she moaned. 'Annie and Chrissie bugger off to bed by nine and I'm not hiking up to Sheila's. No, I'm quite happy here, thank you.'

'Talking of which,' she said, completely changing the subject, 'that Penelope Keith's on the telly tonight in some rubbish called *Goodbye to the Seventies*. D'ya think she's really that posh or is she just putting it on? She makes the Queen sound like she was dragged up in Back Exmouth Street.'

'No, I think she talks like that all the time. Anyway, I haven't rung up to talk about Penelope Keith, I'm ringing to wish you all the best before I go out.'

'Oh, aye. And where are you off tomcatting it tonight, may I ask?'

'Oh, just a pub with Alan and a couple of friends in Camden Town.'

'Camden Town, eh? You're certainly living the highlife down there. Well, enjoy yourself. Just make sure you keep out of trouble.'

'I'm only going for a drink.'

'Exactly. You could get into trouble in an empty house. It's your middle name.'

'Happy new year, Mam.'

'Happy new year, son.'

Outside the Black Cap a fairly well-dressed man standing at the bus stop was berating the revellers as they queued to get in.

'You're all living on borrowed time,' he roared. 'The day of reckoning will soon be upon you, forcing all sodomites to repent their sins.'

'Good luck to you,' a chirpy little Irish queen shouted back from the queue.

'Look at them,' he ranted. 'Blind, every one of you, as blind as the poor fools on the *Titanic*, playing games, blissfully unaware that the ship is about to go down.'

'Ah, shut your mouth and go home, you're pissed,' someone shouted out.

'You're all doomed, can't you see? Doomed,' he carried on, unabashed. 'The storm clouds are looming, death is imminent.'

'Now let me guess,' a familiar voice said in my ear. 'She's either a) blind drunk or insane, probably both; b) a religious fanatic; or c) a journalist for the *Daily Mail*.' It was Reg, dragging a suitcase and two bin-liners containing wigs and costumes behind him. 'Make yourself useful, de-ah, and help me in with this lot instead of standing there listening to this maniac. Go home, de-ah,' he shouted to the drunk, 'you're making a fool of yourself.'

'No, it's you who's the fool,' he muttered ominously, making a drunken sign of the cross. 'You're on a sinking ship.'

'Where the fuck do you think you are, darling, Wapping?' Reg shouted back to the amusement of the queue. He picked up a binliner, leaving the other heavier looking one and the suitcase for me to carry.

'Shall we purchase our ticket then, my de-ar,' he said grandly, turning to me as he swept into the pub, 'for our passage aboard the Ship of Fools?'

At that moment something walked over my grave. Shivering in the cold night air I followed him in.

A SHORT GLOSSARY OF POLARI TERMS

Bona: good
Cod: naff
Eek: face
Jarry: food
Lallies: legs
Latty: flat, room
Naff: bad
Omi: man
Omi palone: gay man
Palone: woman
Pots: teeth
Riah: hair
Slap: make-up
Varda: look
Vogue: cigarette

INDEX

340

INDEX

341